ECOWAS REGIONAL INTEGRATION

The West African Monetary Zone Experience

ECOWAS REGIONAL INTEGRATION

The West African Monetary Zone Experience

Prof. Ngozi E. Egbuna

PYXIDIA HOUSE PUBLISHERS

ECOWAS REGIONAL INTEGRATION:
The West African Monetary Zone Experience

Request for information on this title should be addressed to

Prof. Ngozi E. Egbuna
Email: ngegbuna@yahoo.com
dr.eunicengoziegbuna@gmail.com

Library of Congress Cataloging-in-Publication Data

Prof. Ngozi E. Egbuna
ECOWAS REGIONAL INTEGRATION:
The West African Monetary Zone Experience
ISBN-13: 978-1-946530-42-4 (Paperback)
ISBN-10: 1-946530-42-5 (Paperback)
1. Economics - Finance - Non-fiction 1. Title
Library of Congress Control Number: 2023940172

Edited by Winnie Aduayi

Published in Dallas Texas by Pyxidia House Publishers. A registered trademark of Pyxidia Concept llc. www.pyxidiahouse.com
info@pyxidiahouse.com

Printed in the United States of America

To the founding fathers of ECOWAS Integration,
your dreams are valid.

To the present generation, an integrated ECOWAS
is possible; go for it.

To the generation to come, the future of ECOWAS
integration is full of boundless possibilities;
stay the course.

ACKNOWLEDGEMENTS

This book is my resolve to chronicle my views and experiences at the West African Monetary Institute (WAMI) so that the periods 2011 to 2013 and 2017 to 2021 would not be lost in the ECOWAS integration history. Writing this book would not have been possible without the staff of WAMI, who worked so hard to support the vision and mission of the Institute. I want to single out Mr. Lamin Jarju, who provided research support for this book. Thank you, Lamin.

I am eternally grateful to my boss, Mr. Godwin Emefiele, Governor, Central Bank of Nigeria, and Deputy Governors – Drs. O.J. Nnnanna and Kingsley Obiora for trustily seconding me to WAMI. That gave me unimaginable opportunities; I hope I have not disappointed you all. They exposed me to the discipline of leading a diverse group; I truly had no idea where it was leading up to.

Although the period of my career was filled with many ups and downs, my time at the Central Bank of Nigeria and WAMI was worth it. My time in these great institutions would not have been made possible without the management and staff who taught me the honest central bank game.

To Prof Akin Omotayo, who took a chance on a woman hungry for knowledge and insisted that I work of Cross border Trade Issues in ECOWAS for my Doctorate thesis even against my protests; he saw what I did not see, now see how far that has taken me. He never saw my age, my experiences at the Central Bank of Nigeria, or my initial lack of interest in the topic; he just saw a woman hungry to learn, grow, and earn a degree. He never stopped me; he only encouraged me.

A very special thanks to the Heads of State, Ministers of Finance and Central Banks of the West African Monetary Zone, who demanded professionalism and gave me all the needed support to achieve results. Thank you for introducing me to the regional integration process and exposing me to ECOWAS people.

Writing a book about the West African Monetary Zone is a surreal process. I am indebted to Pyxidia House Team –Winnie, Sam, Craig, Rick, and Okiemute for their editorial help, keen insight, and ongoing support in bringing this book to life. It is because of their efforts and encouragement that I have an odyssey to pass on where one did not exist before.

To Parents - Dan and Victoria, my siblings - Victor, Nkoli, Ofo, Chinwe, and Ekwunife and their families who ceaselessly support me with prayers and good wishes; it is a blessing to be a part of you. My family-in-law, you are the best.

To my family. My husband, Engr. Ik Egbuna: for always being the person I could turn to during those dark and desperate days. You sustain me in ways that I never knew that I needed. To my children, Chukwumaife, Chukwuderah, Chukwudumebi, Chimdi, Chiamaka, and Justin: thank you for putting up with me all these years. So thankful to have you in my life. My grandchildren, Sochikaima and Reya, you give me so much joy, and my world is beautiful because of you.

Finally, to God alone be the glory!

Contents

Preface

I am a central banker seconded to the West African Monetary Institute (WAMI) as the first female Director General from August 4, 2017, to February 1, 2021. My primary responsibilities included the implementation of the WAMZ work programs and policies, providing administrative and technical leadership, manage the human and financial resources available to the Institute towards the attainment of its mandate of undertaking preparatory activities leading to the establishment of a monetary union in the West African Monetary Zone (WAMZ) and Economic Community of West African States (ECOWAS). Then engage with WAMZ authorities (Heads of member states, Ministers of Finance, Governors of Central banks, and the President of ECOWAS Commission) as well as drive engagements with the Institute's key external development partners (African Development Bank (AfDB), International Monetary Fund (IMF), Afrieximbank, African Economic Research Consortium (AERC), and customers (World Bank, Economic Researchers).

This book is an analytical account of my eventful tenure and the need to highlight the macroeconomic environment from 2017 to 2021 characterised by the COVID-19 pandemic and enormous technological innovations like FinTechs and the Pan-African Payment and Settlement System (PAPSS) as well as the establishment of African Continental Free Trade Area (AfCFTA) amongst others.

In the course of carrying out these assignments, I have come to see the WAMZ as an inimitable regional entity uniquely established in the year 2000 to fast-track integration in ECOWAS as a monetary zone by non-WAEMU (West African Economic and Monetary Union (also known by its French acronym, UEMOA) members. The current members of WAMZ are The Gambia, Ghana, Guinea, Liberia, Nigeria, and Sierra Leone. The main aim of creating WAMZ is to unify WAEMU and non-WAEMU countries in ECOWAS, launch a common currency – Eco, for the entire ECOWAS region, and establish a single Central bank to be called the West African Central Bank.

Since my meritorious retirement from both the service of the bank and WAMI, I have been writing this book to provide a comprehensive study into the promotion of zonal integration for the sole purpose of fast-tracking regional integration as a central pillar of intra and extra-ECOWAS relations with the rest of the world. It is a strategy to deal with a core socioeconomic challenge: the transformation of conflicts, particularly civil wars, and conflicts. Yet to also highlight to what extent the promotion of regional integration has been successful in transforming the economies. This volume offers a comprehensive assessment of the integration process irrespective of the track of approach for promoting integration. In my view, it is imperative to write a book designed as a practical and analytical guide for policymakers and academics; this book will also be of interest to scholars and students of international trade.

These integration phases are being implemented progressively, and major strides are being made to establish a solid economic bloc. The WAMZ Protocol is a key milestone on the road to a single currency area upon fulfilment of the key macroeconomic convergence targets. Economic integration benefits the WAMZ countries through increased efficiency and productivity, and entry into a single currency will eliminate bilateral foreign exchange risk, reduce transactions and accounting costs for intraregional trade, and foster financial integration. This is to facilitate the expansion of regional trade and investment, which will promote economic growth and cross-border financial transactions, resulting in economic cohesion, which should make it seamless to merge with the integrated WAEMU countries to form a strong and viable ECOWAS. The achievement of the aforementioned aims and objectives of WAMZ and ECOWAS have been fragmented depending on who is discussing it. Nevertheless, the economics of WAMZ and ECOWAS integration is very important. The political objectives will only be met if economic integration is fruitful and placed on a sound economic footing, especially in the post covid era.

This is where my role as a central banker comes in; I have no opinion on the steps to be taken in the integration process – that belongs to the realm of politics and is also market-driven. However, this book is written to point out the conditions that must be met for certain steps to be taken safely. The reverse is also true: the central banker and central banks are, for their part, influenced by the integration process, and the greater the level of integration in the financial or monetary system, the greater the impact upon them. The Central bank and the central banker are operating in an environment affected by the ongoing integration process – this has to be taken into account; besides, the question arises as to whether a single monetary policy ultimately calls for further integration in other areas. Hence, the motivation for this book is to chronicle regional integration in the WAMZ to highlight past, ongoing, and future initiatives in this direction that significantly impact economic policymaking and economic outcomes in the zone and ECOWAS region. The member states are also among the fastest-growing economies in sub-Saharan Africa since the post-covid era and have achieved average per capita income growth higher than most Regional Economic Communities (RECs). Generally, the countries are making significant progress toward financial integration, including the harmonisation of supervisory arrangements and practices and the modernisation of monetary policy frameworks. However, much remains to be done, like the removal of nontariff barriers, which is essential for the full functioning of the customs union. The launch of a timetable for the elimination of the sensitive products list and the establishment of a supranational legal framework for resolving trade disputes are also important reforms that should foster regional integration.

This book comes at an auspicious time when critical economic reforms are being undertaken in fiscal, monetary, and exchange rate policies to achieve the post covid cohesion and macroeconomic convergence criteria, which are a major basis in the WAMZ and ECOWAS currency union arrangement. The book catalogues recent developments and presents fresh ideas for the way forward on harmonisation and coordination of fiscal, monetary, and financial policies, including strengthening and harmonising the institutional framework underpinning these policies, as well as statistical harmonisation and public financial management and trade issues as a spinoff of the AfCFTA.

ECOWAS and its institutions, especially WAMZ, have variously been criticized for their supposed ineffectiveness, slowness in responding to various challenges, lack of transparency in decision making and lack of democratic legitimacy. However, all those who make such criticisms have forgotten that many of the weaknesses of the ECOWAS institutional setting arise from its voluntary character and the seeming reluctance of member countries to transfer more powers to the Union. Besides, the region has been beset with political tensions, e.g., coups, structural macroeconomic bottlenecks like fiscal indiscipline as well as environmental crises like Ebola and COVID 19 pandemic. Nevertheless, it is in the interest of all member states to have an effectively functioning union that will deliver West African public goods to its citizens. Therefore, the member states should be ready to repair, reset, and rebrand the ECOWAS architecture, even at the cost of sharing more sovereignty.

Introduction

The Economic Community of West Africa States (ECOWAS) was established in 1975 to promote economic integration and eventually graduate to a monetary union for the sub-region. ECOWAS consists of 15 countries that were colonised by the British, French, and Portugal. There are some marginal gains; however, creating a monetary union was not achieved even after over 45 years of existence. It must be noted that the Franco-phone economies are integrated under the West African Economic and Monetary Union (WAEMU) with common Currency (CFA), one central bank, Banque Centrale des Etats de I'Afrique de l'Ouest (BCEAO) and several approved protocols. In 2000, in order to fast-track integration in ECOWAS, another monetary zone known as the West African Monetary Zone (WAMZ) was established by Anglophone countries that are non-WAEMU members. The current members of WAMZ are The Gambia, Ghana, Guinea, Liberia, Nigeria, and Sierra Leone. The main aim of creating WAMZ is to unify WAEMU and non-WAEMU countries in ECOWAS, launch a common currency, Eco, for the entire ECOWAS region, and establish a single central bank to be called the West African Central Bank.

Over 20 years of creating WAMZ, the core objectives are not achieved. The deadline for the introduction of a single currency has been shifted many times. The last deadline for the single currency was 2020/2021. While the Heads of State and Governments appear to be optimistic on the one hand, the technocrats, on the other hand, are pessimistic, insisting that the primary criteria must be met by all the countries for integration to take place. Can the political consideration be ignored? What can be done? Can we learn lessons from EU and ASEAN integration; which of the models would best suit WAMZ and ECOWAS at large?

This book is a compendium of historical and technical initiatives in pursuit of economic integration in the West African Monetary Zone and in ECOWAS at large. It is inspired by ongoing initiatives in this direction that have formed a major part of the region's economic policymaking and economic outcomes. WAMZ countries are making significant progress toward financial integration, including the harmonisation of supervisory arrangements and practices, the modernisation of monetary policy frameworks, and contemporary issues of the payment system infrastructural developments. However, much still remains to be done.

The costs and benefits of regional integration and monetary union are well documented in other regional blocs except for the WAMZ, hence the dire need for this book. It is argued in economic literature that common markets and currency unions reduce transactions and accounting costs for intraregional trade leading up to real convergence by lowering tariffs and eliminating bilateral foreign exchange risk. Regional trade and investment expand under a monetary union, promoting economic growth and cross-border banking operations. This then boosts financial sector competition, integrates financial markets, and could help lower interest rates. Different studies have estimated the impact on the expansion of intraregional trade flows to be huge, ranging from 30 percent (*Rose & Stanley, 2005*) to as much as 200 percent (*Rose & Frankel, 2000*).

The book examines a number of issues ranging from organization, operation, and institutional structure of WAMZ in chapter 2, to prospects and challenges of actualizing WAMZ objectives in chapter 3; opportunities and challenges of economic diversity in WAMZ in chapter 4; sociocultural diversities and political dynamics in WAMZ in chapter 5; the readiness of WAMZ countries for the introduction of a single currency in chapter 6; harnessing the potentials of informal entrepreneurial sector to enhance integration in WAMZ in chapter 7; financial sector development and financial integration in WAMZ in chapter 8; assessment of trade integration in WAMZ in chapter 9; the implications of insecurity on the integration agenda in WAMZ in chapter 10; the implications of African Continental Free Trade Area (AfCFTA) in WAMZ integration in chapter 11; Africa Export and Import Bank (AFREXIMBANK) influence on trade promotion in WAMZ in chapter 12; financial integration experiences in EU & ASEAN: Lessons for WAMZ in chapter 13; and Integration in WAMZ: An Insider's Perspective in chapter 14.

The book is divided into three sections. The first section is made up of four chapters, which provide the prospects and challenges of integration in WAMZ. This section is made up of chapters 2 to 5. The second section is made up of five chapters, chapters 6 to 10. This section documents the potential and benefits of integration in WAMZ. And the third section is made up of four chapters, chapters 11 to 14, and these chapters discuss international experiences and insider perspectives.

Chapter two provides a historical account of the evolution, operational, and institutional structures of the West Africa Monetary Zone (WAMZ). The head of States and governments of Anglophone countries in ECOWAS consider the creation of a second monetary union in the ECOWAS region to fast-track the introduction of a common currency and single ECOWAS central bank. The WAMZ sub-region union consists of a big country like

Nigeria, which is the most populous country in Africa with a land area of 923,768 km2, a population of over 200 million, and a GDP of $440 billion, as well as a small country like the Gambia with 11,295 km2, population of 2 million, and $2 billion. Therefore, the interest and choice of Nigeria are critical to the success of the WAMZ union. The institutions that oversee the technical and administrative functions of WAMZ are the West African Monetary Institute (WAMI), Authority of Heads of States and Government (AHSG), Convergence Council of Ministers and Central Bank Governors (CCMCBG), Technical Committee (TC), and Stabilization and Cooperation Fund (SCF).

The level of integration, which is the core objective of creating WAMZ, is assessed in chapter three. The efforts, challenges, and prospects towards actualizing the objective of WAMZ are examined in this chapter. The main objective of WAMZ is to progressively unify all countries in West Africa into one integrated economic area with a single currency, one central bank, and a common monetary zone. Many efforts were made to modernise the payment system in four member countries, integrating the financial systems, including the banking sector, capital market, and non-bank financial sector. Despite these efforts, intra-regional trade is still low in the zone, and there are still some restrictions on the movement of people across borders. There are many challenges hindering the full actualization of WAMZ countries; among them are the inability to meet the convergence criteria; the existence of barriers to trade; socio-political factors, the persistence of colonial tiers and fear of losing central bank autonomy of individual countries. However, there are some prospects which reassure the hope of actualizing the objectives of WAMZ, the advent of stable democracy, the implementation of the payment system project, and the strengthening of the financial institutions, among others.

Chapter four explains the concepts of economic diversity, the extent of diversity across WAMZ countries, factors that influence the level of diversity, the opportunities embedded in economic diversity, and the challenges posed by diversity. Economic diversity, which is referred to as variation in economic structure across different countries, is essential to economic integration among nations. The structural composition of economies in WAMZ indicates that there is much more diversity across WAMZ member countries. Services and agriculture sectors are dominant in all the countries, while industry and manufacturing sectors contribute the lowest. Several factors are identified as responsible for the non-diversification across the WAMZ countries; among them is colonial history that structured African countries to produce primary products, poor macroeconomic policies and institutional quality, and inadequate public infrastructure. Economic structural transformation into manufacturing economies with a specialisation is imperative to diversification and economic integration in WAMZ.

Chapter five examines the sociocultural diversities and political dynamics in the WAMZ. The discussion in the chapter captures the conceptualisation of sociocultural diversity, political dynamics, and integration in WAMZ, as well as the nexus between sociocultural diversity and integration of the countries in WAMZ. Analysis in the chapter reveals that countries in WAMZ union are heterogeneous in terms of diversity in ethnic, religious, linguistic, legal origin, and political systems, among others. Sociocultural diversity may constitute constraints to integration in the forms of trade barriers. Despite observed sociocultural diversity in WAMZ, there is always a sense of communalism and oneness among West Africans whenever they meet themselves in a foreign land outside the West Africa region, implying that the sociocultural diversity of West Africa can inherently provide opportunities for the integration of the zone if properly explored. The West Africa integration has viable prospects if the sociocultural diversity of the region is effective and positively explored.

Chapter six assesses the readiness of WAMZ member countries for the introduction of a single currency in the Zone and ECOWAS at large. The assessment is based on the primary convergence criteria that all members are required to satisfy. The analysis in the chapter revealed that the countries have difficulty meeting the macroeconomic convergence criteria. Macroeconomic volatility, rising fiscal crisis, and absence of full autonomy of monetary authority are the key factors responsible for the countries not meeting the convergence criteria. The macroeconomic in the WAMZ zone is highly volatile due to the vulnerability of these economies to external shocks, with little or no ability to withstand global price changes, because of the large volume of imports of goods and services, the concentration of exports on few primary commodities, and heavy reliance on foreign aid and debt. Therefore, there is a need for governments and monetary authorities of all WAMZ member countries to take specific actions and decisions by way of fiscal and monetary policies that will sustainably ensure the meeting of the four primary macroeconomic convergence criteria: single-digit Inflation rate (end-period); less than or equal to three percent (3%) Fiscal Deficit or GDP (comm. it basis including grants); less than or equal to ten percent (10%) Central Bank Financing of Fiscal Deficits, and greater than or equal to three Months Gross External Reserve (Month of Imports) in-country as well as within-region. However, the feasibility of all the countries meeting all the convergence criteria at the same time is gloomy; hence the emphasis may be directed to the two big countries in the Zone, Nigeria and Ghana, such that if these two countries meet the criteria, the single currency can be implemented.

Chapter seven evaluates the size and characteristics of the informal sector in West Africa; the economic and welfare impacts of an informal entrepreneur; the possibility, the challenges and the benefits of formalising informal entrepreneurial activities. The informal sector contributes, on average, between 35% to over 50% of GDP in West African countries. However, given the features of the informal sector with ease of entry and little or no regulations by the government, there are no adequate statistical data on the operations of informal entrepreneurs in West Africa. Most of the operators in the informal sectors face a lot of constraints, including limited access to information, advanced skills and technologies, limited access to different sources of finances, limited access to business infrastructures, and low productivity with little or no legal protections. The formalisation of the sector is proposed to harness the benefits of the informal entrepreneurial sector. It is recommended that support programmes be established, and an appropriate legal framework be formulated to facilitate the formalisation of informal entrepreneurial activities.

In chapter eight, the concept of financial integration is reviewed, the extent of financial integration in WAMZ is examined, the level of financial development in WAMZ countries is assessed, and challenges, as well as the way forward, are discussed. Access to broader financial markets, better governance, international inflows of investment and growth, risk-sharing, and efficient financial resource allocation are some of the benefits derivable from regional financial integration. Financial development in each country of the union is critical to the success of financial integration; hence the level of financial development is assessed in the chapter. Nigeria's financial sector is the most developed, followed by Liberia and Ghana. However, the banking sub-sector dominates the financial system in all the countries in WAMZ, with commercial banks accounting for more than 50 percent. Poor information gathering, high cost of cross-border financial transactions, weak monitoring and supervision, heterogenous capital market operation and development, low penetration of insurance sub-sector and small size of non-bank financial sub-sector are the major challenges facing the process of financial integration in WAMZ and ECOWAS at large. It is recommended that more investment should be committed to financial infrastructure, and the laws and regulations should be harmonised across the sub-region.

The extent of trade integration in WAMZ is assessed in chapter nine. The trade profiles of the six countries in WAMZ are provided in the chapter. There is generally negative merchandise trade balance over the years across all the countries, with just the exception of Guinea and Nigeria for a few years. Unfortunately, member countries of WAMZ are not top trading partners of each other. For instance, the five top trading partners to the Gambia are China, India, Senegal, Chile, and the Korean Republic; Ghana's top trading partners are Switzerland, China, South Africa, Netherlands, and India, while India, Spain, China, Netherlands, and Indonesia are the top trading partners to Nigeria. A number of barriers restricting trade among the WAMZ countries are identified in the chapter. These include dissimilarities in the regulatory and supervisory arrangements across the member countries, restrictions on foreign ownership of domestic equities, and regulatory arbitrage also serves as a barrier. A number of trade-promoting policies have been adopted; among them are the ECOWAS customs clearance and documentation procedures, the Pre-Arrival Assessment and Report System (PAARS) and the single window clearing process to ensure speedy clearance at the ports. Nigeria also uses Integrated Custom Information System (NICIS) to monitor trade, while WAMZ member States equally adopted the Inter-State Road Transit of Goods (ISRT) and the formation of the National Road Transport and Transit Trade Facilitation Committees. However, the execution of the agreement remained a problem across the Zone due to the continued presence of roadblocks, lack of weighbridges as well as unpleasant activities by some uniformed personnel along some transit routes. Other challenges are the lack of a clearly defined regulatory framework and institution, unstable exchange rate, weak regional payment and transfer systems, large informal sector, and limited formal intra-regional trade. Therefore, it is recommended that the monetary, fiscal, trade and exchange rate policies be strengthened and harmonised across all member states.

Chapter ten provides an overview of the security situation

in WAMZ and examines the factors responsible for insecurity as well as the implications of insecurity on the integration Agenda of the WAMZ. A successful economic integration agenda in the West African Monetary Zone (WAMZ) can hardly be achieved in an atmosphere devoid of peace and security of lives and property. The intensity and incidence of internal and external conflicts in WAMZ countries were moderate till around 2018, when violent crimes increased. The global peace index shows that West Africa has recorded a slight fall in peace in 2021 and 2022. The index further reveals that terrorism remains a serious threat in WAMZ, accounting for not less than 48 percent of total deaths in the zones, while Nigeria is the major affected country. A number of factors have been identified to explain the persistence of insecurity and violent crimes in the zone. These include the inter-ethnic struggle for political power; weak institutional structure; poor governance; religious extremism; scuffling for natural resource control; and persistent socioeconomic inequalities. The prevalence of insecurity affects integration directly by increasing the costs of international exchange and also indirectly by negatively influencing productive activities and trade-supporting assets.

The role of the Africa Export and Import Bank (AFREXIMBANK) in the promotion of trade in WAMZ and ECOWAS at large is examined in chapter twelve. The bank provides a number of programmes and facilities to promote African export as well as intra-Africa trade.

Among the facilities are different funded and unfunded credits to banks involved in trading activities, such as export-import financing facilities, pre- and post-export financing, and reimbursement guarantee facilities, among others. The bank also provides direct pre- and post-export financing to firms, particularly those firms with financial statements of not less than US $2 million and an annual trade volume of not less than US $10 million. The bank equally provides risk-sharing and risk-bearing programmes. The Pan African Payment Settlement System (PAPSS) was launched in Ghana by AFREXIMBANK; it is expected this system will significantly reduce the cost, time, and duration of cross-border trade. It is recorded that between 1993 and 2021, the bank approved over US $97.7 billion in loans and advances on trade financing activities in Africa. Despite the progress made in trade financing, the following are identified as challenges facing trade financing – weak local banking system, inadequate coverage of trade financing activities by the poor insurance scheme, high level of uncertainties in the financial sector, frequent changes in regulatory policies and policy discrepancies, and high cost of compliance, among others. Therefore, efforts should be directed by the different stakeholders to tackle these challenges so as to maximize the full benefits of the trade financing programmes and facilities by AFREXIMBANK and other financial institutions.

Chapter thirteen provides an overview of the financial

integration experiences in the European Union (EU) and Association of Southeast Asian Nations (ASEAN), while lessons are drawn for the WAMZ integration agenda. Financial integration in the EU and ASEAN are among the major milestone experiences in the world. Although an economic bloc among European countries has been in existence since the 1950s as a measure to prevent the reoccurrence of World War II experience, the process of financial integration in Europe started around the 1990s. The Delors Committee Report of 1989 outlined a plan for the resurrection of the EMU, which led to the 1992 Treaty that eventually led to the establishment of the single currency and the European Central Bank (ECB). The announcement of the Financial Services Action Plan (FSAP) in May 1999 was a significant milestone for financial integration in the EU. The FSAP's goal was to remove legal and market barriers that impede cross-border financial services supply and the free movement of money inside the EU, as well as to provide a fair playing field for market players. The Euro, which is the common currency in the EU, was initially established as book money in 1999, pending the introduction of Euro banknotes and coins in January 2002. Given a transition period, which spanned between January 1999 and December 2001, the use of the Euro was based on the principle of "no compulsion, no prohibition".

As for the experience of the Association of Southeast Asian Nations (ASEAN), the bloc was founded on August 8,

1967, in Bangkok, Thailand, with the signing of the ASEAN Declaration (Bangkok Declaration) by the founding five countries: Thailand, Singapore, the Philippines, Malaysia, and Indonesia. Brunei Darussalam joined on 7 January 1984, followed by Vietnam on July 28, 1995, Lao PDR and Myanmar on July 23, 1997, and Cambodia on April 30, 1999, forming what is now ASEAN's ten member states. Since the Asian financial crisis of 1997 – 1998, the ASEAN bloc has worked tirelessly to improve the framework of financial integration and ensure regional financial stability. The following regional policy arrangement facilitated monetary integration in ASEAN, The ASEAN Preferential Trading Agreement (APTA), ASEAN Industrial Projects (AIPs), ASEAN Industrial Complementation (AIC), and ASEAN Industrial Joint Ventures were among them (AIJVs). The most important of the four was APTA, which was the first attempt to increase intra-ASEAN trade through institutional integration and regional trade preferences. The AIPs, on the other hand, was intended to construct a large-scale, inter-governmental initiative in each member country. The AIJVs and AICs were established to encourage specialisation in complementary goods and to allow resource pooling. Rapid economic growth and development were recorded in ASEAN countries for more than three decades, which was also instrumental to the integration of the sub-region.

The EU monetary integration was established irrespective

of disparities in political and economic structure as well as economic development. There was also a gap between required coordination and institutional capability in the EU countries. This provides a lesson for WAMZ's financial integration agenda. The experience of the EU shows that rigidity in timelines and macroeconomic convergence criteria efforts is not necessary; rather, political and economic institutions that will be in charge of implementing regional integration initiatives should be emphasised. The ASEAN experience indicates the possibility of attaining financial integration in WAMZ. The two sub-regions have some similar characteristics; specifically, they are similar in the areas of economic, political, demographic, cultural, and linguistic, as well as colonial historical diversity.

Chapter fourteen presents the perspectives of the author based on the experience gathered first as Director of the Financial Integration Department between 2011 to 2016 and later as Director General West African Monetary Institute between 2017 to 2021, in six areas that will propel economic integration efforts in WAMZ. The six areas are (i) the link between technological advancement and single currency agenda; (ii) the need for a regional regulatory sandbox in WAMZ; (iii) the need to transform WAMI into a commission; (iv) the harmonisation of statistics among member countries; (v) the need for women empowerment; and (vi) the need to estimate informal cross-border trade. It is argued that technological advances and a single currency in an economic union are not substitutes for each other; instead, they can complement each other. Technology can facilitate the operationalisation of the single currency agenda of countries striving to promote regional economic integration. Therefore, technology can serve as a facilitator in achieving a single currency objective in the WAMZ sub-region. The second area is the need to establish a regulatory sandbox as a response to rapid innovations in the financial sector and the consequences of challenges in WAMZ. This will provide an avenue for engagement with FinTech firms in the payment space, which will further increase the potential for advancing the financial inclusion of those who are hitherto excluded and the underserved customers. The WAMZ Convergence Council in 2014 proposed the establishment of a Commission to provide a platform to make meaningful dialogue on issues of common interest among the Member States of the WAMZ and to speed up the economic integration process in ECOWAS. Following the review of the cost implications of establishing the proposed Commission, it is, however, proposed in this chapter that WAMI should be transformed into a commission rather than establishing a new commission as a separate organisation.

The chapter also contributes to the need to harmonise statistics in WAMZ. Though WAMZ countries have made some progress over the past two decades to strengthen statistical systems towards improving the production and dissemination of comparable economic, financial, and social statistics, the supply of harmonised and comparable statistics from member states has been less than satisfactory to date. The major challenges facing this effort include differences in data collection instruments and methodologies, limited institutional and financial capacity, and inadequate use of modern information technology. Thus, there is a need for more collaborative efforts to strengthen statistical systems and develop a project to support the efforts of National Statistics Offices. The author equally emphasises in this chapter the need to empower women so as to close the gender financial inclusion gap in WAMZ and promote the integration agenda. Economic empowerment of women would mean more income for women and more access to the financial sector. When more women are able to access and use financial services, their ability to invest and undertake productive activities increases. It is recorded that both fiscal and monetary authorities in WAMZ countries intensify efforts toward women's economic and financial empowerment. Finally, a substantial amount of cross-border trade in the WAMZ sub-region is informal and mostly unrecorded. The low intra-regional trade is partly attributed to significant unrecorded cross-border trade, among other issues. It is recommended that all countries in WAMZ conduct Informal Cross-border Trade (ICBT) survey to provide comprehensive and reliable data as well as information on external trade.

Section One
Prospects And Challenges Of Integration In WAMZ

Chapter I

Evolution, Operation, And Institutional Structures Of West Africa Monetary Zone

The economic integration initiatives among African countries started in 1960 when African Union was established for the economic and political integration of the continent (*Kennes & Dinka, 2007*). In line with the mission of promoting economic cooperation, the countries in the west of Sub-Saharan Africa came together in 1975 to form the Economic Community of West African States (ECOWAS). The current member states are Benin, Burkina Faso, Cape Verde, Côte d'Ivoire, The Gambia, Ghana, Guinea, Guinea-Bissau, Liberia, Mali, Niger, Nigeria, Senegal, Sierra Leone, and Togo. Afterwards, the West African Economic and Monetary Union (UEMOA among the Francophone countries) was established in

1994, while the West African Monetary Zone (WAMZ) was established in 2000 among the Anglophone countries.

The West African Monetary Zone (WAMZ) is a regional monetary and financial institution that was created by a group of five West African countries – The Gambia, Ghana, Guinea, Nigeria, and Sierra Leone while Liberia joined in 2010, making the number six. All the members of the group are from English-speaking countries, except Guinea, which is Francophone. The main purpose of WAMZ is to achieve full economic and monetary integration of the member countries and, eventually, full economic integration in the ECOWAS sub-region. The group had a plan of introducing a common currency to be called the "Eco" by the year 2003, but this has been postponed many times.

The statute establishing WAMZ made provisions for the establishment of the West African Monetary Institute (WAMI) with the mandate to make necessary preparations for the introduction of a unified currency, "Eco", among the WAMZ sub-region and the establishment of the West African Central Bank (WACB) for the coordination and management of the financial and monetary activities of the member countries.

The main aim of WAMZ is to integrate both the economic and financial activities of the members through full capital account liberalisation, cross-listing of stocks, regional currency convertibility or quoting and trading in WAMZ currencies, banking supervision, and cross-border payment systems. To achieve the broad aims of WAMZ, the member states intended to unify monetary and economic policies, liberalise regional commerce, monitor members' payment balances, give members better access to resources from the major international organisations, and give the community a more effective tool at the global collective bargaining fora. However, the commencement of full monetary union in WAMZ was premeditated on the fulfilment of primary and secondary convergence criteria. Due to the inability of the member countries to fulfil the convergence criteria, the commencement dates of introducing the single currency have been postponed five times – January 2003, July 2005, December 2009, January 2015, and 2020 (West African Monetary Institute, 2022).

According to WAMI (2002), the primary convergence criteria are as follows:

- Achievement of the moderate inflation rate.
- Achievement of sustainable and moderate budget deficit to GDP.
- Moderation of finance of budget deficit by Central Bank.
- Maintenance of good foreign exchange reserve.

The secondary convergence criteria required are as follows:

- Maintenance of minimal public borrowings.
- Maintenance of robust tax revenue to GDP ratio.
- Maintenance of a minimum wage bill to tax revenue ratio.
- Maintenance of stability of exchange rate.
- Maintenance of robust public investment-to-tax revenue ratio.
- Achievement of positive interest rate.

This chapter is meant to provide an evolutionary and structural composition of WAMZ. Therefore, apart from the introductory section, the remaining part of the chapter contains the profile of the member countries and the institutional and operational structures of WAMZ.

Profile Of WAMZ Member Countries

In this sub-section, a summary of the geographical, political, and economic profiles of the six member countries of WAMZ is presented.

Geographical, Historical And Economic Profile Of The Gambia

The Gambia is a West African country located on the Atlantic Coast and surrounded by Senegal. The country has a land area of 11,295 km^2, with a projected population of over two million in 2021. The country gained independence on 18th February 1965, with the capital city at Banjul and the official currency as Dalasi. The country is a member of ECOWAS and a founding member of WAMZ. About 50% of the country's population lives in urban areas, while approximately three-quarters of the population is engaged in traditional subsistence agriculture. The services sector is the largest part of the economy, accounting for over 63% of the GDP, with tourism and banking services being the major contributors. Agriculture is the second largest, contributing about 21.4% of the GDP. Over 75% of the population depends on the sector, where peanuts, rice, millet, sorghum, corn, sesame, fish, palm kernels, vegetables, forestry, livestock, and fishing are the major agricultural products. Gambia has a GDP of over $2 billion (US Dollars) and a growth rate of 5.63% in 2021.

The strong macroeconomic operation helped to minimise the financial deficit, escape debt slavery, and bring international reserves closer to prudential situations (*African Development Bank Group, 2022a*). The country's profitable growth was strong at 6.2 in 2019, supported by improving confidence and record tourist arrivals. The COVID-19 outbreak brought about a 0.2 percent decline in economic growth and a minimal 3.0 percent increase in real GDP per capita, reversing the progress made on eradicating poverty. But after that, economic growth began to increase, with an estimated 5.6 percent increase in GDP (2.6 in terms of per capita) in 2021. All industries expanded as tourist arrivals exceeded expectations, and record-high remittances kept the construction and distribution industries afloat.

Consumption by households and public investment confirmed growth on the demand side. The monetary environment remained favourable in 2020 and 2021. In 2021, inflation rose to 7.5 from 5.9 in 2020 as a result of high energy and freight costs. The financial deficit expanded from 2.2 percent of GDP in 2020 to 4.0 percent of GDP in 2021 as a result of higher spending in the health sector and subsidies to households and government-run businesses to lessen the COVID-19 shock. Public debt decreased from 85.0 percent of GDP in 2020 to 82.9 percent in 2021 leading to a very high risk of debt unsustainability and financial crises in the country.

The current account deficit increased from 3.3 of GDP in 2020 to 9.3 of GDP in 2021 due to a decline in exports and an increase in imports; this expansion was largely supported by FDI and capital transfers, which also helped stabilise the Dalasi. Gross sanctioned reserves climbed from $352.1 million in 2020 to $496.50 million in 2021, thanks in part to the Special Drawing Rights grant of $85 million, which was utilised to pay for national expenses incurred during the COVID-19 pandemic. Despite the blow from COVID-19 weakening asset quality, the financial sector continued to be profitable, liquid, and well-subsidised. By mid-2021, the ratio of Non-Performing Loans (NPLs) to gross loans had worsened to 5.6 from 4.5 in June 2020. Due to COVID-19, the poverty rate, as determined by the World Bank's $3.20 per day 2011 PPP line, remained high at 35.5 in 2020 and 35.1 in 2021. Hence, macroeconomic parameters indicated that the Gambia needs to rejig the economy to meet the criteria needed to achieve the objectives of WAMZ.

Geographical, Historical And Economic Profile Of Ghana

Ghana is located in the West Africa sub-region of Africa, bordered by Burkina Faso in the North, Togo in the East, and Ivory Cost in the West. It has a land area of 239.46km^2 and a population projection of over 31 million in 2021. The county gained independence from the British on 6th March 1957 and has about 50% of its population living in urban areas. The country's capital city is Accra, with Cedi as the official currency for domestic transactions. The country is a member of ECOWAS and a founding member of WAMZ. The county has a GDP of over $77 billion (US Dollars) and a GDP growth rate of 5.36 percent in 2021. The major mineral resources available in the country are gold, timber, diamonds, bauxite, manganese, and fish. The county also flourishes in agricultural items like cocoa, timber, pineapples, cashew, spices, and rubber. The country earns her foreign earnings mainly from gold and cocoa.

Ghana faces a serious risk of a high debt burden as the state debt climbed to 81.1, and the overall fiscal deficit doubled to 15.2 in 2020. According to preliminary financial figures for the first half of 2021, the government may have reduced spending to make up for earnings issues. 5.1% of GDP was the overall fiscal deficit. In the first half of 2021, headline inflation equalled 7.8 and concluded at 10.0 as a full-time standard. This was brought on by increases in exchange rates, food and non-food prices, and it has persisted through the first quarter of 2022. Inflation hit 15.7 as of the end of February 2022, the highest level since December 2016. In early 2021, exports rose more slowly than imports due to the domestic recovery, although constrained global demand for goods persisted. As a result, the current account deficit is predicted to decrease from 2.3 of GDP in 2020 to 2.4 of GDP in 2019.

Over the medium term, it is anticipated that Ghana's economy will continue to grow quite strongly due to rising export prices for essential goods and robust domestic demand. In 2022, growth was anticipated to reach 5.5. It is projected that growth will be broadly based, driven by services, assiduity and husbandry sub-sectors of the economy. The government's ambitious economic policies have increased profit from 16 percent in 2021 to 20 percent in 2022. By taking some stringent financial measures, it is expected that the deficit will drop from 12 in 2021 to 4.5 in 2024.

Geographical, Historical, And Economic Profile Of Guinea

Guinea is a West African country boarded by the Atlantic Ocean in the West, Senegal in the North, and Liberia in the South. The country has a land area of 245,860 km^2 and a projected population of over 13 million in 2021. The country gained independence from France on 2nd October 1958, with the capital city at Conakry and the official currency as the Guinea Franc. The country is a member of ECOWAS and a founding member of WAMZ. The country had a GDP of over $158 billion (US Dollars) and a GDP growth rate of 3.12% in 2021. The country gets about 95% of her export earnings from the mining sector, while the remaining 5% is contributed by agriculture. Major mineral products produced by the country are petroleum oil, aluminium, bauxite, diamond, and a vast quantity of untapped iron ore. The major agricultural products available in the country are rice, cassava, coffee, banana, potatoes, pineapples, sheep, goats, timber products, and cattle.

Guinea is blessed with abundant natural resources, particularly those related to mining and hydropower, which have the potential to generate considerable wealth.

Experience has shown, however, that mining and hydropower can have substantial adverse effects on biodiversity and the environment, both directly and indirectly. Gender disparities in employment, inadequate human capital, low productivity in agriculture, a dearth of high-quality agricultural inputs, restricted access to finance, and high severance are additional significant challenges that hinder the country's economic growth. Some of these challenges hinder the extent of women's involvement in the country's growth and development trajectory.

Agriculture is the nation's primary source of employment and is essential for the elimination of poverty and the development of pastoral communities. Even though the country has favourable weather and climatic condition suitable for sustainable development, Guinea needs to embrace inclusive governance to fully realise her growth potential and to accelerate the level of her structural transformation process. Furthermore, with the increase in average temperatures and a drop in the volume of rainfall, especially in the North-Western and North-Eastern regions, Guinea is becoming more vulnerable to the problem of climate change.

The economic growth was approximately 10% in 2016 and 2017 and then slowed to 5.8% in 2018, though growth is still strong and is being supported by FDI in the mining industry. The mining industry expanded at an approximately 50 percent annual rate in 2016 and 2017, whereas the non-mining industry recorded a 5.4 percent growth rate in 2018 due to robust structural investment and continued growth in the primary and tertiary sectors. Due to rising energy and electricity costs, the inflation rate in 2018 was 9.8, approaching double-digit conditions. The financial balance position of the economy moved from -2.1 of GDP in 2017 to -1.1 of GDP in 2018 due to lower energy price subsidies, rising electricity costs, and restrictions on public sector hiring and promotion.

Geographical, Historical, And Economic Profile Of Liberia

Liberia is a West African country bordered by Guinea in the North, Ivory Coast in the East, and the Atlantic Ocean in the South-East. The country has a land area of 111,369 km^2, and a population projection of over 5 million in 2021. The country emanated as the settlement of freed slaves from the United States in 1822 and gained independence on 26th July 1847, becoming the first African country to obtain independence. The country's capital city is Monrovia, and its currency is the Liberian Dollar. The country is a member of ECOWAS and officially joined WAMZ in 2010. The country is categorised as a low-income country by World Bank. Over 70% of the population, and three-quarters of the rural population, participate in the agricultural sector, producing rubber, cocoa, coffee, and palm oil.

The country also has a vast number of mineral resources like diamond, gold, iron ore, and tin.

The nation has abundant natural resources such as iron ore, diamonds, gold, fertile soil, fisheries, and forestry. Real GDP growth is anticipated to reach 3.6% in 2021, indicating the first increase in per capita GDP since 2016. Nevertheless, it is projected that poverty will marginally rise as per capita consumption continues to decline, with imports of goods driving the increase. In view of the successful efforts of the government, inflationary pressures have been reduced. By July 2021, the rate of inflation had slowly decreased to 7.1 due to falling food prices and the Central Bank of Liberia's cautious financial position.

The first five months of 2021 saw an improvement in Liberia's financial situation because of higher profits and spending. The Liberian government established a special budget to cover financial operations from July 1 to December 31, 2021. The new Public Financial Management (PFM) statute would require Liberia to align its financial time to the scheduled time by 2022. Between July 1 and December 31, 2021, total earnings and subventions are expected to be $429 million, or 12.7 percent of GDP, with domestic profit accounting for 70 percent of public coffers.

The special budget is expected to have a fiscal deficit of 0.9 percent of GDP, which will be entirely covered by loans from outside. It is projected that Liberia's current account deficit will decrease in 2021. In contrast to resurgent global demand, the price recovery of the major import items has increased export value and improved the trade balance. Liberia's frugality is expected to rise by a typical 4.9 points between 2022 and 2023. Both the mining industry and outside demand will play a significant role in driving growth. Construction, farming, and mining activity are expected to rise as a result of structural improvements. By 2023, it is predicted that the per capita GDP will be back to pre-COVID-19 levels (*African Development Bank Group, 2022d*).

Geographical, Historical, And Economic Profile Of Nigeria

Nigeria is located in West Africa, bothered by Niger in the North, Cameroun in the East, and Benin in the West; it is the most populous African country, with over 250 ethnic groups, a land area of 923.km^2, and a population projection of over 211 million in 2021 (*World Bank, 2016a*). The country gained independence from the British on 1st October 1960, with 36 states, Abuja as the federal capital, and Naira as the official currency. Nigeria has been a founding member of ECOWAS since 1975 and of WAMZ since 2000. The country is the largest economy of WAMZ, with a GDP of over $440 billion (US Dollars) and a GDP growth rate of 3.65% in 2021. The country's vast population is spread across agriculture, mining, manufacturing, and industrial sectors. The country largely depends on petroleum for foreign exchange earnings, with the agricultural sector playing second fiddle.

A vast range of underutilised mineral resources is also present in Nigeria, including coal, bauxite, tantalite, gold, drum, iron ore, limestone, niobium, lead, and zinc. Despite significant natural resource deposits, Nigeria's mining industry is still in its infancy. The nation still has significant developmental problems, such as the need to diversify its frugality and lessen its reliance on oil, repair its weak institutional framework, create strong and efficient institutions, and handle governance issues and public fiscal operating systems. Poverty reduction has been adversely impacted by inequality, which is still widespread in terms of income and job opportunities. The root cause of widespread poverty, native inequality, and social and political unrest is a lack of employment opportunities. High pricing and high affectation in 2020 are expected to have forced an additional 7 million Nigerians into poverty.

Nigeria's economy increased by 3.6 percent from a contraction of 1.8 percent in 2020 to an expansion of 4.4 percent in the non-oil sector versus a contraction of 8.3 percent in the oil sector of the economy. Due to a small increase in earnings, the financial deficit decreased from 5.4 of GDP in 2020 to 4.8 of GDP in 2021. Also, in 2021, the public debt was US$95.8 billion, or roughly 22.5 percent of GDP. Periodic average inflation increased to 17.0 in 2021 from 13.2 in 2020, exceeding the central bank's intended range of 6 to 9. In December 2021, the ratio of non-performing loans to total loans was 4.9, while the capital-acceptability rate was 14. The above statistics show that the macroeconomic environment of the country needs a great deal of restructuring and reforms for the realisation and achievement of the lofty objectives of WAMZ.

Geographical, Historical, And Economic Profile Of Sierra Leone

Sierra Leone is a West African Country bothered by Liberia in the South-East and Guinea in the North. The country has a land area of 71,740 km2, and a projected population of over 8 million in 2021. The country gained independence on 27th April 1961 from the British; its capital city is Freetown, and its official currency is Leone. The country is a member of ECOWAS and a founding member of WAMZ. The country has a GDP of over $4 billion (US Dollars) and a GDP growth rate of 3.05 in 2021 (World Bank (2016b). The country is rich in mineral resources, has one of the largest deposits of rutile in the world and is among the top ten diamond-producing countries. The country's major mineral resources are platinum, gold, bauxite, iron ore, titanium, chromite and manganese. Over 80% of the country's population engages in substance agriculture producing rice, cocoa, palm kernels, peanuts, cashew, poultry, cattle, sheep, and fish. The sector contributes about 71% of the GDP and about 25% of the export earnings. As a result of the COVID-19 epidemic, which caused global force chain disruptions and lockdown measures, Sierra Leone's economy shrank by 2 percent. The year 2020 saw a 4 percent decline in GDP per capita, thereby affecting the poverty reduction programmes of the government. Real GDP was projected to increase by 4.2 in 2021 as a result of the government's policy to ameliorate the negative consequences of the pandemic and the relaxation of COVID-related limitations. In March 2021, headline inflation was 8.9; however, by the end of June, it had sharply risen to 10.2, reflecting a spike in the cost of food and energy. In June 2021, food inflation was 17.1, far more than the 9.9 pre-COVID-19 level. The COVID-19 epidemics were compounded by inadequate access to vaccines, a sluggish immunization effort, and a resurgence of the epidemic.

Quantitative Comparison Of WAMZ Member Countries' Profile

The demographic (proxied by population size), geographic (proxied by land mass), and economic (proxied by GDP) weights of WAMZ member countries were computed as a ratio of West Africa. The economic implications of the parameters are discussed. Each parameter was calculated using the formula:

$$\text{Demographic Weight (\%)} = \frac{\textbf{Total Country Population}}{\textbf{Population of ECOWAS Region}} \times \frac{100}{1}$$

$$\text{Geographical Weight (\%)} = \frac{\textbf{Total Country Geographical Area}}{\textbf{Total ECOWAS Geographical Region}} \times \frac{100}{1}$$

$$\text{Economic Weight (\%)} = \frac{\textbf{Country Gross Domestic Product}}{\textbf{ECOWAS Region Gross Domestic Product}} \times \frac{100}{1}$$

As shown in Table 1, Nigeria is the strongest member of WAMZ. The country's demography is more than triple the sum of the remaining members of the union. The geographical weight of the country is more than half of the remaining countries. It can also be seen that the economic weight of the country far out-weight that of other countries added together. This implies that the realisation of WAMZ objectives relies heavily on the economic and political performances of Nigeria.

FIGURE 2.1: DEMOGRAPHY WEIGHT (%)

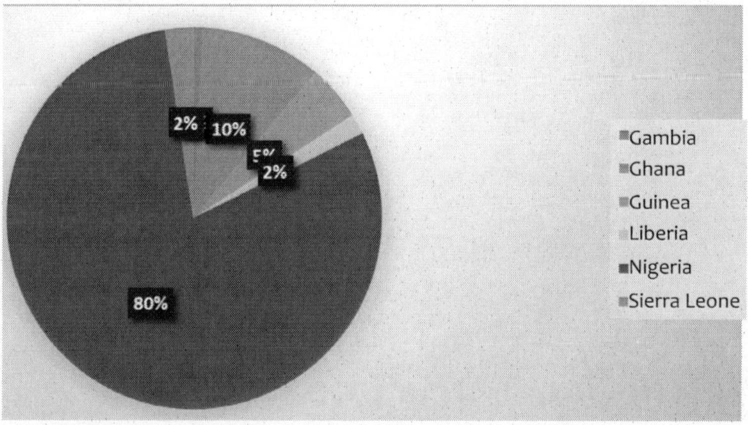

Figure 2.2: Geographic Weight (%)

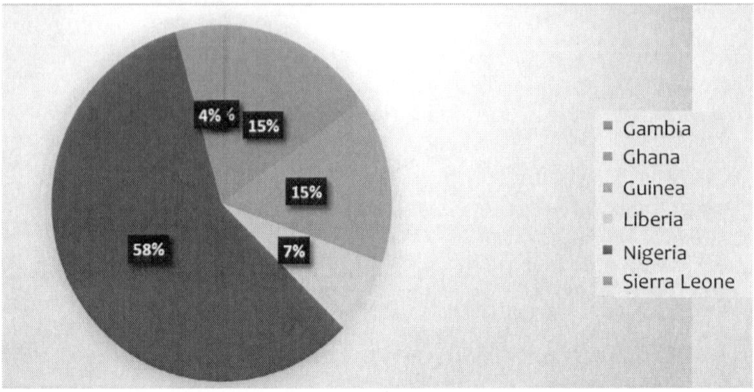

Figure 2.3: Economic Weight (%)

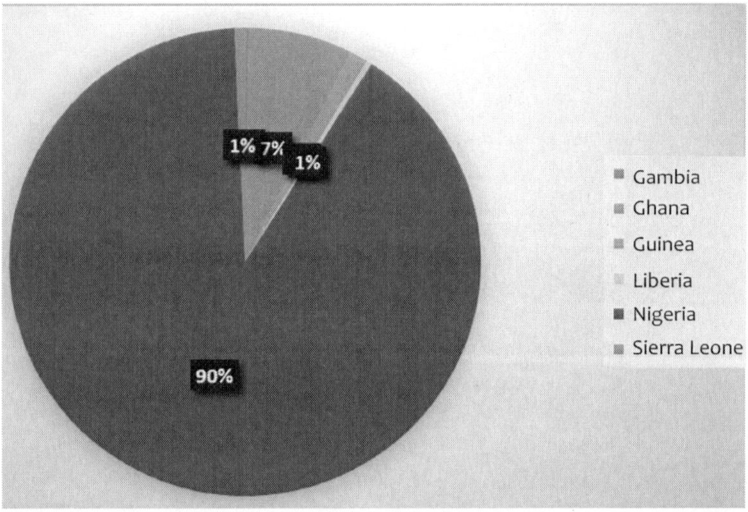

Institutional Structure Of WAMZ

Six institutions have been created under the WAMZ Agreement to facilitate arrangements for the eventual introduction of a single currency in the zone. The institutions are as follows: The West African Monetary Institute (WAMI); the Authority of Heads of States and Government; the Convergence Council of Ministers and Central Bank Governors; the Technical Committee; and The WAMZ Stabilization and Cooperation Fund (SCF).

The West African Monetary Institute (WAMI) is an organization set up in 2001 in Accra, Ghana, to articulate policy and institutional frameworks for the optimum operation of WAMZ. WAMI, since March 2001, has opened for business. The main purposes of WAMI are:

- Keeping track of member countries' macroeconomic performance and progress toward confluence and acting accordingly by complying with applicable laws and offering recommendations;
- Facilitating the harmonisation of the agreement and WAMZ bills with the various member nations' fiscal and banking legislation and regulations. When a shared central bank is established, the the adjustment would be beneficial in the administration of fiscal policy;
- Formulating the procedures and evaluating the peculiarities involved in creating a shared central bank and a common currency;
- Increasing public awareness of the financial integration process and eventual introduction of the single currency in the zone;

- Increasing public awareness of the financial integration process and eventual introduction of the single currency in the zone among the people of member countries.

The Authority of Heads of State and Government is the zone's political and governing body, and it is ultimately in charge of ensuring that the WAMZ's goals are accomplished. It is made up of the chairpersons and heads of the member nations. The WAMZ and its institutions are under the control of the Convergence Council of Ministers and Central Bank Governors. The Council consists of the Central Bank Governors and representative Ministers from the member nations. Its duties include making recommendations to the Authority of Heads of State and Government. The Technical Committee is made up of specialists from the member nations. The Committee collaborates with WAMI and examines and contributes to the completion of technical and policy materials created by the institute to facilitate integration. Its duty is to provide the Convergence Council with policy suggestions and guidance. The WAMZ Stabilization and Cooperation Fund (SCF) is established to provide financial support to members whose balance of payments may experience brief disequilibrium. Member nations contribute their $100 million (US Dollars) capital base in two instalments of $50 million (US Dollars).

Operational Structure Of West African Monetary Zone

The operational framework of WAMZ is based on the payment methods that are built to ensure hitch-free monetary and financial transactions within and among member countries. The operational mechanisms are financial products and strategies that were developed and tested in some of the member countries. According to WAMI (2022), the payment systems are based on the fulfilment of the following objectives:

- Ensuring that financial transactions among the member countries are risk-free.
- Ensuring a robust exchange of funds and securities among the members.
- The transition from cash and paper-based payments to electronic modes of payment.
- Ensuring that government bills are effective and an accepted means of payment.
- Improvement of the WAMZ National Central Banks' (NCBs) financial operation capabilities.
- Alignment of the legislative framework of WAMZ member nations to their internal and cross-border payments.

The achievement of the above objectives is premised on the e-payment system, tagged Payment System Development

Project, funded by the African Development Bank and is being experimented in The Gambia, Liberia, Guinea, and Sierra Leone. The project is meant to upgrade and automate the payment systems of the aforementioned countries to the level available in Ghana and Nigeria. For smooth financial and monetary systems in the member countries, the following payment systems were implemented:

- Real Time Gross Settlement (RTGS) System.
- Scripless Securities Settlement System (SSSS).
- Automated Clearing House System.
- Automated Cheque Processing System.
- Core Banking Application for the Central Banks, and
- Pan Africa Payment and Settlement System.

The Financial Integration Department (FID) of WAMI is another operational room wherefrom many activities are coordinated. The major functions of the unit are as follows:

- Participating in the draft of the Zonal Multilateral Convergence and WAMI Annual Reports.
- Supervision of the payment system and infrastructure projects in the WAMZ.
- Collaboration with development partners in capacity building and financial sector development programmes.

- Collaboration with the legal department in representing WAMI at the Legal and Institutional Issues Committee (LIIC) of the WAMZ.
- Publication of the study that relates financial activities of WAMZ.

FID is dedicated to fulfilling its primary responsibilities, which include ensuring that the financial sectors are integrated and encouraging Member States of the WAMZ to enhance their payments infrastructure. The pension market is still the only industry that hasn't been included in the WAMZ financial integration setup.

Conclusion

WAMZ is a sub-regional financial and monetary union that is meant to harmonise and unify the financial and economic activities of the member countries. However, the unfavourable economic realities of the member countries have made it difficult to satisfy the primary and secondary convergence criteria, which are needed for the economic stability and equivalence of the member countries. This has led to the postponement of the adoption of a singular uniform currency in the sub-region five times. The current economic situations of most member countries make the realisation of lofty objectives difficult in the nearest future.

Chapter 2

Actualizing WAMZ Objectives: Challenges And Prospects

It is common for nation states that share geographical borders to form themselves into integrated regional blocs in order to take advantage of the close proximity and to promote trade in goods and services, as well as encourage labour flows among themselves (Bah, 2015). In pursuance of the integration agenda, nations go into monetary unions where countries would agree to give up their national currencies for a single and shared currency. According to Bayoumi and Ostry (2010), a monetary union is formed when member countries of an integrated economic region agree to sacrifice their individual monetary autonomy in preference for a monetary union. The main argument for the creation of a monetary union is that sharing the same currency reduces the cost of trade between member nations, given that the transactions are made in the same currency. Equally, uncertainty related to trade costs would reduce with monetary union. In addition, the risk of the exchange rate varying between the time of purchase and the time of payment would disappear when countries use the same currency.

In 1975 countries in West Africa came together to form the Economic Community of West African States (ECOWAS) to promote economic cooperation among member states to raise living standards and promote economic development. The current member states are Benin, Burkina Faso, Cape Verde, Côte d'Ivoire, The Gambia, Ghana, Guinea, Guinea-Bissau, Liberia, Mali, Niger, Nigeria, Senegal, Sierra Leone, and Togo. When the objective of creating a monetary union with a single currency in ECOWAS could not be realised, seven members regrouped in 1994 to establish a monetary union called the West African Monetary and Economic Union (also known under the French acronym UEMOA). Members of the union adopted Franc CFA as a common currency which is controlled by one central bank, Banque Centrale des Etats de l'Afrique de l'Ouest (BCEAO). The member countries are Benin, Burkina Faso, Côte d'Ivoire, Mali, Niger, Senegal, and Togo. It is important to note that all the member states are Francophone countries. The treaty that established the union came into force in 1994 after member states ratified the treaty. Guinea Bissau joined the union in 1997, making the membership eight in total.

The level of success attained by WAEMU in terms of integration among members and the stability enjoined in the union make members unwilling to forgo WAEMU for a larger ECOWAS full economic integration objective. This further frustrated the objective of creating a single central bank and common currency in ECOWAS. Hence, non-WAEMU countries pushed for the creation of a second monetary union. Consequently, the West African Monetary Zone (WAMZ) was established in December 2000 by the Authority of the Heads of State and Governments of Gambia, Ghana, Guinea, Nigeria, and Sierra Leone, who were not members of WAEMU, with a mandate to coordinate regional efforts aimed at achieving full ECOWAS regional monetary integration. In 2010 Liberia joined the union bringing the membership of WAMZ to six.

A two-stage implementation approach (medium and long term) was agreed upon for the ECOWAS region's full monetary integration. In the medium term, WAMZ is to integrate the non-WAEMU countries (Gambia, Ghana, Guinea, Liberia, Nigeria, and Sierra Leone) into the West Africa monetary union (WAMU), form one common central bank (Central Bank of West Africa) and introduce a single common currency (ECO) (Balogun, 2009). In the long run, WAMZ is to be merged with WAEMU to form a single monetary union in ECOWAS with a central bank and a single common currency.

The main objective of the West African Monetary Zone (WAMZ) is to progressively unify all West African countries into one integrated economic area with a single currency, one central bank and a common monetary zone. The target of WAMZ members was to create a common currency for all countries in ECOWAS by January 2003 and to work towards merging WAMZ and WAEMU into a single monetary union by January 2004 (Asante & Masson, 2001). The target of creating a single currency in 2003 has been postponed many times, first to 2005, then to 2009, 2015, 2020, and now to 2022.

These targets could not be met after over two decades of the existence of WAMZ. The actualisation of the objectives of WAMZ is fundamental if full integration must be achieved in the ECOWAS region. Therefore, this chapter aims to identify the key challenges responsible for the non-actualisation of WAMZ objectives as well as the prospects of WAMZ. The remaining parts of this body of work are divided into:

- Efforts towards actualizing WAMZ objectives in section 2.
- Assessment of integration in WAMZ in section 3.
- Challenges of actualizing WAMZ Objectives in section 4.

- Prospects of actualizing WAMZ objectives in section 5.
- And section 6 concludes the chapter.

Efforts Towards Actualizing WAMZ Objectives

To achieve full economic and monetary integration in WAMZ and ECOWAS, several steps have been taken to promote integration among member countries in trade, banking and finance, capital market, insurance, as well as policies and regulations. After the creation of WAMZ in 2000, the first step was the establishment of the West African Monetary Institute (WAMI) in 2001 as a technical body to undertake measures for the creation of a full monetary union with one central bank and single currency. Hence, the institute has the mandate to monitor the progress of member countries in meeting the convergence criteria and to take measures that will facilitate trade integration, financial integration, integration of payment systems and harmonisation of statistics across countries. Since its inception, WAMI has made significant efforts directed at actualising its mandates. These include initiating the modernization of the payment system in 2004, the establishment of the College of Supervisors of the West African Monetary Zone (CSWAMZ) in 2010, the West African Capital Market Integration Council (WACMIC) was also established in 2013, and more recently, the College of Supervisors for Non-Bank

Financial Institutions (CSNBFI) was inaugurated in 2019, and at the meeting of West African Insurance Supervisors Association (WAISA) held in February 2019, it was agreed that the College of Supervisors that will monitor and standardize the operations of the insurance sector be constituted.

To eliminate restrictions in cross-border payment, clearing and settlement systems and eradicate risks involved in the payment process in WAMZ, WAMI started the modernization of the payment system in WAMZ by setting up an e-payment system development project in four countries – The Gambia, Guinea, Liberia, and Sierra Leone. The project, which was completed in 2016, aims to develop and automate the payment system infrastructure. The project consists of different payment system components, which include Real Time Gross Settlement (RTGS) System, Scripless Securities Settlement (SSS) System, Automated Cheque Processing System, Automated Clearing House System, and Core Banking Application (CBA) for the Central Banks.

The Gambia was the first country among the four countries to operationalize all the components of the WAMZ Payments System Development Project in 2012. Guinea and Liberia implemented the project in 2016, and Sierra Leone also completed the introduction of rules and procedures for the operation of the RTGS, ACH, and CSD with a robust pricing mechanism for the use of the systems in the same year. After observing that the four countries have completed the implementation of the WAMZ Payment System Development Project, then the effort is directed to upgrading infrastructure in the form of Local Area Network (LAN) reconfiguration and Metropolitan Area Network (MAN). The MAN and the use of internet technologies provide a dedicated inter-bank communication backbone system for the operation of the RTGS, SSS, ACH, and ACP systems. The project also built Disaster Recovery sites in each of the four countries at a safe distance that does not share the same risk of disaster with the Main Sites.

The CSWAMZ was established in 2010 to provide a common platform for regulators from the WAMZ countries to come together to discuss how to oversee individual and cross-border financial institutions in the zone. Over the year, CSWAMZ made efforts to ensure a safe and stable financial system in the zone via effective exchange and cooperation of information, as well as cross-border supervision. CSWAMZ equally implemented Risk Based Supervision (RBS) in all member states. In 2019, the College of Supervisors for Non-Bank Financial Institutions (CSNBFI) was inaugurated to provide a platform for the exchange of knowledge and information, harmonisation of the legal and regulatory framework, and reviewing developments in the non-bank financial institutions (NBFI) sectors in all member countries of WAMZ. CSNBF also has the mandate to promote financial inclusion and address the risks involved in cross-border transactions of NBFI.

The West African Capital Market Integration Council (WACMIC) was established in 2013 in order to facilitate the integration of capital markets in the sub-region. The Council adopted a three-phased approach to capital market integration, namely – Sponsored Access (Phase 1), Qualified West African Broker (QWAB) (Phase 2), and Fully Integrated West African Securities Market (WASM) (Phase 3). The Council is saddled with the responsibility of managing the processes that will facilitate the formation of an integrated capital market in ECOWAS. The Council, therefore, tried to harmonise the rules and regulations for the issuance and trading of financial securities across countries in ECOWAS. The need for the integration of the insurance sub-sector was identified after revising the roadmap for the actualisation of the single currency agenda. Hence, at the meeting of the West African Insurance Supervisors Association (WAISA) in February 2019, it was recommended that the College of Supervisors that will monitor and standardize the operations in the insurance sub-sector be established. This recommendation is premised on the fact that cross-border operations by insurance companies in the WAMZ are increasing significantly.

Series of meetings are often held to review progress and

design or revise the roadmap to actualise WAMZ objectives.

Assessing The Level Of Integration In WAMZ

The core objective of WAMZ is the attainment of full economic and monetary integration among member countries and ECOWAS at large. Therefore, in this sub-section, the extent of integration in the zone since inception is assessed. An attempt to examine the progress of a regional or sub-regional economic union is not new in literature (*African Union Commission, 2016; Egbuna et al., 2018; Huh & Park, 2017*). Generally, this assessment is based on the extent to which certain criteria have been met. In relation to the WAMZ zone, this study assesses the level of integration in the zone in terms of the following key areas, which are reported to be crucial for the integration of countries within the union (*Egbuna et al., 2018*): trade integration, macroeconomic and financial integration, compliance with the ECOWAS protocol on the free movement of people and goods, institutional integration, and infrastructure integration.

Trade Integration

Trade integration is a key requirement for a successful economic union. Typically, an economic union's trade integration is measured in terms of four key indicators:

- the level of customs duties on imports,
- the share of intra-regional goods imports,
- the share of inter-regional goods exports, and
- the share of intra-regional goods trade as a percentage of total inter-REC trade (*Egbuna et al., 2018*).

The performance of all six countries in the union determines the level of trade integration in the zone. To begin with, available data indicate that intra-regional trade among countries in the zone is still low, possibly due to the similarity in their export and import products (West African Monetary Institute, 2021). In particular, the countries' exports are mainly primary products, while all the countries mainly import manufacturing goods, which are lowly produced by countries in the zone due to lower capacity to manufacture goods. As demonstrated in Table 3.1 below, intra-regional export of the zone expressed as a percentage of the GDP of member countries remains at a low level, and the trend analysis of the statistics suggests no remarkable improvement since the year 2015 as the average intra-WAMZ trade only increased from 0.16% in 2015 to 0.23% in 2020.

The available data on the intra-WAMZ imports even suggests a much worse outcome as the level of importation among member countries remains at a very low level and recorded a slight decrease trend from 0.07% in 2015 to

0.03% in 2020. In terms of the total trade among the member countries expressed as a percentage of their GDP, the countries in the zone record low intra-WAMZ trade, which was 0.26% in 2020. A historical study of the intra-WAMZ trade data suggests that no remarkable improvement has been recorded since 2015, as the trade to GDP only increased by 0.03%, from 0.23% to 0.26%. The implication is that the level of trade integration in WAMZ remains low, and the current trend does not suggest that there is likely to be any remarkable improvement in trade relations among the member states in the shortest possible time.

TABLE 3.1: INTRA-WAMZ TRADE BETWEEN 2015 AND 2020 AS A PERCENTAGE OF GDP

Indicator	Year					
	2015	2016	2017	2018	2019	2020
Intra-WAMZ Export	0.16	0.24	0.168	0.182	0.829	0.229
Intra-WAMZ Import	0.07	0.08	0.06	0.06	0.07	0.03
Intra-WAMZ Trade	0.23	0.32	0.23	0.24	0.90	0.32

Source: *Compiled by the author using WAMZ 2020 report on Trade Integration*

Macroeconomic And Financial Integration

The other key area that is central to the attainment of economic integration by WAMZ countries is macroeconomic and financial integration. This is based on the premonition that a non-integrated macroeconomic system will subject the economies of other members to the negative effect of bad macroeconomic policies from any member states. As part of strategies aimed at tracking the zone's progress toward macroeconomic integration, the WAMZ established a set of macroeconomic convergence criteria, which are divided into primary criteria consisting of four indicators, including single-digit inflation, fiscal deficits of less than 4%, central bank deficit financing of less than 10%, and external reserves that must meet at least three months of the import bill, and secondary criteria consisting of a stable exchange rate that is not more than 10% and total debt to GDP ratio of not more than 4%.

None of the member countries fulfils all the four primary macroeconomic convergent criteria, as Ghana only fulfils two of the criteria (inflation and reserve), the same as Guinea (inflation and fiscal deficit), The Gambia (inflation and central bank financing), and Nigeria (Fiscal Deficit and Reserve), Liberia (Fiscal Deficit), and Sierra Leone (Reserve) fulfil only one criterion each, suggesting that the zone performed below average in 2018. Three of the countries – Ghana, Guinea, and Nigeria fulfilled all the two secondary convergence criteria in 2018, while the other two countries, The Gambia and Sierra Leone, only fulfilled one, indicating good performance with regards to the attainment of secondary convergence criteria. The overall WAMZ performance in primary criteria for the year is 41.6%, while that of secondary is 66.7%. There was a remarkable improvement in the macroeconomic convergence of the zone in 2019 as the overall performance in primary convergence criteria improved from 41.6% in 2018 to 66.7% in 2019. Two countries, the Gambia and Guinea, fully met the primary convergence criteria. The performance on the primary macroeconomic criteria recorded a decline in 2020 from 66.7% to 45.8%, while it remained at 45.8% in 2021, suggesting that countries in the zone are below average in meeting the macroeconomic convergence criteria. Hence, macroeconomic integration in the zone is low.

In terms of financial and fiscal integration, the establishment of a common central bank is essential to the attainment of economic integration in the zone in order to achieve a common currency that would facilitate trade and financial transactions among the member states. The attainment of a single currency among European countries was made easy by the European Central Banks, which coordinate the monetary and economic policies of the member states. The establishment of a common central bank in the zone is yet to be realised, while an attempt to achieve a common currency to be named ECO is equally far from being attained. There is the problem of variation in indirect taxation among the member states. For instance, the value-added tax (VAT) varies substantially across the zone. For the five member countries that use VAT, VAT ranges from 5% in Nigeria to 12.5% in Ghana, 15% in Sierra Leone, 15% in Gambia, and 18% in Guinea. The Gambia, Ghana, Guinea, Nigeria, and Sierra Leone all make use of VAT for revenue generation. In Liberia, the passage of the VAT Bill, which was intended to replace the

Goods and Services Tax (GST), was awaiting legislative approval. The VAT would replace the existing Goods and Services Tax (GST), which was set at 10.0%. The VAT system must be harmonised among the member states to achieve full economic and trade integration in the zone.

Free Movement Of People

At the core of the economic integration of the WAMZ countries is the free movement of people, which aligns with the ECOWAS protocol on the free movement of persons, the right to reside and to establish. There are still observed impediments to the free movement of people as it is believed that there must not be an obstruction to the movement of people within the union. This is based on the expectation that obstruction to free movement would impede the transfer of knowledge and ideas within the zone, which can limit the ability of the zone to increase its productivity. Over the years, there have been commitments from member countries to ensure the removal of restrictions on the movement of people within the zone, except in the case of an emergency where such a restriction is key to the socio-economic existence of the countries, such as during the outbreak of the COVID-19 Pandemic and Ebola. However, few of the countries-imposed restrictions for reasons unrelated to unforeseen circumstances. Nigeria, for example, has closed its border since 2017 and will only reopen it in 2022 – also, Guinean border closures following their presidential elections in 2020 also restricted trade, particularly with the Gambia. In addition, customs at border posts of the member countries have also yet to demonstrate the will to promote the free movement of people, as citizens within the region are often harassed unnecessarily. Many roadblocks are also mounted by customs, which makes the movement of people and goods across the zone difficult. The restriction on the movement of people in the zone is also fuelled by the threats of organised crimes in some member states, among which are the proliferation of light weapons, especially from Libya to Nigeria, which is often linked to the unending terrorism activities in the country, and the incidents of human and drug trafficking and kidnapping in many of the countries in the zone. The restriction is also influenced by the incessant threat to maritime security, including increased pirate attacks along coastal lines, especially along the Gulf of Guinea, where 22 separate attacks on vessels were recorded in 2020, resulting in the kidnapping of 135 crew members.

Table 3.2: Performance on the Compliance to ECOWAS Protocol on Free Movement

	Free Movement of People		**ETLS**	
Countries	**2019**	**2020**	**2019**	**2020**
WAMZ	75	75	58.3	58.3
The Gambia	70	70	50	50
Ghana	60	60	50	50
Guinea	90	90	50	50
Liberia	60	60	75	75
Nigeria	90	90	75	75
Sierra Leone	80	80	50	50

Source: *compiled by the author using WAMZ Trade Integration Report, 2020*

There are some challenges to the free flow of goods as there are still non-tariff barriers to the movement of goods within the zone, which range from the imposition of bans on some selected products to quotas and administrative systems among member states. There is also non-compliance with ECOWAS regional protocols that would have promoted the free flow of goods, such as the ECOWAS Trade Liberalisation Scheme (ETLS) and the Inter-State Road Transit (ISRT), which are expected to expand duty-free trade of approved products. Some Member States continued to impose barriers to trade on goods along transit corridors in the zone. Some members of the union equally fail to grant zero-rate duties on some of the ETLS-approved products, which impedes the free flow of goods among the member countries. Although tariffs represent one of the major ambits of integration, the tariff structure in the zone remains discriminatory, as reflected in the existence of different tariff arrangements with differing rates of customs duties in the zone. Each member still uses its own customs tariff at the border as against a common tariff among the member states, which would have deepened intra-regional trade for the members. According to the world trade reports, for instance, only Ghana and Nigeria, among the six member states, have fully harmonised their customs clearance and documentation procedures in tandem with ECOWAS and World Trade Organization (WTO) standards. On the other hand, customs clearance and documentation procedures are yet to be fully harmonised with the

ECOWAS and WTO standards, and this negatively impacts the free flow of goods among the member states.

The performance of each of the member countries and the zone on the adherence to the free movement of people and ETLS is summarised in the table based on data obtained from the WAMZ trade integration report. From the table, the average performance on the free movement of people was 75% in 2019 and 2020, ranging from 60% in Ghana in both years to 90% in Nigeria and Guinea in both years. The implication is that the zone has made substantial progress as related to the free movement of people among member countries. The performance on the adherence to the ECOWAS protocol on ETLS is 58.3% in 2019 and 2020, ranging from 50% in The Gambia, Ghana, Guinea, and Sierra Leone to 90% in Nigeria. The implication is that compliance with the ECOWAS protocol on ETLS needs to be intensified among the countries in the zone to attain full economic integration in the zone.

Institutional Integration

Institutional integration is also central to the success of economic integration. In this respect, WAMZ countries have made promising progress in certain areas of institutional integration, while no progress has been made in some areas. An area where there is substantial progress is the entrenchment of democracy among the countries in the zone, as each country has consistently practised a presidential system of government, resulting in uniform institutionalised democracy in the zone. For instance, democracy is highly entrenched in Ghana, and the recent improvement in the electoral process in Nigeria, in which the voting process now reflects the choice of the people at the polls (though vote buying is still prevalent), has improved the democratic experience in the country. Under this, countries in the zone have continued to record uninterrupted democratic dispensation.

On the contrary, corruption remains highly prevalent among the countries in the zone as the countries are lowly ranked in terms of transparency in public service. The report from the Transparency International corruption perception index reveals that countries in the zone are below average in terms of transparency in the public service, with a percentage transparency score ranging from 43% in Ghana, 37% in Gambia, 29% in Liberia, 25% in Guinea, 24% in Nigeria, and Sierra Leone 34% (*Transparency International Corruption Index 2022*), while in comparison to other countries, none of the countries in the zone is ranked among the first 100 transparent countries in the world. Ghana, which is the most transparent in the zone, is ranked 72 in the world, followed by Gambia at number 110, Liberia at number 142, Guinea at number 147, Nigeria at number 150, and Sierra Leone 110 out of 180 sampled countries (*Transparency International, 2021*).

Internal conflicts among the member countries pose a threat to institutional integration in the zone and full economic integration by extension. For instance, Sierra Leone was recently entrenched in a civil war in addition to the conflict in Liberia, while the potential election crisis rented up the air in the Gambia. There is also a prevalence of jihadist war in Northern Nigeria states, which reportedly results in the take-over of some local governments by Islamic fundamentalists. This is in addition to the recent armed bandit surge in the Northern states, including Abuja, the country's capital. There is also a herdsmen-farmer crisis which spreads from the North to the Southern part of the country, while secessionist agitation in the South-East and Southwestern Nigeria for Biafra and Oduduwa republics, respectively, poses a threat to political stability and institutional integration in the zone. Another major threat to institutional integration is the surging cases of kidnapping for ransom in Nigeria, which is now more pronounced in both the Northern and Southern parts of the country and has led to the loss of many lives, including businessmen, politicians, and students. The preponderance of such bitter conflicts in the zone stretches the military capacity in the countries and takes away a large number of resources that would have been used for integration-promoting activities by the affected countries. The conflicts also affect the socio-economic landscape of member countries as they result in certain instances of drought, famine, refugee problems, destruction, diseases, etc.

Infrastructure Integration

Central to the attainment of full economic integration of WAMZ countries is infrastructure integration. Infrastructural support is indispensable for effective trading activities to take place within and among countries. Some of this infrastructure includes ICT, transport, and power infrastructure. The availability of good infrastructure is expected to increase the competitiveness of the products produced by member countries in the WAMZ zone through a reduction in the cost of production. However, the existing stock of infrastructure in WAMZ is inadequate, and there have not been significant changes in the level of infrastructure in recent times. Relying on the data from the World Economic Forum (WEF) competitiveness index, the infrastructure level in WAMZ countries is low compared to those required for successful economic integration. From the statistical database of the WEF, it was found that none of the member countries in the zone recorded an average in terms of infrastructure stock. Compared to the other countries in the world, none of the WAMZ countries is ranked among the first 100 in terms of infrastructure stock, as shown in Table 3. All the countries in the zone are equally ranked outside the best 100 countries in utility infrastructure, while all countries in the zone except Guinea are ranked outside the best 100 countries in transportation infrastructure. Equally, only Ghana ranked among the best 100 countries in terms of ICT infrastructure, while others are outside the best 100. Hence, the level of infrastructure integration in WAMZ is lower than what is required for meaningful economic and trade integration.

TABLE 3.3: SELECTED INFRASTRUCTURE INDICATORS OF WAMZ COUNTRIES IN 2019

Countries	Free Movement of People		ETLS	
	2019	2020	2019	2020
WAMZ	75	75	58.3	58.3
The Gambia	70	70	50	50
Ghana	60	60	50	50
Guinea	90	90	50	50
Liberia	60	60	75	75
Nigeria	90	90	75	75
Sierra Leone	80	80	50	50

Source: *Compiled by the author using WEF Competitiveness Report, 2019*

Challenges To Actualisation Of WAMZ Objectives

The actualisation of WAMZ objectives has been delayed beyond stipulated dates due to a number of factors that hinder full economic and monetary integration. The challenges include:

- The inability of member countries to meet the convergence criteria.
- Limited financial integration.
- Social and historical factors.
- Barriers to trade.
- Infrastructural deficit; political factors.

- Weak policies and regulations, among others.

According to Adelakun (*2020*), the most critical challenge to actualising WAMZ objectives is the inability of member countries to meet the macroeconomic convergence criteria. To date, none of the countries in WAMZ has been able to meet all the convergence criteria; even the primary criteria are yet to be met. For instance, as of the second quarter of 2021, only The Gambia, Ghana, and Guinea recorded inflation of less than 10%, while none of them met the fiscal deficit criteria. Similarly, Ghana, Guinea, and Nigeria satisfied central bank deficit financing as of 2021. However, most of the countries met the external reserve criteria except Liberia.

For financial integration in terms of the payment system, harmonisation of capital markets, insurance markets, and general banking system unification, some progress has been made in harmonising the payment system in cross-border business transactions in WAMZ. However, the payment system is yet to be harmonised across member countries. There are still a number of challenges hindering full financial integration in the zone. Some of the challenges are difficulty in cash settlement due to differences in currencies, the absence of a common forum for information sharing, and even the development of the financial sector across countries. For instance, Nigeria and Ghana have more developed capital markets than other members.

Social and cultural differences across member states serve as a hindrance to cross-border trade in the zone. The social-cultural divide yields divergent social trajectories such that people can easily interact within their social group but most often find it difficult to relate with people outside the group. Similarly, the persistence of colonial tiers severed the objective of full economic integration in the ECOWAS sub-region. The relationship with the former colonial masters significantly influences the administrative and political systems of the countries, leading to diverse and distinct local and foreign interests across countries. The Francophone countries have strong historical ties with France such that the CFA used by WAEMU members is fixed in parity with the Euro, and their reserves are domiciled in Paris with certain conditions. The Francophone countries, however, enjoyed relative macroeconomic stability due to this arrangement. Thus, if the Francophone countries disconnect from France, it may result in a macroeconomic crisis such as price instability.

Several factors serve as a barrier to trade, hence, restricting the process of full economic integration in WAMZ and ECOWAS at large. These factors include poor inter-countries infrastructure such as road, rail, telecommunication, and energy, non-implementation of trade agreements, conflicts and political crises, inability to harmonise the tariff arrangement, and difficulty of currency convertibility, among others. Transport infrastructure is very imperative to the promotion of the movement of goods, services, and people across countries. The countries in WAMZ are largely connected by road; meanwhile, the road infrastructure is not adequately functional. According to Ogunkola (*2005*), the absence of functioning inter-countries transport infrastructure, including the lack of free residence right of citizens of different countries, impede the free flow of goods and persons. The countries in WAMZ mostly depend on revenue from import duties; therefore, they are not willing to harmonise the tariff, leading to divergent tariff arrangements in the zone. Another factor hindering trade integration in WAMZ is the pockets of conflicts across different countries in the zone. All these can inflict on the free flow of trade across countries.

The fear of threat to central bank autonomy of individual countries as well as national sovereignty is one the reasons why most countries in WAMZ and ECOWAS are yet to consent to full monetary union with one central bank and single currency. Therefore, there exists a high level of complacency among the central banks of WAMZ countries in taking decisive action leading to the establishment of the planned single central bank for non-CFA countries. Meanwhile, the existence of a common central bank is the same as the creation of a monetary union. The WAEMU monetary union is successful due to the existence of the common Central Bank of West Africa States (BCEAO).

Prospects Of Actualizing WAMZ Objectives

Despite the inability of WAMZ countries to achieve full economic and monetary integration for more than two decades since its conception due to several challenges, there are some developments that give hope of actualising WAMZ objectives. Some of these prospects are elucidated subsequently.

To begin with, the advent of some level of stable democracy in most WAMZ countries, particularly in Nigeria and Ghana, which are the dominant economies of the sub-region, offers some hope for the potential of WAMZ to attain full economic and monetary integration. For instance, Ghana has implemented a number of programmes and policies aimed at intensifying citizens' participation in politics while their rights are fully protected in order areas. These have been made possible through the establishment of good electoral management and a political party code of conduct, which make the elections free and fair, and the establishment of affirmative action policies that guarantee the protection of citizens' rights. Nigeria has also made progress in deepening its democracy as the rule of law has recently improved in the country. Several judicial pronouncements in recent times have favoured the opposition parties at the expense of the ruling party. In addition, the credibility of the electoral process has greatly improved as the perception that their votes would count has increased through the introduction of electronic devices such as BVAS in the voting process. This is evident in the defeat of the ruling party in the sub-national elections in the country. The government has also passed freedom of information acts in the country, which protects the rights of citizens to air their opinions on any public matter. All these are expected to improve institutional integration in the WAMZ zone.

The second prevailing development in the zone, which gives prospects to the attainment of full economic integration in WAMZ, is the existence of integration among the citizens in the zone, as reflected in the ability to move between the countries, notwithstanding the challenges. For example, a sizable number of Nigerians are currently living in Ghana and conducting business there, while a sizable number of Ghanaians are also in Nigeria and conducting business there. The currencies of the member countries are also traded in member countries to a great extent. For instance, the Nigerian naira is accepted in most markets in Ghana, while the Ghanaian cedi is accepted in the Balogun Market in Nigeria.

The WAMZ payment system development project is aimed at making four countries — Gambia, Guinea, Liberia, and Sierra Leone — close to the level of development achieved by Ghana and Nigeria. The WAMZ payment system was completed in Gambia in 2012, Guinea in 2016, Liberia in 2016, and Sierra Leone (BSL) in 2016. These bridge the gap in the payment systems of those countries with Ghana, which has an Interbank Payments and Settlement System (GhIPSS), and Nigeria, which has its own Interbank Payment and Settlement System (NIBSS) and other financial technology (FinTechs) in the two countries. This has led to a gradual shift to an electronic payment option against the hitherto widely practised cash economy. The step towards a unified payment system in the zone would enhance the capacity of the member states in the day-to-day operational management of the payment system, which would guarantee simple, low-cost, and risk-controlled payment, clearing, and settlement systems. It is also expected to provide an alternative to the prevailing high-cost and lengthy correspondent banking relationships in the zone, which would promote trade and other economic activities among the member countries and formalise some of the unrecorded trade due to the prevalence of informal cross-border trade in the zone.

The strengthening of the capacity of financial institutions in the sub-region through the successful implementation of banking sector consolidation in most WAMZ countries has substantially increased the capital base of the banks in the zone and increased their ability to reduce the possibility of systemic crises in the zone. The ability of Central banks to maintain short-term interest rates near a target level would also be enhanced as there would be increased coordination among the banks in the zone. In addition, the ability of the consolidated banks to establish branches across the zone would increase the tendency to achieve full monetary integration.

The adoption of the African Economic Commission (AEC) treaty and the revision of the ECOWAS treaty suggests that West Africa possesses the institutional framework necessary to move forward with regional integration. However, the future course and success of that process cannot be taken for granted. In addition, the signing of the African Continental Free Trade Agreement (AfCFTA) by member countries, commenced operations in 2020, with Ghana being an active participant, as two companies in Ghana have so far been able to ship goods under the scheme.

In addition, member states of WAMZ have also fully implemented the brown card third-party vehicle insurance scheme. This strengthens the prospects of the member states to achieve improved trade integration. The implication of the scheme by the member states, which is similar to the European Union's Green Card scheme, will guarantee the absorption of risk arising from the road. An attempt has been made in this chapter to examine the challenges and prospects towards accidents and other damages suffered by non-resident citizens within the WAMZ in a prompt and fair manner.

Conclusion

Actualising the WAMZ objectives, which is full economic and monetary integration: It was revealed in the chapter that substantial efforts have been made among the member countries towards actualising the WAMZ objectives since its conception in the year 2000. These include, among others, the setting up of WAMI with the mandate to undertake measures for the creation of a full monetary union with one central bank and a single currency, the establishment of the West African Capital Market Integration Council (WACMIC) in 2013 to facilitate the integration of capital markets in the sub-region, and the West African Insurance Supervisors Association (WAISA) for the integration of the insurance sub-sector.

Despite the commitments demonstrated by the member countries and huge efforts directed at the actualisation of full economic and monetary integration in the zone, the level of integration in WAMZ is still low. Trade integration is very low, as suggested by the low level of intra-WAMZ import and export and intra-WAMZ trade in general. Macroeconomic integration in the zone is equally low as the member countries have yet to meet the macroeconomic convergence criteria set by the WAMI, with a performance rate of about 45% in 2021. There is, however, substantial progress regarding financial integration as reflected in the consolidation of banks in member countries, the implementation of the West African payment system and the full implementation of the brown card insurance scheme. The countries also perform poorly in infrastructure integration like road, ICT, and utility infrastructure in the zone remain poor, preventing the attainment of improved connectivity in the zone. There is also a low level of institutional integration despite the continued entrenchment of the democratic system among member states. This is reflected in the poor performance of the countries in the Transparency International Corruption Perception Index and the upsurge of internal conflicts in member countries, with implications for political stability in the zone. Even though there is significant compliance with the ECOWAS protocol on the free movement of people and goods, there are still a few cases of restrictions to the free flow of people and goods within the zone.

It was also demonstrated in the chapter that the inability of the zone to achieve full economic integration is due to a few factors, which include the persistent presence of tariff and non-tariff barriers to trade in some member countries, infrastructural deficits including road, port, power and ICT infrastructure, political factors, and weak policies and regulation, among others. Despite the stated challenges, certain conditions exist in the zone, which gives prospects for the actualisation of WAMZ objectives of economic and trade integration. Some of these include the stable democracy in some countries in the zone, the implementation of bank consolidation policies by member countries, the adoption of the WAMZ payment system development project in some WAMZ countries, the full implementation of the brown card third-party vehicle insurance scheme, and the signing of the ECA agreement as well as the signing and commitment to the African Continental Free Trade Agreements.

It is therefore advocated that member countries should intensify efforts towards integration by removing tariff and non-tariff barriers to intra-WAMZ trade. More commitment to full compliance with the ECOWAS protocol on the free movement of goods and goods by member countries should be shown. In addition, countries should review and harmonise their macroeconomic policies to move towards attaining the macroeconomic convergence criteria set for full economic and monetary integration in the zone. There is also a need to reduce infrastructure deficits in the zone through efficient infrastructure investment spending. The institutional environment in the zone should also be improved upon through a reduction in the incidence of corruption and the amicable resolution of internal conflicts among member states. Efforts should equally be geared towards the attainment of common customs and monetary union to increase cross-border trade and financial transactions among member states while trying to formalise the process of currency convertibility within the zone such that member currencies would be quoted in other members' banks.

Chapter 3

Economic Diversity In WAMZ: Opportunities And Challenges

Diversity in economic structures relates to the relative importance of different economic activities for aggregate output. Differences in economic activities across countries would yield the production of different goods and services across countries. The differences in the relative importance of activities reflect countries' specialisation in the production of various goods and services. If different countries in an economic union focus on certain sectors or products, this will lead to international specialisation. As each country specialises in the production of certain goods and services, production would increase, leading to a rise in the supply of those goods and services beyond domestic demand. The excess supplied would be exported to other countries within the union; then goods and services in which other countries specialise are imported. These differences in economic activities across countries pave the way for trade integration among member countries since domestically produced goods and services would be traded among member countries. Hence, economic diversity across countries in any given economic union is expected to promote trade among member countries.

Besides fostering trade among member countries, economic diversity across countries has other benefits. A diversified regional economy would lead to sustainable regional integration; hence, it provides new opportunities in terms of employment, income generation and wealth creation across an integrated economic region. Thus, economic diversity is expected to promote economic growth and development in the region. In addition, the economic volatility of an economic region can be sufficiently reduced with increased participation of the real sector through economic diversification, thereby improving macroeconomic stability and convergence within the region.

Several factors can account for economic diversity across countries, including differences in natural endowment, geographical location, demographic structure, institutional framework (including the legal framework, fiscal and monetary policies) and consumption patterns, among others. The natural endowment varies from country to country, and the nature, type, quantity, and quality also vary across countries. This variation creates differences in comparative advantage in the production of goods and services. Similarly, differences in terms of geographical conditions, such as vegetation, weather, climatic variables, topography, soil quality, access to the sea, and others, provide a variety of opportunities for production as well as distribution of goods and services. Since all these geographical factors are not the same across countries, thus, the opportunity cost of producing goods and services varies across different geographical locations. Diversity in demographic structure in terms of composition and distribution would yield differences in demand and production capability. For example, a country with a large population of children would need more goods and services to satisfy children's needs. In such a country, the need for education-related goods and services, toys, and children's wear would be high. This high demand for children's goods and services would push entrepreneurs to the production of more children's goods and services. This would be different from a country where a large proportion of the population is old age people. The point is that demographic structure and distribution could lead to divergent opportunities and, in turn, create economic diversity across countries. The government or policymakers of a country may decide to direct policies and efforts toward the promotion of certain priority sector(s). This would lead to better performance in the priority sector(s). If different countries in an economic union choose different priority sectors, there would be economic diversity across countries in the union.

Therefore, this chapter examines the extent of economic diversity across countries in WAMZ. Following this introductory section is Section 2, which clarifies the concept of economic diversity, Section 3 presents the overview of economic diversity in WAMZ; factors that promote or hinder diversity in WAMZ are discussed in Section 4; how diversity can serve as an opportunity for integration in WAMZ is in Section 5. Section 6 presents how the current status of diversity in WAMZ can be a challenge to integration, and finally, Section 7 concludes the chapter.

Concept Of Economic Diversity

The concept of economic diversity can mean different things to different people depending on the context it is used. In this chapter, economic diversity is referred to variation in the economic structure of countries in a particular integrated economic union. Different countries may specialise in the production of different goods and services; thus, countries differ from each other in terms of production, distribution, and consumption of goods and services. Therefore, economic diversity is the extent of structural variation across countries of a region or sub-region or structural differences across different regions.

There are indicators to measure the economic diversity of a country, such as the HHI index, but there are no indicators yet to measure the level of diversity across countries in West Africa. What researchers often do is compare the concentration of economic activities across countries. If major economic activities between two different countries differ significantly, then it is said that there is economic diversity between them. For example, one country specialises in the production of agricultural goods, and another country specialises in the production of manufactured goods. These two countries can benefit themselves since there is diversity in what they produce.

Overview Of Economic Diversity In WAMZ

The extent of diversity across the countries in WAMZ is examined in this sub-section. The structural composition of each economy in the union is examined and then juxtaposed across countries. One way that economists measure the structural composition of an economy is by decomposing aggregate national income into value-added by economic activities. A sector with higher value-added output implies that there are more activities in such a sector than in the other. Therefore, in this section, the value-added output of four key sectors, viz agriculture, industry, manufacturing, and services, are presented, discussed, and compared across the six countries in WAMZ. Table 4.1 presents the value added as a percentage of GDP, while Table 4.2 presents the value added as current US dollars. The data in Table 4.1 depict the relative contribution of each sector to the national income, and the data in Table 4.2 depict the relative size of each sector.

TABLE 4.1: VALUE ADDED AS PERCENTAGE OF GDP BY SECTOR, 2021

Sectors	The Gambia,	Ghana	Guinea	Liberia	Nigeria	Sierra Leone	Zone's Average
Agriculture, forestry, and fishing	19.70	19.71	25.50	37.21	23.36	59.49*	30.83
Industry (including construction)	19.52	28.26	27.70	18.36	31.41	5.24*	21.75
Manufacturing	2.90	10.70	9.56*	2.28	14.61	1.88*	6.99
Services	51.11*	45.93	35.96	37.04	43.79	30.98*	40.80

Source: *Computed by the author from WDI, *Data are as at 2020*

TABLE 4.2: VALUE ADDED (CURRENT BILLION US$), 2021.

Sectors	The Gambia	Ghana	Guinea	Liberia	Nigeria	Sierra Leone	Zone's Average
Agriculture, forestry, and fishing	0.41	15.29	4.04	1.30	102.95	2.42*	21.07
Industry (including construction)	0.41	21.93	4.39	0.64	138.44	0.21*	27.67
Manufacturing	0.05	8.30	1.35*	0.05	64.40	0.08*	12.37
Services	1.06*	35.64	5.70	1.29	193.01	1.26*	39.66

Source: *Computed by the author from WDI, *Data is as at 2020*

The structures of the economies in WAMZ are generally similar, with little differences across countries. The composition of the economy in terms of value-added by sectors is represented in Table 4.1. In the Gambia, the services sector is the dominant sector with value added as a percentage of GDP of above 50%. Agriculture and Industry jointly contribute less than 40%, while the Agricultural sector value-added is 19.70% as of 2021, and Industry value-added is 19.52%. The Manufacturing sector has the least contribution, with just 2.90% value added.

Looking at the structure of Ghana's economy, the story is similar to the structure in the Gambia. The services sector also dominates in Ghana, taking about 45.93% of the total value-added. However, the performance of the Industrial sector in Ghana is a little above the performance of the Agricultural sector. The Industrial sector contributes 28.26%, while the Agricultural sector contributes 19.71%. The value added from the Agricultural sector in Ghana is almost the same as the sectors' contribution in the Gambia. Though the Manufacturing sector is the least-performing sector in Ghana, with a value-added of 10.70%, this is relatively high when compared across the countries in the zone. Ghana's manufacturing value-added is the second highest after Nigeria in the Zone.

In Guinea, Agriculture, Industry, and Services are nearly proportional in size. The share of the agriculture sector in national income is about 25.50%, while the share of industry is 27.70%, and the share of Services is 35.96% as of 2021. Though relative across the three sectors,

Services has the highest value-added, followed by Industry, and Agriculture value-added is slightly below that of Industry. As it is in the Gambia and Ghana, the Manufacturing sector has the lowest value-added, which stood at 9.56% as of 2021. Meanwhile, the value-added of the manufacturing sector in Guinea is the third highest in the zone. Only Nigeria and Ghana have higher Manufacturing value-added than Guinea.

The structure of the economy in the case of Liberia presents a situation where the agriculture sector and Services sector contributed approximately equal value-added. The agriculture sector has 37.21% value-added, while services have 37.04%. On the other hand, Industry contributed 18.36% value-added, and Manufacturing had the least value-added, which stood at just 2.28%. Liberia scarcely produces manufacturing goods, just like the Gambia and Sierra Leone.

The structural composition of the Nigerian economy is not much different from other member countries of WAMZ. The services sector dominates with 43.79% value-added as a percentage of GDP. Immediately after the services sector, the next biggest contributor to national income is the industry sector, with 31.41% value added. The agricultural sector contributes 23.36%, and Manufacturing contribution is 14.61%. Though Manufacturing value-added is the lowest among the four sectors, it is the highest among all the members of the union.

It is only in Sierra Leone that the services sector does not have the highest value-added; rather, it is the second highest after the Agriculture sector. The Agriculture sector contributes 59.49% of value added to the national income. The services sector, which is the second largest sector in the Sierra Leone economy, contributes 30.98%. The country has the lowest value added in the Industry and Manufacturing sectors in the union. The value added as a percentage of GDP in the Industry sector is only 5.24%, while that of the Manufacturing sector is 1.88%.

The aggregate economic structure in the zone, as presented in the last column of Table 4.1, shows that the Services sector is the dominant sector in the union. Following the Services sector is the Agriculture sector, and the third biggest sector in the union is the Industry sector, while the Manufacturing sector contributes the lowest to the economy of the union. The average value-added in the West African Monetary Zone (WAMZ) is 40.80% in the Services sector; it is 30.83%, 21.75%, and 6.99% in Agriculture, Industry, and Manufacturing sectors, respectively.

In terms of structural composition, there is not much diversity across the countries in WAMZ; manufacturing value-added is generally low across all the countries in the union. The Services sector dominates in almost all the countries in the union, and Agriculture is the second largest sector in all the countries except Sierra Leone, where it is the biggest sector. However, the size of the sectors varies across countries. Table 4.2 above presents the relative sizes of each sector across all the countries in WAMZ.

Analysing the size of the sectors across the countries, it is evident that Nigeria dominates in all the sectors. The size of the Services sector in Nigeria is about $193.01 billion (US Dollars), while the size of the Industry, Agriculture, and Manufacturing is $138.44 billion (US Dollars), $102.95 billion (US Dollars), and $64.40 billion (US Dollars), respectively. In Ghana, the size of the Services sector is about $35.64 billion (US Dollars), the Industrial sector is $21.93 billion (US Dollars), the Agriculture sector is $15.29 billion (US Dollars), and the Manufacturing sector is $8.30 billion (US Dollars). The size of the Services, Industry, Agriculture, and Manufacturing sectors in Guinea is $5.7 billion (US Dollars), $4.39 billion (US Dollars), $4.04 billion (US Dollars), and $1.35 billion (US Dollars), respectively. Similarly, the sizes of the sectors in Sierra Leone are $2.42 billion (US Dollars) for Agriculture, $1.26 billion (US Dollars) for Services, $0.21 billion (US Dollars) for Industry, and $0.08 billion (US Dollars) for Services. In Liberia, the sizes are $1.3billion (US Dollars), $1.29 billion (US Dollars), $0.64billion (US Dollars), and $0.05 billion (US Dollars) for Agriculture, Services, Industry, and Manufacturing sectors, respectively. Finally, the size of the largest sector in the Gambia, which is services, is about $1.06 billion (US Dollars), the size of the

Agriculture and Industry sectors are equal with value-added of about $0.41billion (US Dollars) each, while manufacturing is the smallest in size with just about $0.05billion (US Dollars) value-added.

The linear addition across the Gambia, Guinea, Liberia, and Sierra Leone of the value added in the Agriculture, Industry, Manufacturing, and Services sectors, respectively, sum up to $8.17billion (US Dollars), $5.65 billion, $1.53 billion (US Dollars), and $9.31billion (US Dollars). The total sum of value added from these four countries is less than the value added in Ghana for all the sectors. Equally, adding up the four countries along with Ghana does not measure up to half of the size of Nigeria's value added for any of the sectors. This implies that the disparity of diversity in terms of size is disproportionately skewed towards Nigeria and Ghana.

Factors Influencing Diversification In WAMZ

In spite of the recognition attributed to economic diversity as the driver of sustainable growth as well as the commitment of policymakers in developing countries, including those in WAMZ, the economic structures of countries in WAMZ remain highly concentrated on the primary sectors and service sectors. In contrast, the share of the manufacturing sector significantly remains low. These situations may be attributed to a number of challenges that face diversification efforts among the countries in the zone, among which are:

- Levels of human capital development.
- A history of colonialism.
- Macroeconomic management policies.
- Public infrastructure, among others.

Level of Human Capital Development

Inadequate human capital development is a key factor that has hampered the successful diversification drive in the zone. Economies that are trying to move to a more diverse production form must develop the know-how required to manufacture high-value-added products and provide services. Human capital constitutes the main channel through which the know-how is built. This human capital is essential for the development of modern industrial and service sectors that will move the economy away from overconcentration. A manufacturing sector and other value-adding activities require high-level skilled manpower. The sector also requires adequate fundamental scientific knowledge, which can be attained through investment in research and development (R&D). However, the level of human capital development among the countries within the zone is inadequate.

The Global Human Capital Index revealed that countries

in the zone's ability to capture their human capital potential is below average, except for Ghana, with a 50% score. Other countries recorded below-average performance, with Nigeria, Gambia, Guinea, and Sierra Leone recording a human capital index of 40%. Liberia, on the other hand, recorded a lower human capital index of 30%. The country's performance is lower compared to the industrialised countries' average (WDI, 2021). The observed inadequate human capital development in the zone hampers the economic diversification drive as it limits the domestic capacity of these countries to create new technologies or reduces their absorptive capacity to assimilate imported technologies. This has largely been responsible for the markedly lower total factor productivity (TFP) performance of the manufacturing sector in the zone. The low level of human capital makes the countries in WAMZ remain trapped in traditional "low-tech" activities characterised by a limited level of productivity. The countries' capacity to provide the skilled labour force required in skill-intensive industries and the use of technological advancements is hampered by the low level of human capital development. In addition, the low level of human capital development in the region prevents manufacturing firms in the secondary sector from adopting production systems that align with the more advanced segments in the global value chains.

Insufficient education support facilities like research laboratories, computers, libraries, classrooms, and various equipment impede effective skills development in the zone. In addition, technical and vocational education, which are now being considered prerequisites for improved industrial productivity and competitiveness, in the zone do not receive adequate attention. Hence, the development of technical and vocational skills remains at a lower level than required for successful structural transformation. The educational systems of the majority of countries in the zone remain patterned along outdated curricula, while the efforts at modernising them, in a few cases, are at variance with the needs of the economy and society as a whole. In general, the educational system in the zone technically deviates from the needs of industry, which stymies the zone's transformation from the primary sector to the manufacturing sector.

There is also very low investment in research and development, which is essential for developing the 'Science-Technology-Innovation" trilogy. Available data reveals that the spending on research and development among the countries in the zone is below 0.5% of the GDP, which is far from the average of between 2.5% and 4% in developed economies (US, Japan, China, South Korea, and Germany) and the average of between 0.7% and 1.2% in transition economies (Brazil, India, and Malaysia). The inadequate potential for skill development is reflected in the rankings of the universities in the zone, where no university from the zone could be ranked among the world's 200 universities. In fact, no university in the

WAMZ zone is among the top ten ranked in Africa; universities in South Africa and Egypt dominate this top ten ranking.

The Colonisation of the Countries

The mode of the economy created and bestowed on various colonies by the colonialists is also responsible for the slow pace of diversification in the zone. At the advent of the industrial revolution, the colonialists needed raw materials since the agriculture sector in their home countries could not meet the demand for raw materials by the emerging industries. Hence, they colonised countries outside Europe, including those in West Africa, to harness their raw materials for the use of their industries. Most of the economic development plans during the period of colonial rule were tailored towards increasing raw material production and exportation to their home countries. In addition, the public infrastructure investment by the colonialists was focused on achieving smooth exportation of raw materials to the European countries instead of linking towns and increasing communication and connectivity. The level of education introduced to the countries in the zone was aimed at training low-level manpower, which would help them exploit the African continent's rich resources at the expense of those that would stimulate technological development for the take-off of industrialization in the region. The mode of education brought by the Europeans displaced the prior education plans, which were rooted in indigenous

African technology. Before colonialism, for instance, African countries were generally involved in non-primary activities, including cloth weaving, while some others were successful carvers, sculptors, and blacksmiths, among others.

The colonial system also introduced and entrenched classes in African society. The African bourgeoisie class created by the colonial system were used by the colonialist to exploit and siphon the economies of the countries in the region. These African bourgeoisie inherited political power after the independence, and they maintained a relationship with the former colonial masters; thus, they continued with the economic structure left by them, which gave room for the exploitation of the peasant and the proletariat classes. Since the primary sector, which includes the extraction of natural resources, gives room for rent-seeking, of which the proceeds are being used by the leaders to influence the outcome of the election and hold on to power, there continued to be little incentives to diversify the economy. This makes the countries in the zone remain trapped in an economic structure that is highly concentrated in the primary sector.

Macroeconomic Management Policies

The absence of sound macroeconomic management is another factor that has impeded the attainment of economic diversity in the WAMZ countries. A case to illustrate the imperative of sound macroeconomic policy is that of Malaysia, whose diversification drove from 70% primary export and 5% manufacturing in the 1970s to about 70% manufacturing output in the 2000s was attributed to sound macroeconomic management. The exchange rate system in the zone is largely unstable and regulated in most cases. The interest rate remains high in the zone, which restricts access to credit by domestic investors. This has continued to retard the business capacity development, which would have helped to shift the economy away from the dependency on primary products. The restricted access to credit and generally low business capacity development hamper the attainment of a competitive and dynamic business ecosystem, which would have triggered the creation of new ventures and facilitated improved productivity growth in the existing modern businesses. There is a general lack of macroeconomic policies directed at supporting entrepreneurship and small business development in the zone. Available statistics from the World Economic Forum (WEF) competitiveness index indicate that members of WAMZ perform below average in terms of macroeconomic stability (*WEF, 2019*). The unstable macroeconomic environment may impede the diversification drive of the countries as investors will face a higher level of uncertainty, which may drive them away from investing in the zone. The data from the WEF competitiveness index indicates that countries in WAMZ are ranked outside the first 100 in terms of macroeconomic stability. While Ghana is ranked 132nd in the world, Gambia is ranked 125th in terms of macroeconomic stability. Guinea is ranked 123rd, while Nigeria is ranked 130th.

Level Of Foreign Direct Investment

Member countries of WAMZ have attracted relatively low FDI, which is mainly concentrated in the primary sector, which is resource-driven. Nigeria's five-year average FDI as a percentage of GDP is found to be 0.8%, while that of Gambia is 1%. Only Ghana and Guinea recorded relatively high inward FDI inflows of 5.8% and 6% of GDP, respectively. A higher foreign direct investment inflow, especially in the secondary sector, such as manufacturing, is expected to integrate the economies of these countries into the global supply chain through improved quality of the output such that it will meet international standards. This will not only trigger the diversification of these countries' imports but also diversify their trading partners. The case of Vietnam comes to mind on the role of FDI in economic diversification as the country's diversification of exports and trading partners was reportedly facilitated by FDI buoyed by aggressive trade-policy reforms, including liberalisations of foreign exchange access, domestic prices, and external trade, among others.

The inability to attract foreign investment is also triggered by a poor business environment, as the countries are not suitable for foreign investors to thrive. The ease of doing business rank of these countries tells the story of the poor business climate in the zone. Figure 4.1 below depicts the ease of doing business score and rank of WAMZ members. Ghana and Nigeria, which recorded the best-doing business score in the zone, with a respective score of 59.96% and 56.88%, are ranked 118th and 131st in the world, while Gambia, Guinea, Sierra Leone, and Liberia are respectively ranked 155th, 156th, 163rd, and 175th.

FIGURE 4.1: SCORE AND RANK OF DOING BUSINESS

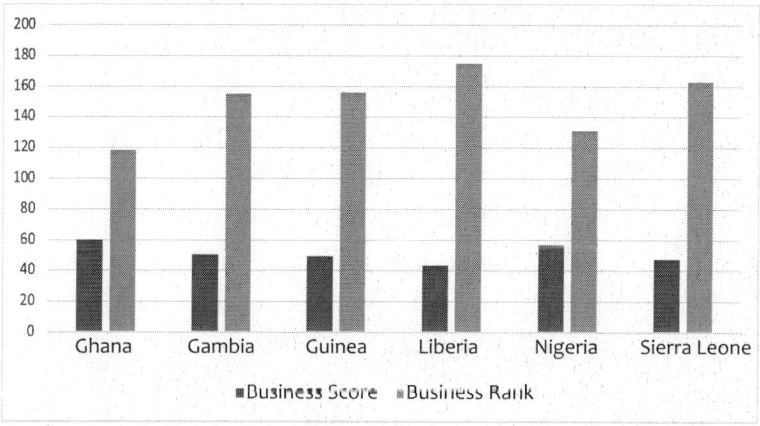

Source: *Compiled by the author from WDI, 2021*

Public Infrastructure

It has been widely demonstrated in various discussions that successful diversification efforts are closely linked with the quality of infrastructure, including roads, electricity, logistics, and water (*Adebowale, 2018; Nnyanzi et al., 2022; Umofa et al., 2018*). This is because secondary sectors in which the economy must be transformed heavily rely on high-quality infrastructure. In the countries in WAMZ, generally, public infrastructure is deficient as the public infrastructure is inadequate in terms of quantity and quality. Public infrastructure, in terms of ports, railways, roads, and public utilities, is undoubtedly indispensable for the production of industrial and manufacturing outputs. The World Bank Logistic Performance database indicates that WAMZ countries are poorly ranked in terms of logistic performance as Ghana and Nigeria, which are the best performers in the zone with an LPI score of 2.565 and 2.532, respectively, out of 5, are ranked 106 and 110, respectively, out of the 168 countries included for assessment. Gambia is ranked 127 with an LPI score of 2.4, Liberia is ranked 143 with an LPI score of 2.22, Guinea is ranked 145 with an LPI score of 2.20, while Sierra Leone is ranked 156 with an LPI score of 2.08 out of 5. The WEF's competitiveness report equally revealed that members' countries have an inadequate stock of infrastructure, as Ghana, with a score of 46.6%, is ranked 118th in the world. These countries are outside the world's first 100 in terms of infrastructure quality. None of the member countries is also within the first 100 ranked in terms of utility and transport infrastructure, while ICT infrastructure is not in any way different as only Ghana is ranked 90th while others are ranked outside the first 100.

The low quality of infrastructure and higher cost of

energy in the zone make the cost of doing business unfriendly to domestic and foreign investors, which has, in recent times, culminated in the relocation of many foreign enterprises away from the zone.

Institutional Quality

The quality of institutions in an economy is also argued to be crucial for a successful diversification drive (*Nnyanzi, et al., 2022*). Inadequate property rights and the incidence of corruption are major trademarks of typical African countries, including those in WAMZ. The incidence of corruption remains entrenched in the socio-economic systems of the countries in the zone. According to the Transparency International report for 2021, as shown in Figure 4.2, all six countries have a high perception of corruption, with Ghana, Gambia, Liberia, Guinea, and Nigeria having corruption perception scores of 43%, 37%, 29%, 25%, and 24% respectively, with corresponding ranks of 73, 102, 136, 150, and 154 out of the 180 countries assessed. The performance of the countries in the zone was poor compared to the highest score of 88 per cent recorded by Denmark, Finland, and New Zealand. The laws and regulations guiding business and socio-economic systems in the zone are equally fragile. The rule of law, which captures the public perception of obeying or disobeying the rules of society among the countries in the zone, is still at a lower level than needed for successful diversification to take place. Before investing in any country, investors must be assured that the law will protect their investment.

In Nigeria, for instance, the incidence of corruption remains high among public workers, especially in the judiciary, police, and government ministries and agencies. The appointment of presiding officers into government agencies and the recruitment process are largely based on political patronage at the expense of economic pragmatism. The legislature and political officeholders are now taking charge of recruitment into government agencies. More worrisome is that the legislature (Senators and House of Representatives members) boasts of good performance in terms of employment into government agencies they influence (including employment into universities). The implication of these practices is public-sector inefficiencies, which makes it difficult to develop and successfully implement policies that can adequately bring about the structural transformation of the economy.

In addition, poor-quality institutions give room for rent-seeking to thrive, and in such a scenario, the policy decisions are at the mercy of political patronage, which does not create an incentive for the political elite to pursue diversification. In resource-rich countries, when the institutional quality is poor, politicians over-extract the natural resources to influence the outcome of elections in favour of their parties, which starves the diversification-driven sectors of the needed funds. It has been reported in several quarters that better governance is crucial for economic diversity (*Nnyanzi, et al., 2022*). Hence, for the attainment of economic diversity in the zone to be realised, standard structural reforms that address government failures and improve institutional quality are inevitable.

FIGURE 4.2: CORRUPTION PERCEPTION SCORE

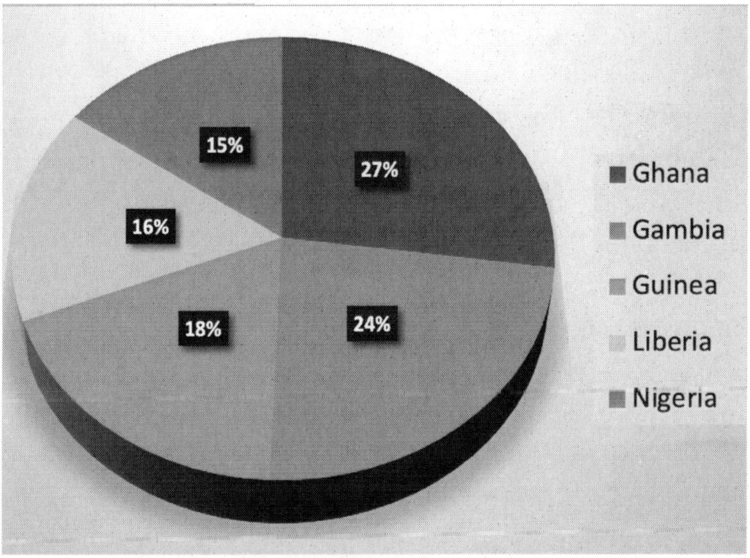

Source: *Compiled by the author from WDI, 2021*

Economic Diversity As Opportunity For Integration in WAMZ

The trade among the member countries remains low, which has been retarding the economic integration of the zone.

The union can leverage economic diversity to increase trade among the member states. In particular, the structural transformation of the economies into manufacturing sectors with specialisation within the zone will reduce reliance on European countries for the importation of manufactured products. According to available statistics, as summarised in Table 4.4, the majority of countries in the zone export primarily primary products while relying heavily on manufactured outputs from developed economies. None of the member countries is among Gambia's top five trading partners in terms of imports and exports. Though Ghana's exports exceed its imports, primary products account for most of its exports, with few manufactured goods, and its top trading partners are countries outside the WAMZ. Guinea is shown to be a net exporter with a higher export than import, though the export commodities are primary products, while manufactured goods constitute the key import commodities. In addition, the top trading partners in export and import are outside the zone.

TABLE 4.3 (A): INTERNATIONAL TRADE RELATIONS OF WAMZ COUNTRIES

Countries	Total Export				Import			
	Total (US$)	Africa	Top three Commodities	Top Three Trading Partners	World	Africa	Top Three Commodities	Five Trading Partners
Gambia	24	18 (75%)	Mining, Wood and Food and Animal	Mali, Guinea Bissau, China	488	108 (22.1%)	Mining, Manufacture Produce, Vehicles and Parts	Cote d'Ivore, India and Brazil

Source: Extracted by the author from AFDB Statistical Yearbook, 2020

Table 4.3 (B): International Trade Relations of WAMZ Countries

Ghana	16705	2948 (17.65)	Natural Pears and imitation jewellery, mineral resources, cocoa, and cocoa products	China, Switzerland , and India	10486	1078(10 .3%)	Vehicles, Nuclear reactors, and mechanical appliances, electrical and electronics	China, United States, United Kingdom
Guinea	2481	469	Mining resources, Ships and floating structures, Agriculture produce, nuclear reactors, machinery, and mechanical appliances	China, United States,	4553	227	Mineral resources, nuclear reactors, machinery and mechanical appliances and Vehicles	China, Netherlands, Belgium

Source: *Compiled by the author from WDI, 2021*

TABLE 4.3 (C): INTERNATIONAL TRADE RELATIONS OF WAMZ COUNTRIES

Liberia	112	24	Rubber, Animal products, Cocoa, and wood	US, Sierra Leone, Belgium	1147	276	Mineral resources, Cereals, Electrical machinery, and equipment, Vehicles	India, China and Cote-d'Ivoire
Nigeria	62633	12801	Mineral Resources, Ships and boats, Agriculture produce	India, Spain, and Netherlands	54431	3572	Machinery and mechanical appliances, Mineral products distillation, vehicles	China, India, and US

Source: *Extracted by the author from AFDB Statistical Yearbook, 2020*

TABLE 4.3D: INTERNATIONAL TRADE RELATIONS OF WAMZ COUNTRIES

Sierra Leone	472	324	Vehicles, Rubber and cocoa, iron and steel	UAE, Anguilla, and Amenia	5980	1762	Electrical and electronics, Machinery and mechanical appliances, vehicles	China, South Africa, US

Source: *Extracted by the author from AFDB Statistical Yearbook, 2020*

On the other hand, Liberia is a net importer whose imports are dominated by vehicles and primary products, and its major imports are manufacturing products. None of the countries in the zone is equally among the top trading partners of Liberia in terms of imports and exports. Though Nigeria is a net exporter (exports outnumber imports), primary products are the main export commodities, while manufactured goods are the main imports. Nigeria's top trading partners in export and import are also countries outside the zone. Sierra Leone is a net importer because it lacks abundant mineral resources and must rely on a few manufacturing products and agricultural produce for exportation, while manufacturing products are its major import commodities. The top trading partners of the country are also outside of Africa. The trading positions of the countries illustrated show that economic diversification, especially into the manufacturing sectors, would deepen intraregional trade among the WMAZ members as virtually all the countries presently rely on countries outside the zone to meet their demand for manufactured products.

Economic Diversity As Challenge To Integration in WAMZ

The current economic structure is characterised by the concentration on the primary products, which are mainly mineral resource extraction, mining, and agricultural production. The implication is that the level of diversity in the WAMZ is low, with implications for the integration of the zone.

Low diversity in the zone results in low trade among member countries as the basis for trade is dim. For instance, the major trading commodity of Nigeria is crude oil, which is exported to countries with refining capacity. However, member countries in WAMZ lack the technical know-how and technological capability to refine the crude oil. The implication is that Nigeria's crude trading to member countries in WAMZ could not take place. In addition, most of the countries in the zone are rich in similar mineral resources and mining products, which means they have to look for trading partners outside the zone since there is no value addition to the extracted resources, which would have created an opportunity for trading among the member states. The countries are also abundantly rich in agricultural production due to their similar geographical conditions. For instance, Nigeria and Ghana produce cocoa in sufficiently large quantities, which implies that trading of such a commodity could not take place between the countries. Similar scenarios exist among other countries since they are all highly involved in agricultural production and trading with very limited value addition that would have created a basis for trade and economic integration among the member states. Therefore, the production of similar products that are in primary sectors implies a limited basis for trade among the countries. This condition could only be reversed by creating value addition to the primary product, which could, in turn, create the basis for trade. As demonstrated earlier, this accounts for very low trade among countries within the zone, as none of the member states is among the top importers and exporters of Gambia, Ghana, Liberia, Guinea, Nigeria, and Sierra Leone. Over-concentration on the primary sector also implies the existence of limited technological differences among the countries, which would have promoted trade integration.

The low level of economic diversity in the zone equally affects trade integration in WAMZ through its impact on each of the criteria for macroeconomic convergence. Four primary convergence criteria were set for the integration of the WAMZ countries, which is to be monitored by the West African Monetary Institute (*WAMI, 2021*). These convergence criteria include:

- the attainment of less than 10% inflation in the member countries,
- a fiscal deficit that is below 4%,
- a less than 10% central bank deficit financing, and
- the ability of the external reserve to meet not less than three months of importation.

Countries in the zone generally have a high level of inflation, which is above 10%. A diversified economic structure which reduces the dependency of the countries on those outside the zone is less prone to imported inflation, which is outside the control of the countries. The low level of diversity in the zone reduces the tax revenue generation that would have come from the secondary sectors and utilised to meet the spending requirements of the government. The low level of economic diversity among the countries subjects them to importation from countries outside the zone, which often results in a negative trade balance, which has implications for the external reserve of the member countries. This may also limit the ability of the countries to meet integration convergence criteria and, thus, prevent economic integration among member states.

Diversity equally affects trade integration in the zone by exposing the countries' economies to external shocks attributed to concentration in primary products. The volatility that always accompanies the primary commodities and minerals that the zones depend on for export, directly or indirectly, affects some other macroeconomic fundamentals essential for trade integration in the zone. One of these is the continuous trade imbalance, which would make it difficult for the countries in the zone to put in place the required soft and hard infrastructure, which is hugely in deficit. Tax revenue in the zone, for instance, remains very low at less than 15% of the GDP (WDI, 2021), compared to an average of about 35% in OECD countries, which could be attributed to the low concentration of economic structure in the primary sector, which is difficult to tax.

Conclusion

The critical role of economic diversity in sustainable growth is well recognised among developing countries, including those in the WAMZ. In particular, economic diversity reduces the exposure of developing countries to world price shocks or fluctuations. Hence, the majority of the developing plans and other policy documents in these countries have been tailored towards attaining a more diverse economic structure. In spite of the awareness of its crucial role and commitment towards the structural transformation of their economies, countries in WAMZ continued to be characterised by highly concentrated economic structures. In particular, it was found (as shown in the earlier sections of this chapter) that countries in the zone have economic structures that are highly concentrated in the resource-based primary sector and the services sector, while the share of the manufacturing sector remains low in all the countries in the zone. The inability of the countries in the zone to attain a diverse economic structure can be linked to a number of factors, among which is the poor quality of infrastructure, which makes the cost of doing business unfriendly to domestic and foreign investors and forces the relocation of few existing foreign enterprises, and the poor institutional quality, which creates uncertainty for investors who often need to be guaranteed of the law that will safeguard their investment. Other factors that have been the stumbling blocks for successful diversification drives are the colonisation of the countries in the zone, which has deterred them from developing indigenous technology that would have driven economic diversity, and inadequate human capital development, which prevents the acquisition of fundamental scientific knowledge needed for structural transformation of the economic structures of member states.

Attainment of a diverse economic structure presents an opportunity for economic integration in the WAMZ as it will promote the participation of the zone in the global supply chain and increase the tendency of the zone to move from its present small open economy towards a large open economy. In addition, intra-regional trade among the member countries would be enhanced as the manufacturing output being sourced from countries outside the zone could be replaced by the manufactured products within the zone. In addition, the ability to coordinate the economies of the zone would be enhanced as the dependency on countries outside the zone would be reduced. More importantly, it will accelerate the capacity of the member states to meet the convergence criteria for WAMZ economic integration. On the contrary, the failure of the countries to achieve a diverse economic structure has potentially negative consequences, including the vulnerability of the members' economies to external shocks, low capacity to manage exchange rate systems, and the possibility of persistent imported inflation.

In line with the established factors that hinder economic diversity, it is recommended that countries in the WAMZ should embrace standard structural reforms that address government failures and improve institutional quality. In addition, these countries should give more attention to technical and vocational education, which is more relevant to manufacturing activities, while the educational system in the zone should be tailored towards the needs of the industry to accelerate the transformation from the primary sector to the manufacturing sector. There is equally a need for the entrenchment of sound macroeconomic management policies, which would result in an interest and exchange rate that is manufacturing sector friendly. The provision of various types of infrastructure, including power, road, and telecommunication infrastructure with high quality, should be intensified by countries in the WAMZ to attract more competitive advantage to the products of the countries.

Chapter 4

Sociocultural Diversities And Political Dynamics In West African Monetary Zone

West Africa is socioculturally diverse in terms of ethnicity, culture, tradition, language, and religion. These diversities can constitute a major challenge or create an opportunity for full integration of the West African subregion in general and the realisation of the core tenets of the West African Monetary Zone (WAMZ) in particular. It is established in the literature that, depending on effective management, sociocultural diversity can be a threat to unity or an opportunity to ensure unity and peaceful co-existence. However, a deep understanding of the concept and context of the diversity in question is essential for its proper management. So, to exploit the potential and surmount the challenges of sociocultural diversity concerning the achievement of the objectives of the WAMZ, it is imperative to discuss the concept of diversity and its nexus with the political dynamics of the sub-region and integration of the WAMZ countries. Therefore, this chapter captures the conceptualisation of sociocultural diversity, political dynamics, and integration in WAMZ and the nexus between sociocultural diversity and integration of the countries in WAMZ. The discussion centres on sociocultural heterogeneity as a barrier or potential for integration in WAMZ.

Concept Of Sociocultural Diversity

Diversity is derived from the Latin word diversus, which means more than one of different kinds. The concept of diversity has been defined differently by different scholars. It refers to all forms of differences – visible and invisible, which include ethnicity, disability, sexual orientation, education, age, social class, rank, etc. (Daya, 2014). Richter (*2014*) sees diversity as the variety of differences and similarities (dimensions) among people, including their culture, personality type, nationality, education etc. In this context, sociocultural diversity implies the different kinds of ethnicities, languages, cultures, religions, and socioeconomic statuses. It concerns the multiplicity of ethnicities, languages, cultures, religions, different income groups, and other sociocultural factors, such as beliefs, values, demographics, social classes, sexuality, and attitudes in society. Therefore, sociocultural diversity concerns the aspects of culture that can influence an individual's interactions with others of different backgrounds. Furthermore, it can influence how individuals and groups participate in an organisation; thus, critical in the integration of the WAMZ countries.

Overview Of Sociocultural Dynamics Of The West African Monetary Zone

Generally, West Africa is diverse in culture, religion, ethnicity, language, tradition, and even income distribution. These diversities are equally eminent in all the members of the West African Monetary Zone (The Gambia, Ghana, Guinea, Liberia, Nigeria, and Sierra Leone). On average, Nigeria and Liberia are the 7th and 11th most diverse (heterogenous) countries, respectively. Also, Ghana is the 20th most fractionalised (diverse); Sierra Leone is the 22nd, Guinea is 37th, and the Gambia is the 45th most diverse country in the world, respectively. This implies that the WAMZ countries are among the top 50 most ethnically, linguistically, and religiously diverse countries in the world (Alesina et al., 2003). This portrays huge sociocultural diversity, which is critical for the integration of the WAMZ. Thus, the overview of the sociocultural diversities in the WAMZ is discussed as follows.

TABLE 5.1: FRACTIONALIZATION INDEX

Diversities	The Gambia	Ghana	Guinea	Liberia	Nigeria	Sierra Leone
Ethnic Fractionalization	0.7864	0.6733	0.7389	0.9084	0.8505	0.8191
Rank	19	45	26	2	9	12
Linguistic Fractionalization	0.8076	0.6731	0.7725	0.9038	0.8316	0.7634
Rank	17	42	25	2	14	27
Religious Fractionalization	0.097	0.7987	0.2649	0.4883	0.7421	0.5395
Rank	193	6	149	99	15	86
Average Fractionalization	0.56367	0.71503	0.5921	0.76683	0.80807	0.70733
Rank	45	20	37	11	7	22

Source: *Alesina et al., 2003*

Ethnic And Cultural Diversities

The WAMZ is home to numerous ethnic groups with diverse cultures. The fractionalisation index, reported in Table 5.1, indicates that Liberia is the second most ethnically diverse (fractionalised) country in the World, while Nigeria and Sierra Leone are ranked the ninth and twelfth most ethnically diverse countries in the World, respectively. Also, Gambia is ranked Nineteenth, while Guinea and Ghana are ranked 26th and 45th, respectively. Fractionalisation "is a measure of the likelihood that two randomly selected people in a given country will be from two different groups (ethnicities, languages, religions, etc.) or speak two different languages" (*Alesina et al., 2003, pp 158*). In its initial form, a fractionalisation is a number between 0 and 1, with 0 meaning no variation (no diversity) and 1 meaning complete variation (numerous diversities).

The closer the fractionalisation value to 1 (one), the more diverse the country or territory is, and vice versa. Thus, the fractionalisation scores of the WAMZ countries show that the countries are remarkably diverse in terms of ethnicity, language, and religion.

The six countries harbour numerous ethnic groups. For instance, Nigeria is home to more than 300 tribes with major ethnic groups, including Hausa, Fulani, Igbo, and Yoruba. Other ethnic groups in Nigeria include Nupe, Bariba, Tiv, Igala, Ijaw, Urhobo, and Ibibio, to mention a few, organized into many autonomous ethnic nationalities (CIA, 2022). In Ghana, the largest group is the Asante; then there are the Ewe, Ga, Fante, Gurma, Dagomba, Bimoba, and Anyi of the coast etc. The Mende, Temne, Loko, Kono, Limba, Susu, Kissi, and Vai are some of the ethnic groups in Sierra Leone. Liberia is also home to many ethnicities, including the Kru, Krahn, Loma, Bassa, Kpelle, Gola, Gbandi, Grebo, and Kissi. The Wolof, Kissi, Mandinka, Manjak, Jola, Biafada, Bassari, Bubi, and others are ethnic groups in The Gambia and Guinea (*CIA, 2022*)

Despite the wide diversity of cultures in the West African Monetary Zone, the people extensively shared similar dress, cuisine, music, and culture. Hence, ethnic diversity can be a great potential for exploiting the gains of the WAMZ. However, due to the long history of ethnic clashes in the WAMZ countries, ethnic diversity can pose a major threat to the integration of the WAMZ, resulting from the fear of domination among the ethnic groups.

Religious Diversity

Religious plurality is the main characteristic of the six member countries of the West African Monetary Zone. Islam, which is the biggest religion of the most populous ethnic groups in the zone, is the predominant religion in the Gambia (96.4%), Guinea (89.1%), and Sierra Leone (78.5%), while a greater proportion of the population in Ghana (71.3%) and Liberia (85.6%) practice Christianity (*see Table 5.2*). In the case of Nigeria, the people are almost evenly distributed between the two religions, with more people practising Islam (53.5%) than Christianity (45.9%). Few people are animists, practising indigenous religions – Traditional African Religion, while some are atheists in all the six countries of WAMZ. The rules of the religions guide the lifestyle, values, dress, and cultures of the people in the zone, so much so that the concept of tribalism is less observed by the religious groups across the member countries of WAMZ. Religious teachings encourage inter-ethnic marriages, and shared cultural icons are established through a superseded commonality of beliefs or faith organisations (*Tollnek & Baten, 2017*).

However, Traditional African religions (noting the many different belief systems) are the oldest belief systems among the populations of this region and include the

Akan religion, Yoruba religion, Odinani of Igbo, and Serer religion (Larkin et al., 2006). They are spiritual but also linked to the historical and cultural heritage of the people. Although traditional beliefs vary from one place to the next, there are more similarities than differences.

Christianity was largely introduced from the late 19th century onward when missionaries from European countries brought the religion to the region. West African Christians are predominantly Roman Catholic or Anglican; some Evangelical churches have also been established. Christianity has become the predominant religion in the central and southern parts of Nigeria and the coastal regions stretching from southern Ghana to coastal parts of Sierra Leone. Like Islam, elements of traditional African religion are mixed with Christianity. Therefore, the WAMZ is characterised by religious diversity, which can play a vital role in the proposed integration of the region.

TABLE 5.2: RELIGIOUS, ETHNIC, AND LINGUISTIC DIVERSITIES IN WAMZ

	The Gambia	Ghana	Guinea	Liberia	Nigeria	Sierra Leone
Religions						
Christianity	3.5%	71.3%	6.8%	85.6%	45.9%	20.4%
Islam	96.4%	19.9%	89.1%	12.6%	53.5%	78.5%
Others	0.1%	8.8%	4.1%	1.8%	0.6%	1.1%
Number of Ethnic groups and languages						
	The Gambia	Ghana	Guinea	Liberia	Nigeria	Sierra Leone
Ethnic groups	8	> 70	24	16	>250	16
Languages	10	> 80	22	20	>525	25

Source: *Computed by the author using data from World Factbook – Central Intelligence Agency*

Linguistic Diversity

West Africans primarily speak Niger-Congo languages, belonging mostly, though not exclusively, to its non-Bantu branches, though some Nilo-Saharan and Afro-Asiatic speaking groups are also found in West Africa. However, the six countries of the WAMZ are highly multi-lingual. For instance, Table 5.2 shows that there are over 500 languages spoken in Nigeria and over 80 languages in Ghana, while Guinea, Liberia, and Sierra Leone have at least 20 languages each. Gambia is the most linguistically homogenous in the zone, with ten different languages. The Niger–Congo-speaking Yoruba, Igbo, Fulani, Akan, and Wolof ethnic groups are the largest and most influential. The Hausa and Tiv people are found in Nigeria. Songhai, Kanuri, and Zarma are found in the zone. Colonial languages also play a pivotal cultural and political role, being adopted as the official languages of most countries in the region, as well as linguae Franca in communication between the region's various ethnic groups. For historical reasons, Western European languages such as French and English are adopted by Guinea and the other five countries (Gambia, Ghana, Liberia, Nigeria, and Sierra Leone) as their official languages, respectively. So, Guinea is the only francophone country in the WAMZ. Therefore, the zone is linguistically diverse. Unfortunately, the multiplicity of languages in the zone has had the unfortunate potential of dividing the people of the region, who see each other as different and immutable. It also poses a language barrier, which makes commercial transactions difficult and threatens the integration of the zone.

Political Dynamics And Integration In WAMZ

West Africa was broadly affected by the colonial activities of France and Britain, the positive and negative legacies of which can be felt to this day. Colonial powers, France and Britain, ventured into Africa to claim colonies. Slavery impacted West Africa in many ways. Many West African groups were instrumental in capturing and holding West Africans as slaves to trade with European merchants.

By 1900, European colonial powers claimed most of Africa. Only the Kingdom of Ethiopia and the area of Liberia, which was established as a home for freed slaves, remained independent. In 1884, Otto von Bismarck of Germany hosted the Berlin Conference, which to a great degree, determined how Africa was colonized (*Boahen, 1985*). This conference included fourteen colonial European countries and the United States, and its purpose was to divide Africa and agree on colonial boundary lines. Germany had few claims in Africa; thus, Bismarck was hoping to benefit by playing the other countries against each other. At the time, more than 80 percent of Africa remained free of colonial control. On a large map of Africa, claims were argued over, and boundary lines were drawn according to European agreements.

There was little regard for the concerns of the sociocultural dynamics of Africa. Colonial boundaries divided close-knit communities into separate colonies. Ethnic boundaries were disregarded as often-warring groups were placed together in the same colony. The Europeans, seeking profits from cheap labour and resources, did not consider the culture of the people and often employed brutal measures to subdue the local people. Most of the current borders in West Africa are a result of the Berlin Conference, and many of the geopolitical issues that confront West Africa today can be traced back to this event specifically and to colonialism in general (*Larkin et al., 2006*).

European colonialism remained strong in West Africa until the end of World War II, which left many European countries economically exhausted. In 1945, the United Nations (UN) was established. One of the primary UN objectives was to oversee the decolonisation of European colonies. Still, colonialism in West Africa lingered on. It was not until the 1990s that the last colony was finally freed. The transition from a colony to an independent nation itself caused conflict – civil wars were fought over who would control the country after the Europeans were pushed out. The transition to full independence has exacted a heavy toll on West African countries but has resulted in stronger political structures and greater democratic liberties in many cases. The first country to gain independence in West Africa was Ghana in 1957.

During the era of independence after World War II,

the Cold War between the United States and the Soviet Union enticed many of the West African countries to support one or the other of the superpowers. The political pressure that divided West African countries during the Cold War has persisted and is the basis of some of the current political problems. The European countries extracted raw materials and minerals from their West African colonies, as well as slave labour. Varying degrees of attention were given to education, medical care, or infrastructure development. The dependency that a colony, especially the Francophone countries, had on European countries for economic income in some cases continued long after independence and may continue today (Bundu, 1997). On the other hand, major technology transfers from Europe to Africa infused greater efficiencies into West Africa's economic activities. The imperial nature of colonialism and the divisive Cold War did bring about, in an unfortunate manner, the benefits of structured institutions and economic and political systems patterned towards those of France and Britain that are not in touch with the sociocultural dynamics of the people of West Africa.

From Colonialism To Independence

The transition from a European colony to an independent state has not necessarily been a civil transition for West African countries, as they have struggled to create stable governments or peaceful conditions. In nearly all cases, removing the colonial powers from West Africa was only half the battle toward independence. The other half was establishing functional, effective institutions and economic and political systems that are consistent with the sociocultural dynamics of the people (*Adetiba, 2019*).

Though each West African country has taken a slightly different path, most former colonies have endured civil unrest, conflict, or warfare in their push for stable institutions, economies, and governments due to the underground disruption of their former colonial masters (France and Britain). Coups, fraudulent elections, military regimes, and corruption have plagued the political leadership in many West African countries with the tacit support of either France or Britain. Civil unrest usually precedes a change in leadership: political power regularly changes hands by undemocratic means. Developing and maintaining effective governance institutions and economic and political systems has been the most challenging. Political leaders have come and gone, many have been replaced before their terms were over, and many have instituted themselves for long years after their terms ended. In most cases of supposed leaders being elected democratically, it is common to have widespread accusations of corruption, voter fraud, or ballot box scandals due to the institutions of governance being weakened and compromised by corrupt politicians. Such governments are customary for mismanagement, lack of transparency and accountability, and institutionalisation of corruption.

The vacuum left by retreating colonial powers at times has been filled by authoritarian dictators or by leaders who assumed control of the government and then proceeded to pillage and plunder the state for personal gain or the enrichment of their clan or political cronies. After the colonial era, it was not uncommon for new leaders to be connected to the old colonial power and to adopt the language and business arrangements of the European coloniser. This gave them an advantage over their competitors and provided a means of income gained by the support of their former European colonial business partners, which often wanted to keep ties with their colonies to continue to exploit their resources for economic profits. Many of these leaders stayed in power because of military backing or authoritarian rule funded by the profits from selling minerals or resources to their former colonial masters.

A few countries are still struggling to bring about some type of order and unity, and despite all the negative issues, there have been democratic and relatively stable progressive governments in Africa that have emerged from the transition in recent years, which is a hopeful trend for the long term.

It is important to note that the objective of colonialism was to connect a colony with the mother country, not to connect African countries. As a result, little cooperation occurs between African countries. Each country interacts more with its European colonial counterpart concerning trade, economics, and cultural dynamics. European colonialism has isolated African countries from their neighbouring countries and does not contribute to unity within or among African regions. Colonial powers often built new port cities to extract goods and resources from their colonies and transportation systems from the new ports to the interior to collect the resources and bring them to the port. However, the colonial powers did not build a network of transportation systems that connected the region as a whole. Colonial powers were intent on continuing dependence on the mother country so their colonies could be controlled and dominated.

The current wave of globalisation based on corporate colonialism continues to encourage the same pattern of discouraging interaction between countries and instead encouraging trade with more economically powerful non-African countries. Most of the interaction between countries results from crisis or warfare, in which case large numbers of refugees cross the border into neighbouring countries for personal survival or security. In order to begin to work together and promote trade, common transportation, security, and industry, fifteen West African states came together in 1975 to create the Economic Community of West African States (ECOWAS). Since then, various African countries have signed additional political and economic agreements. In 2001, the more expansive African Union was created to help African states compete in the international marketplace.

Institutional, Economic, And Political Dynamics Of West Africa Integration

Bundu (1997) gave an appraisal of ECOWAS and the future of regional integration of West Africa and, thus, categorically posits that for regional integration to flourish as an instrument of economic development in ECOWAS, there must be the restructuring of national and institutional arrangements. The importance of regional integration requires that a key ministry be established in each country to act as a focal point. It should be mandated to assume the coordination of all forms of regional integration and cooperation and should ensure that national development policies and decisions are cast from a regional perspective. Although attempts of this sort have been made in several member states, such arrangements are not effective anywhere in the region. Instead, one finds small coordination units created in certain ministries as token gestures representative of how peripheral regional integration remains on the national economic agenda. Such deficiencies have a deleterious effect on the attention accorded to regional integration matters and the level of preparation and participation at ECOWAS meetings.

After the deep decline of the early 1980s, national economies are only now barely achieving a measure of stabilisation. Unfortunately, there is little evidence that the reforms have had the desired effect of restructuring the region's economies, and the need to transform and diversify the regional economic base is more acute than ever. The establishment of a more stable economic environment capable of encouraging long-term investment and development should be one of the preoccupations of the ECOWAS Consultative Forum mentioned earlier.

The wave of reforms currently sweeping the region in favour of political pluralism and economic liberalism should help to narrow political and ideological differences among member states. This tendency may be reinforced by the Community's adoption in 1991 of the Abuja Declaration of Political Principles, which enshrines a minimum set of democratic principles as guidance to member states in their quest for a well-established democratic society. This is a modest beginning of political cooperation but constitutes a vital step nonetheless. The revised Treaty also envisages the establishment of a West African parliament to promote grassroots involvement and popular participation in regional integration and cooperation. The more democratic rule should bring about a more stable and congenial political atmosphere, which is a sine qua non for regional integration (*Bundu, 1997*).

The dynamics that exist among the Francophone and

Anglophone countries in West Africa can be looked at majorly from three different perspectives – institutional, economic, and political. The Francophone countries are still controlled by their colonial masters in terms of having control over their institutions, such as their central bank and using the currency of the colonial masters, thereby controlling the economy and, by extension, the political system. Whereas some of the Anglophone countries have their indigenisation policy which has given them control over their institutions and economy. These dynamics have made it difficult for the West African states to have a common front in terms of the actualisation of regional integration.

Francophone And Anglophone Relations In West Africa

West African countries were colonised by both the French and British colonial masters. The French are known for their policy of assimilation, while the British are exploitative. The Francophone and Anglophone countries came together for economic reasons since no country can be an island in the international system. The world, being a global village, collaboration and cooperation amongst the Francophone and Anglophone colonies became imperative. It is important to mention that the Organization of African Unity (OAU), now the African Union (AU), formed in 1963 and brought together many African countries wasn't initially the idea of the colonial masters (*Adetula, 2009*).

The West African Sub-region organisation, the ECOWAS, came into being in 1975 and is the corollary of the African Union. These organizations aim at forging unity of purpose in the West African sub-region in particular and Africa in general in the areas of trade, commerce, security, and development amongst the member states for the well-being of the citizens. However, Francophone and Anglophone countries have often differed and sometimes battled on the political field, especially within the Organization of African Unity.

Hence, Chidozie and Abiodun- Eniayekan (*2017*) opine that it cannot be ruled out that there could be some mutual suspicions amongst these nation-states, be it Francophone against Francophone, Francophone against Anglophone, or Anglophone against Anglophone. But it is still in their interest to come together to forge a common purpose. There are some skirmishes among these Francophone and Anglophone countries, especially demonstrated in the usual killings in the Francophone and Anglophone countries, especially between Nigeria and Cameroon at their frontiers, on land, and in the sea by Cameroonian gendarmes. For more than a decade, the Cameroon government of President Paul Biya has responded with repression and human rights violations to attempts by Anglophone political parties and other groups to ameliorate the situation of Anglophones within Cameroon, according to reports from human rights groups, international organizations, and media sources.

The evolving commitment of its elites to three foreign policy principles – la francophonie, regional integration, and conflict resolution suggests the beginning of the bridging of the historical gap between Francophone and Anglophone West Africa. Nigeria's attendance at the Franco-African summit, increased cooperation between the Union Economique et Monétaire Ouest Africaine – The West African Economic and Monetary Union (UEMOA) and ECOWAS, and the settlement of the Liberian civil war are examples of enhanced cooperation within greater West Africa.

Schraeder (*2014*) believes that there is growing Francophone-Anglophone rapprochement among West African elites against the backdrop of rising Francophone-Anglophone tensions at the continental level, such as in the OAU and within the international system, as witnessed by growing tensions between Washington and Paris.

It is not as if there are no skirmishes amongst Anglophone countries in West Africa; for instance, Nigerians were sent packing from Ghana in the early 1960s. In 1969, the Nigerian government retaliated by repatriating Ghanaian nationals. Again, during Shehu Shagari's regime in the second republic, there was a "Ghana must go" drama that played out in the country. This was just to say that there are usual mutual suspicions amongst West African and African States, be they Francophone or Anglophone.

More so, the Nigerian size and seeming "prosperity" makes her vulnerable to attracting envy from some other countries in West Africa.

Consequently, it has been observed that there are mutual suspicions and an attendant lack of trust that mars the relationship between the Francophone and Anglophone countries of West Africa. Consistent with the above, Jooji (*2011*) critically noted that most West African countries share a common historical and political experience, even though there appear to fall within the boundaries of the Lusophone, Francophone, and Anglophone divides.

Therefore, it is worthy to note that it rightly asserts that "ECOWAS was founded to achieve collective self-sufficiency for the member states utilising Economic and Monetary Union, thus creating a single trade bloc (*Jooji, 2011*). This is equally noted in Osagie (*2005*) that proposes a higher level of integration that requires members to surrender national sovereignty over sensitive financial matters, monetary integration where a new currency replaces national currencies.

In comparison to the above assertion, N'zué (*2011*) opines that with the interconnection of the economies amongst themselves (the new world economy), these Eurozone problems would impact, without any doubt all, the economies and, in particular, the economies of

ECOWAS countries. Hence the Francophone members of the ECOWAS have a monetary union called Union Monétaire Ouest Africaine (UMOA) (West African Monetary Union) (WAMU) which is rather closely tied to France, their colonial masters and is not concerned with the ECOWAS monetary arrangements.

In contrast, Faujas (*2014*) notes with dismay that the common currency among French-speaking countries in both West and Central Africa, the CFA Franc, has also, seemingly, been a burden, although it is more protected from inflation than currencies that are not aligned to the Euro.

In terms of relationship and cooperation, Chidozie and Abiodun- Eniayekan (*2017*) reveals that Nigeria, an Anglophone country, has always been at the receiving end of military incursions by its smaller neighbouring Francophone countries. In the spirit of "big brother", Nigeria has always been derided by these small Francophone West African countries. Invariably, these countries have always seen the need to come together because there are benefits that can be derived from peaceful coexistence among the nation-states. In furtherance, N'Zué (*2012*) points out that case studies of selected ECOWAS countries are carried out to address the issue of how Africa can design schemes to enhance its domestic resource mobilisation capacity to push the ECOWAS regional integration Agenda.

It is worthy of mention to note that the ECOWAS has gone beyond its frontiers and is now collaborating with the Economic Community of Central African States to combat piracy and maritime crimes.

Sociocultural Diversity As A Barrier To Integration In WAMZ

In the pre-colonial era, when empires and kingdoms reigned in the West African region, most wars were fought along ethnic, religious, language, or cultural divides. For example, the Civil War in Nigeria (*1967-1970*), Liberia, and Sierra Leone all have ethnic, linguistic, and religious undertones (*Deng, 1997*). Also, during the slave trade era, though there were cases of people in West African communities that sold their relations and kinsmen to slavery, however much of West Africans sold to slavery were mostly captives of wars fought along ethnic or cultural divides. The trend continued during the colonial era, as the colonial masters deployed the "divide and rule" strategy to create enough faultlines in the sociocultural diverse West Africa by creating a sense of distrust, suspicion, and disunity among West African communities, thereby conquering and exploiting them. Unfortunately, the situation seems not to have improved years after all countries of West Africa (including WAMZ) were granted political freedom as their former colonial masters, France and Britain, still indirectly influence the institutional, economic, and political dynamics of countries in the West African region to the disadvantage of the region (Somerville, 2016). This hinders the realisation of the full potential of ECOWAS, which has been existing for the past 47 years without achieving the set objectives. The same reason can hinder the integration of the West Africa Monetary Zone subregion integration.

Specifically, the sociocultural diversity of the West African Monetary Zone constitutes the main constraint to the integration of the subregion. The barriers are numerous but can be discussed under the following: language barrier; persistence of colonial ties; fear of domination by small countries; lack of visionary leadership; poor engagement of key stakeholders; socioeconomic divergence and disparities; rising ethnopolitical tensions; conflict; crisis; and insecurity; inadequate and poor state basic infrastructure; limited access to quality education; and insufficient support to the informal entrepreneurial sector.

- **Language Barrier**

The lack of a common spoken and written language in the West African region constitutes a barrier and complexity in education, trade, and business communication. Though countries in the region have tried to adopt either English or French (based on colonial influences) as a national language, the influences of these two languages have been socioculturally divisive in West

Africa and of negative effects on the expected cooperation towards the attainment of collective emancipation of the sub-region.

- **Persistence of Colonial Ties**

The persistence of colonial ties with France and Britain for the structure and operations of institutions, economy, and political systems is counterproductive to the regional integration efforts in West Africa. These ties are only meant to preserve both local and foreign interests of France and Britain as well as their allies in ensuring the preservation of the status quo of West Africa remaining subjugated.

- **Hidden Fear of Domination by Small Countries**

The unspoken fear of domination by the bigger countries (especially Nigeria) by many small West African countries is another major sociocultural challenge to the realisation of West African integration. No doubt, Nigeria overshadows every other country in the region in terms of population, gross domestic product, industrialisation, and natural resource endowment. But France, unfortunately, given its continued ties with the francophone countries of the region, sees the actualisation of the West Africa integration being championed by Nigeria as a threat to her economic interest in the region. Hence, subtly undermine it by instilling fears of Nigeria's dominance in the minds of political leaders of small countries in the region.

- **Lack of Visionary Leadership**

Many West African countries have been plagued by years of lack of visionary political leadership. No country in the region, even Nigeria, which stands to benefit most from West Africa integration, has shown visionary leadership, and each continues to view the other with suspicion. The sit-tight approach of our leaders towards sovereignty is deplorable, and their continued refusal to "give a bit to gain so much" is also despicable. Nations of the sub-region should develop a new genre toward this untapped strategy, and it is even more incumbent upon the bigger nations in the sub-region, like Nigeria, to step forward and provide leadership; otherwise, the entire project would remain a mirage. Considering that integration involves the cession of a measure of sovereignty, there's no gainsaying that the clear and unfettered commitment of member states beyond lip service and signing treaties or protocols is a sine qua non for the actualisation of true integration of the region.

- **Poor Engagement of Key Stakeholders**

Another socio-cultural challenge of West African integration is that, most often, there is no involvement and engagement of key stakeholders such as civil society groups, non-governmental organizations, the private sector, and advocacy groups in the integration process. No proper enlightenment is given to the citizens of the region as regards the goals of West Africa integration. Proper engagement of key stakeholders is needed for adequate awareness creation, information dissemination, proper understanding, and better collaborations to ensure that the objectives and benefits of the integration are well known within the region.

- **Socioeconomic Divergence and Disparities**

Different growth paths and levels of development in the West African region are other socio-cultural challenges to West African integration. The overall poverty level in the region is high but more endemic in rural communities. Unfortunately, many West African areas are rural. Again, the literacy rate of the region is very low (World Bank, 2021). Surprisingly, a very high percentage of the small population that is educated is unemployed or underemployed (*World Bank, 2021*). Access to basic education, health, potable water, and sanitation is low and poor (*World Bank, 2021*). Also, these create a sense of disillusion and depression among the citizenry as well as loss of faith in their respective countries and, by extension, in the wider West Africa region. These situations often create migration problems that lead to sociocultural disequilibrium.

- **Rising Ethnopolitical Tensions, Conflict, Crisis, and Insecurity**

Lack of good governance and proper management of sociocultural diversities have led to incessant cases of social, political, ethnic, and religious tensions, unrest, and conflicts. Evidence of the above exists, giving rise to a state of ethnic rivalry, religious and political riots, armed robbery, kidnapping, and terrorism. All these compromises weaken the ECOWAS region's sustainable growth and development prospects. The Sierra Leone Civil War, the Liberian conflict, the unconstitutional takeover of government in the Niger Republic, the election crisis in the Gambia, the terrorist activities of Boko Haram and Islamic State in West Africa operating in the north-eastern states of Nigeria and Lake Chad region as well as the rampaging of armed bandits and Jihadist terrorising most North Central and Northwest states of Nigeria are indicators of how raising the state of insecurity to lives and properties is challenging the actualisation of the objectives of WAMZ. The preponderance of these states of insecurity in West Africa has created famine, drought, destruction, refugee problems, diseases, destruction of private properties and physical infrastructure, and in some cases, ethnic cleansing in West Africa, thereby worsening the already bad socioeconomic growth and development dynamics across the West African region.

- **Inadequate and Poor State of Basic Infrastructure**

The lack of adequate infrastructure by way of roads, energy, power, rail, recreation facilities, communications, and information technology for the facilitation of the information gathering and sharing, movement of goods, capital, services, and persons, including the right of access to information poses a major challenge to the actualisation of the integration in West Africa. This has created a situation of weak productive capacity for citizens of West Africa, arising largely from poor and decaying infrastructural conditions. Regional integration demands the aggregation of resources of states in the region to gain comparative advantages within the region. However, the greater challenge in West Africa is that of a region so bereft of infrastructure, which creates sociocultural disequilibrium.

- **Limited Access to Quality Education**

The West African education system lags far behind the systems of other developing countries. The situation is growing worse as people in much of West Africa lose faith in the state school system. With nearly 50% of the population under the age of 15, education should receive much more attention. Education develops economic performance, integrates young people, and transmits new values. The rehabilitation of the school system is, therefore, a major task of utmost urgency but one that will be particularly hard to achieve.

- **Insufficient Support to the Informal Entrepreneurial Sector**

West African societies are still at the stage where individual daily survival depends largely on individualistic informal entrepreneurial activities in subsistence agriculture, petty trading, and arts and crafts services, as more than 70 percent of the West African economy is in the informal sector. Governments and policymakers across West Africa are not providing an enabling environment as well as the much-needed support for the informal entrepreneurial sectors. In this era of globalisation, societies need to have regular information on socio-cultural and economic dynamics around them and the world at large. Existing statistical systems in West Africa is not providing this information.

Sociocultural Diversity As A Potential For Integration In WAMZ

Although the sociocultural diversity of member countries of the West African Monetary Zone constitutes a constraint to the integration of the zone, there is always a sense of communalism and oneness among West Africans whenever they meet themselves in a foreign land outside the West Africa region, implying that the sociocultural diversity of West Africa can inherently provide opportunities to the integration of the zone if properly explored. The West Africa integration has viable prospects if the sociocultural diversity of the region is effective and positively explored, following some of the following options:

Institution Of A Credible, Transparent, And Accountable System Of Governance

The current instability in West Africa's political and economic decline and social discontent reflects a leadership crisis across the region. If this is true of individual countries, it is equally valid for the regional integration process. The emergence of a credible, transparent, accountable system of governance has the prospect of providing the needed re-direction of the sociocultural dynamics in the region, thereby engendering self-sacrifice and commitments on the part of citizens. This is essential in any cooperative endeavour, such as the regional integration of WAMZ. However, not all countries are given the same appreciation of the need for cooperation. It would appear that some have to be encouraged, persuaded, and pulled along by others. West Africa, in reality, has credible men and women with proven capacity, even outside the region, who can do this.

Connecting With The Diaspora Community

Prospects of the integration of WAMZ via the sociocultural dynamics of the zone are viable if and only if some level of strategic thinking and visioning is observed by governments and policymakers in the region. West African Monetary Zone is currently blessed with a high population of educated, informed, and tech-savvy youth population, ready to take on the world around them. Also, years of underdevelopment in West Africa forced many West Africans to migrate to other parts of the world in search of opportunities. Interestingly many did find the opportunities legitimately and are playing strategic roles in the economic systems and processes globally. West Africa needs to take advantage of its vibrant diaspora population in fast-tracking the West Africa integration process by creating the right investment environment that can attract their attention.

Need For New Cooperation and Partnerships With Emerging Economies Of The World

The competitive advantage of the WAMZ in the African continent due to the availability of natural and human resources in the zone makes the zone attractive to the industrial world. There is an opportunity to untie the unfavourable relationships with France and Britain by seeking favourable new economic cooperation and partnerships with the more liberal, newly emerging economies of the world, such as India, Brazil, etc. Through such an arrangement, the WAMZ can protect against the negative manipulation of her sociocultural dynamics by forces outside the African continent.

Engagement Of The Youth Population

The population of the WAMZ countries is dominated by the youths, and the youths have an average education level that is far higher than that of their elders due to the results of efforts undertaken over the past few years in the education sector. With this prospect, there is still a need for strategic thinking to create consistency between the current training systems and the future needs of the youth.

While the proportion of youth that will find jobs in the modern sector will certainly increase, the informal economy is likely to remain a major workplace for young people. The informal sector is also likely to develop faster than in the past because of the average increase in the educational level of its actors. Will the WAMZ countries experience a new form of economy based on enterprises that are mid-way between the informal and formal sectors?

The youths are, more than their elders, connected to the rest of the world. They are attentive and assiduous spectators of global evolutions. As it already happens, families will establish strategies for educating their children according to job "availability in the North", more particularly in the area of caregiving (nurses, medical care providers, etc.), where the prospects are satisfactory due to the ageing of the population in developed countries. Some economic operators in developed countries or West Africa may open specialised training institutions in the region that would primarily be geared toward the northern labour market. Young Africans of today are farther from the colonial past of their region than the previous generations. They have weaker links with the traditional mindsets and ways of doing things that their elders had learned from educational systems designed in former colonial countries. They have greater access to schools of thought broadcast through new information technologies. Unlike their elders, they have known the omnipresent post-colonial era and have more readily turned to the private sector. These will enhance the integration of the WAMZ and facilitate the realisation of the full convergence of the member countries.

Conclusion

The West African Monetary Zone (WAMZ) is unique and crucial for the monetary integration of the West African sub-region. The WAMZ is home to the most populous black country in the world (Nigeria), the oldest republic in Africa (Liberia), the first African country to gain her independence from British colonial rule (Ghana), and the first francophone country to gain her independence in Africa (Guinea). However, the zone is a heterogenous society with diverse ethnic, religious, linguistic, and political orientations and economic conditions. The study of sociocultural diversity and the political dynamics of WAMZ is critical for regional integration. This chapter has revealed the significant importance of taking advantage of the sociocultural diversity of the zone, drawing lessons from the changes in sociocultural dynamics of the region during a different era of her evolution. The challenges and opportunities associated with the sociocultural diversity and political dynamics of the zone were discussed extensively. In conclusion, the discourse in this chapter revealed that irrespective of the socio-cultural and political challenges confronting the integration of the WAMZ, there are still opportunities to fast-track the integration process and actualise the benefits thereof.

The discourse in this chapter identified the advantages of diversity in WAMZ. Thus, it is recommended that the WAMZ countries should take concerted actions at both country and regional levels to exploit the prospects highlighted in this chapter. This can be achieved by engagement of the youth population, cooperation and partnerships with emerging economies of the world, development of strong institutions and accountable systems of governance, and connecting with the diaspora community.

SECTION TWO
Potentials And Benefits Of Integration In WAMZ

Chapter 5

Single Currency Agenda: How Ready Are WAMZ Countries?

One of the fundamental components of a monetary union is the adaption of the common currency as means of payment by members of the union. Successful monetary integration would necessarily lead to a regime of a common currency and a single central bank accepted by all countries in the integrated monetary union (*Cham, 2009*). Scholars agree that similarity in government policy attitude, as well as inflation convergence, are important requirements for a successful monetary union (*Bah, 2015*). A monetary union must be characterised by the homogeneity of policies and regulations and not by internal or external disparities and disequilibria, hence the need for a single currency. The traditional Optimum

Currency Area (OCA) theory identifies macroeconomic convergence as a prerequisite for the introduction of a common currency. Notwithstanding the recognition of the importance of macroeconomic convergence in the process of introducing a single currency by WAMZ members, there is a dearth of empirical studies on the assessment of the level of macroeconomic convergence of WAMZ countries. Therefore, this chapter provides an assessment of the readiness of WAMZ countries in terms of convergence to basic criteria.

More than twenty years after the establishment of the West African Monetary Zone (WAMZ), a single currency has not been introduced in the region (*WAMI, 2020*). The introduction of the single currency has been postponed about six times, from 2003 to 2005, 2009, 2015, to 2020, and 2021. One of the reasons has been the inability to meet the macroeconomic convergence criteria by countries in the region. Efforts aimed at meeting the set criteria of macroeconomic convergence is urgently required in order to fast-track the process of introducing the single currency. Hence, the need for this chapter, which objective is to assess WAMZ country's macroeconomic convergence performances, identify challenges limiting macroeconomic convergence in WAMZ countries as well as make suggestions on possible policy interventions that governments and monetary authorities of each WAMZ country need to take towards meeting macroeconomic convergence criteria. The remaining parts of this chapter are organised into the following: Rationale for the introduction of a single currency; theoretical underpin of monetary integration; assessment of WAMZ countries' readiness for the introduction of a single currency; challenges of meeting the macroeconomic convergence criteria; and finally, conclusion and recommendation.

Rationale For A Single ECOWAS Currency

The single common currency is one of the fundamental components for the smooth function of a monetary union. Thus, to attain full economic integration across countries, the introduction of a single currency is imperative. The adoption of a single currency by member countries of an integrated economic area promotes inter-country trade among member countries. If the prices of commodities across countries are expressed in the same currency, price comparison will be straightforward. This may help firms cut costs, as they will be able to find the cheapest product more easily. It will also encourage greater competition as there is greater transparency in prices. It has equally been documented in the literature that a single currency is expected to result to:

- elimination of currency exchange risk;
- reduction of transaction cost;

- transparency of prices;
- facilitation of market transactions;
- stabilization of prices;
- prevention of competitive devaluation by nation states, and
- promotion of inter-country trade flow, among others.

It is expected that the businesses operating within WAMZ would not have to worry about exchange rate fluctuation if the single currency, "Eco", is introduced. In the absence of a single currency, there is the need to exchange one currency for another in order to trade across countries. There is a risk involved here because, between the period of purchase and payment, the rate of exchange may change. This risk will be eliminated with the introduction of a single currency among the countries. The adoption of a single common currency also helps to reduce transaction costs involved in intra-country trade. Thus, the payment system is made easy, further encouraging trade flows among member countries of the union. Within the single currency union, all prices would be quoted in the same currency facilitating easy price comparison. It will not be possible for firms to translate high local prices into international prices. If, for instance, the proposed single currency, Eco, is introduced in WAMZ and ECOWAS at large, it will be easy for consumers to compare the prices of goods between Ghana and Guinea. This would encourage firms to improve their efficiencies and competitiveness across countries in the single currency area. Lower transaction costs, elimination of exchange rate fluctuations, and price transparency will give incentives for firms to expand their markets within the single currency area. This would also generate investment and employment among the countries of the union.

The introduction of the Eco single currency would yield more stable prices because the value of Eco would reflect the average economic conditions of the whole Zone and not that of a single national economy. A single currency would prevent the need for nation states in the WAMZ to devalue their national currencies to achieve a competitive edge over other nation-states. With a single currency, there would be a need for any country to respond to the devaluation of the currency in another country by devaluating its own currency. Hence, competitive currency devaluation among countries in the Zone would be eliminated.

Theoretical Underpin Of Monetary Integration

Monetary integration and single currency operations are founded mainly on the Optimal Currency Area (OCA) theory. The theory went through about four different phases over time since the pioneering work in the early 1960s. The main aim of the pioneering phase was to propagate the properties of theory and also to show the benefits of the currency area. The second phase emphasised the relative importance of the properties, and the literature in this phase gave more structure to the analysis of the costs and benefits of the currency area. In the third phase, empirical evaluation of the benefits and costs of OCA theory was examined, and there was more emphasis on the benefits of currency area and monetary integration. The last phase is the empirical phase, where the properties of the OCA theory are reviewed in great detail, and the interpretation of each property is made simple.

What is the Optimum Currency Area (OCA) theory, and what are its properties? Optimum currency area theory (OCA) states that specific areas not bounded by national borders would benefit from a common currency. In other words, geographic regions may be better off using the same currency instead of each country within that geographic region using a different currency.

To derive the benefits inherent in the currency area, as an emphasis in OCA theory, four properties are required:

i. There should be free movement of people across members of the currency area such that there is an integrated labour market in the area.

ii. Prices and wages should be flexible, inter-country trade imbalances should be eliminated, and capital mobility should also be flexible.

iii. There should be a centralised or controlled budget to facilitate wealth redistribution from countries with surpluses to countries that suffer due to labour and capital mobility.

iv. All participating members should have a similar macroeconomic condition, that is, a convergence of key macroeconomic indicators.

Assessment Of WAMZ Countries Readiness For A Single Currency

In November 2002, the Forum of Finance Ministers of WAMZ decided to facilitate the harmonisation of fiscal and monetary policies by introducing two sets of convergence criteria, four primary and six secondary criteria, for members. According to WAMI (*2002*), the primary criteria are as follows:

(i) Achieve and maintain price stability by recording single-digit end-of-period inflation rate by 2003 and 5 percent by 2004.

(ii) Ensure sustainable government fiscal position by reducing the ratio of budget deficit to GDP to 4 percent or less throughout the period 2003–2005.

(iii) Limit Central Bank financing of government budget deficit as a percent of the previous year's tax revenue to 10 percent or less throughout the period 2003–2005.

(iv) Maintain a sufficient level of gross official foreign exchange reserves of at least three months of import cover throughout the period 2003 – 2005.

These four criteria are evaluated at the different target dates for the introduction of the single currency. The date for the introduction of the single currency was shifted four times, from 2003 to 2005, 2009, 2015 and 2020 – 2021. Therefore, the readiness of each country is evaluated on these dates.

The basic macroeconomic convergence criteria status of Gambia is presented in Table 6.1, while the status of Ghana, Guinea, Liberia, Nigeria, and Sierra Leone are presented in Tables 6.2 to 6.6, respectively. As of 2003, which is the first date stipulated for the launching of the single currency, the Gambia met only one criterion out of the four criteria. However, in 2005 the country satisfied three of the criteria. This indicates that the government and monetary authorities of the Gambia have shown sufficient commitment towards the preparation of introducing a single currency. In 2009, all four criteria were met in the Gambia. Unfortunately, the country backslid in the area of fiscal deficit, central bank financing of deficit, and gross external reserve in 2015 – this year, only one of the criteria was satisfied. This could be due to the global economic meltdown at that period. In 2020, the country met three benchmarks (inflation, central bank financing of deficit, and gross external reserves criteria) out of the four basic convergence criteria. Only the fiscal deficit criterion was not met, but there is sufficient evidence to suggest that the above may have been due to the impact of Covid-19. The consequences of the pandemic spill over to 2021, and the country failed in two criteria, fiscal deficit and central bank deficit financing.

The second biggest economy in the zone after Nigeria is Ghana; the macroeconomic convergence status of this second giant is presented in Table 6.2. The readiness or preparedness of Ghana for the take-off of the monetary union with a single currency has not been impressive over the years. The country had not met more than two of the criteria (central bank financing and gross external reserve) through all the target dates (2003, 2005, 2009, 2015, and 2020) till 2021, when three benchmarks were satisfied. In fact, only one criterion (gross external reserve) was met in 2009. It is, however, worth noting that Ghana has never missed the gross external reserve. On the other hand, the country always met central bank financing criteria except in 2009.

The convergence status and readiness of Guinea are presented in Table 6.3. As of the first target date, 2003, for the introduction of the single currency, Guinea did not meet any of the four criteria. However, there was a significant improvement in 2005 as the country satisfied two of the criteria (fiscal deficit and central bank financing) out of the four. Meanwhile, the country failed in these two in both 2009 and 2015, while the country made an improvement in the inflation target. The recent effort of the government and monetary policy authorities in Guinea is reflected in the performance of the country in 2020 and 2021. In 2020, the country met two criteria and three criteria were satisfied in 2021.

The convergence status and readiness of Liberia are presented in Table 6.4. Liberia joined WAMZ in 2010; thus, the convergence status and readiness of the country from post-2010. The first target date after Liberia joined was 2015; that year, the country satisfied three criteria out of the four. This was a very impressive beginning for the country but, unfortunately, maintained a progressive failure to meet some of the criteria subsequently. In 2020 and 2021, the country met only one criterion (fiscal deficit); this was probably due to the effect of COVID-19, as observed in almost all the other member states. From the above, the government and monetary authorities of Liberia need to double up their commitment to meeting the primary macroeconomic convergence.

Nigeria's convergence status and readiness are presented in Table 6.5. The performance of Nigeria is critical to the success of the WAMZ and the eventual introduction of a full monetary union in the whole of ECOWAS. As of 2003, Nigeria met two out of the four basic criteria, and the number of criteria satisfaction moved to three in 2005. The performance could not be sustained in 2009 when the country backslid to meet two criteria. Interestingly, Nigeria was fully ready for the take-off of the single currency in 2015, when the country met all four primary convergence criteria. Unfortunately, this performance could not be sustained, as the country met three criteria in 2020 and two in 2021. The unsustainability of meeting the primary macroeconomic convergence by Nigeria is the biggest challenge to the introduction of a single currency in WAMZ and ECOWAS at large. Besides the fact that Nigeria is the biggest economy in the ECOWAS region, it is also expected that Nigeria will derive the highest benefits from the integrated monetary union.

Evidence, as presented in Table 6.6, shows that Sierra Leone is lagging behind in meeting the basic macroeconomic convergence criteria. In 2003, the country did not meet a single criterion out of the four criteria. Sierra Leone was able to satisfy a maximum of two criteria in 2005 and 2015, while for the rest of the stipulated dates, 2009, 2020, and 2021, the country met just one criterion (gross external reserve). Sierra Leone's government and monetary authority need to double efforts to improve macroeconomic performance to meet the basic convergence criteria for the introduction of a single currency.

Table 6.1: Gambia's macroeconomic convergence status at different Target Dates

Primary Criteria	Target	2003	2005	2009	2015	2020	2021
Inflation rate (end-period)	Single Digit	14.8	29.7	7.9	7.3	10.4	9.5
Fiscal Deficit/GDP (including grants)	≤ 3%	-10.5	0	6.8	6.2	3.6	4.7
Central Bank Financing of Fiscal Deficits	≤ 10%	16.1	0	40.1	24.3	5	5
Gross External Reserve (Month of Imports)	≥3 Months	1.8	0.9	2.2	1.3	3.9	4.2
Number of Criteria Satisfied		0	2	1	1	2	3

Source: *Compiled by the author using the WAMI database*

Table 6.2: Ghana's Macroeconomic Convergence Status at Different Target Dates

Primary Criteria	**Target**	**2003**	**2005**	**2009**	**2015**	**2020**	**2021**
Inflation rate (end-period)	Single Digit	23.6	13.9	16	17.7	11	9
Fiscal Deficit/GDP (including grants)	≤ 3%	-7.5	-1.6	-4	4.9	11.4	9.7
Central Bank Financing of Fiscal Deficits	≤ 10%	0	0	26.3	0	2	2
Gross External Reserve (Month of Imports)	≥3 Months	5	4	4.4	3.2	4.5	4.1
Number of Criteria Satisfied		2	2	1	2	2	3

Source: *Compiled by the author using the WAMI database*

Table 6.3: Guinea's Macroeconomic Convergence Status at Different Target Dates

Primary Criteria	Target	2003	2005	2009	2015	2020	2021
Inflation rate (end-period)	Single Digit	14.8	29.7	7.9	7.3	10.4	9.5
Fiscal Deficit/GDP (including grants)	≤ 3%	-10.5	0	6.8	6.2	3.6	4.7
Central Bank Financing of Fiscal Deficits	≤ 10%	16.1	0	40.1	24.3	5	5
Gross External Reserve (Month of Imports)	≥3 Months	1.8	0.9	2.2	1.3	3.9	4.2
Number of Criteria Satisfied		0	2	1	1	2	3

Source: *Compiled by the author using the WAMI database*

TABLE 6.4: LIBERIA'S MACROECONOMIC CONVERGENCE STATUS AT DIFFERENT TARGET DATES

Primary Criteria	Target	2003	2005	2009	2015	2020	2021
Inflation rate (end-period)	Single Digit	14.8	29.7	7.9	7.3	10.4	9.5
Fiscal Deficit/GDP (including grants)	≤3%	-10.5	0	6.8	6.2	3.6	4.7
Central Bank Financing of Fiscal Deficits	≤10%	16.1	0	40.1	24.3	5	5
Gross External Reserve (Month of Imports)	≥3 Months	1.8	0.9	2.2	1.3	3.9	4.2
Number of Criteria Satisfied		0	2	1	1	2	3

Source: *Compiled by the author using the WAMI database*

TABLE 6.5: NIGERIA'S MACROECONOMIC CONVERGENCE STATUS AT DIFFERENT TARGET DATES

Primary Criteria	Target	2003	2005	2009	2015	2020	2021
Inflation rate (end-period)	Single Digit	23.8	11.6	14	9.6	12	10.3
Fiscal Deficit/GDP (including grants)	≤3%	-2	1.3	3.3	-1.5	0.3	3.9
Central Bank Financing of Fiscal Deficits	≤10%	37.6	0	0	0	0.3	0
Gross External Reserve (Month of Imports)	≥3 Months	4.9	11	16.6	5.8	6	6.9
Number of Criteria Satisfied		2	3	2	4	3	2

Source: *Compiled by the author using the WAMI database*

TABLE 6.6: SIERRA LEONE'S MACROECONOMIC CONVERGENCE STATUS AT DIFFERENT TARGET DATES

Primary Criteria	Target	2003	2005	2009	2015	2020	2021
Inflation rate (end-period)	Single Digit	11.3	13.1	12.2	8.9	17.5	15.2
Fiscal Deficit/GDP (including grants)	≤3%	-10	-8.6	8.4	4.3	6	4.2
Central Bank Financing of Fiscal Deficits	≤10%	24.3	0	21.2	20.1	26	15.8
Gross External Reserve (Month of Imports)	≥3 Months	1.7	4.3	7.9	3.4	4.5	3.7
Number of Criteria Satisfied		0	2	1	2	1	1

Source: *Compiled by the author using the WAMI database*

Table 6.7 summarises the macroeconomic convergence performance of all the countries in each of the stipulated years for the introduction of a single currency. As depicted in the table, none of the countries met the four criteria in 2003, 2005, 2020, and 2021. While in 2009, only Gambia met all four criteria, and in 2015 only Nigeria met the four criteria. Meanwhile, in 2003 Ghana and Nigeria had the best performance, while Gambia and Nigeria had the best performance in 2005. The Gambia outperformed all the countries in 2009, and its performance deteriorated to one of the worst performances in 2015. Nigeria took the best performance position in 2015 by meeting all four criteria. In 2020, the Gambia bounced back and shared the first position with Nigeria. Ghana and Guinea overtook Nigeria and Gambia as the best-performing countries in 2021. Evidence from Table 6.7 is that there is no particular year where all the countries satisfy the four convergence criteria. This confirms the argument of Ekpo (*2020*) that it would be extremely difficult, if not impossible, for all the member countries to meet the criteria at the same time.

Comparing the performance by each criterion across countries reveals that the potential to meet each convergent target varies from country to country. For instance, in terms of satisfying the inflation target, the Gambia outperformed the rest of the countries. Gambia always met the inflation at each stipulated date except 2003 which was the first proposed date for the introduction of the single currency. Ghana, Liberia, Nigeria, and Sierra Leone met the inflation target once each. This implies that to harmonise the level of inflation across the countries in the zone, the monetary authorities in these countries, that is, Ghana, Liberia, Nigeria, and Sierra Leone, are required to make concerted efforts on the stability of prices. Guinea met the inflation target three times and missed it three times; hence, the monetary authority in Guinea is also required to improve its price stability strategies.

In the case of maintaining a fiscal deficit to GDP ratio of 3% or less, Ghana and Sierra Leone never met this target at any of the proposed start-off dates. Liberia has never missed this target since the country joined WAMZ. This is the only criterion where Liberia did very well; therefore, efforts should be directed at sustaining this performance. Nigeria was able to meet this target four times out of six, while the Gambia and Guinea met it once; Ghana and Sierra Leone never met this target. The fiscal deficit criterion is the least satisfied target by all the countries except Nigeria and Liberia. Ghana and Sierra need to work on their fiscal institutions so as to promote fiscal discipline. The fiscal authorities in Liberia, Gambia, and Guinea should improve their fiscal rules and institutions in order to improve the fiscal situation in these countries. Nigeria should make a little more effort to improve on her achievement in fiscal discipline.

Ghana and Nigeria satisfied the central bank deficit financing target five times each, while Gambia and Guinea met it three times; Liberia and Sierra Leone met it only once. Finally, Nigeria always met the external reserve criterion, Gambia and Sierra Leone missed it just once, while on the other hand, Guinea met it only once, and Liberia never met it.

Considering the performance of all countries across the four basic criteria, the most satisfied target over the six different proposed dates is the external reserve criterion, followed by central bank deficit financing, then inflation, and the least is the fiscal deficit target. Generally, there is a need to jointly work on improving fiscal discipline across all the countries and then improve on policies and strategies for the stability of prices.

Table 6.7: Number of macroeconomic convergence criteria satisfied by countries at the target years

Countries	2003	2005	2009	2015	2020	2021
Gambia	1	3	4	1	3	2
Ghana	2	2	1	2	2	3
Guinea	0	2	1	1	2	3
Liberia				3	1	1
Nigeria	2	3	2	4	3	2
Sierra Leone	0	2	1	2	1	1

Source: *Author's computation using Tables 6.1 to 6.6*

Challenges Of Meeting The Macroeconomic Convergence Criteria

There are a number of challenges facing the countries in WAMZ and ECOWAS countries at large, which are responsible for their inability to meet the convergence criteria. These challenges include macroeconomic volatility, rising fiscal crisis, and the absence of full autonomy of monetary authority. One of the key reasons why the countries in WAMZ are not meeting the convergence criteria is the high level of macroeconomic volatility, which is due to the vulnerability of these economies to external shocks. Countries in the Zone have little or no ability to deal with global price changes because of the large volume of imports of goods and services, the concentration of exports on a few primary commodities, and heavy reliance on foreign aid and debt. Any little change in international prices would distort the macroeconomic stability of these countries, irrespective of their policy stance. This will have significant implications on the current account balance, external reserve, exchange rate, and even inflation in the domestic economy of WAMZ countries. Public expenditure and debt are rising rapidly across countries in WAMZ and ECOWAS at large. There are theoretical and practical reasons why public expenditure is rising in WAMZ countries, just like most other developing countries. Among these reasons are:

- The need to build basic infrastructure to fill the huge infrastructure deficit; the rising population growth.

- The increase in social security spending due to high levels of poverty and unemployment.
- Rising insecurity which requires more defence spending.
- High cost of running a democratic government.

All these are among the key reasons why government spending is rising in most countries in WAMZ, leading to the fiscal crisis, hence making them fail to meet the macroeconomic convergence criteria. Corruption also contributes to the cost of governance and, in turn, leads to high spending of government.

The lack of full central bank autonomy is another factor responsible for the failure of WAMZ countries to meet the convergence criteria. The fiscal authorities and politicians often interfere with the operation of the central bank, which affects the effectiveness of monetary policies. Fiscal deficit financing by the central bank will lead to a rise in aggregate expenditure, which will further lead to the expansion of aggregate demand. A rise in aggregate demand will result in an increase in the general price level, thus causing inflation and price instability at large.

Conclusion

The adoption of a single currency is imperative to the

attainment of full monetary integration. This chapter assesses the readiness of WAMZ member countries for the introduction of a single currency in the Zone and ECOWAS at large. The assessment is based on the primary convergence criteria that all members are required to satisfy. The analysis in the chapter revealed that the countries have difficulty meeting the macroeconomic convergence criteria. Therefore, for the feasibility of the adoption of a single currency, governments and monetary authorities of all WAMZ member countries must take responsible specific actions and decisions by way of fiscal and monetary policies that will sustainably ensure the meeting of the four primary macroeconomic convergence criteria: single-digit Inflation rate (end-period); less than or equal to (≤) 3% Fiscal Deficits/GDP (including grants); less than or equal to (≤) 10% Central Bank Financing of Fiscal Deficits, and greater than or equal to (≥) 3 Months Gross External Reserve (Month of Imports) in-country as well as within-region. Specifically, the Gambia should make more efforts on fiscal deficit and central bank deficit financing. Ghana should focus more on inflation and fiscal deficit and sustain the efforts on central bank deficit financing and external reserve. Guinea needs to restructure the strategies on fiscal deficit and external reserve, while the efforts on inflation and central bank deficit financing should be doubled. Liberia's fiscal and monetary authorities should reconsider policies targeted at the external reserve, central bank deficit financing and inflation, then strengthen the policy on fiscal deficit.

Nigeria needs to work on its inflation policy, strengthen fiscal policies and sustain its efforts on central bank deficit financing and external reserve. The technical committee of WAMZ may need to assist the policymakers in Sierra Leone to improve their performance in inflation, fiscal deficit, and central bank deficit financing.

Generally, the feasibility of all the countries meeting all the convergence criteria at the same time is gloomy; hence the emphasis may be directed to the two big countries in the Zone – Nigeria and Ghana. If the two countries can satisfy the criteria, the single currency agenda may be introduced, or if the number of countries that meet the criteria is more than those that do not meet them, the agenda can be implemented. The experience in the Euro Zone shows that not all countries met the convergence criteria when the full monetary union was operationalised. Finally, there is a need to harmonise fiscal, monetary, trade, and tax policies. The production base of the countries should be improved so as to increase production in the Zone. There is also a need to diversify the economies in the Zone with an emphasis on expanding the value-addition capacity to produce goods and services. Equally, significant efforts should be made in the area of import substitution policies, as well as promoting intra-WAMZ trading. To improve compliance with fiscal deficit criterion, efforts must be made to diversify the economy, promote private sector participation in the economy, and strengthen tax administration and public financial management, with a focus on boosting revenue and implementing expenditure rationalisation measures. Governments of countries are encouraged to seek additional grant financing for emergency spending from international multilateral organisations, such as the World Bank, African Development Bank, and other development partners, to safeguard debt sustainability. WAMZ states governments need to collaborate as well as remain steadfast with aggressive measures to contain the spread of Covid-19 and lessen its impact on the country's socioeconomic development.

Chapter 6

The Potentials Of The Informal Entrepreneurial Sector For West African Regional Growth

Informal economy was coined by a social anthropologist named Keith Hart in 1971. The informal economy is a survival economic sector for the poor people in which economic transactions and everyday business practices are built around a contextually binding moral fabric. The informal economy is, by nature, not easy to measure because economic agents involved in informal economic activities are hiding so as not to be detected. Formal economy and informal economic sectors are so important in the design of economic policies for meaningful development. Understanding of informal economy will assist in estimating the size of tax evasion and how best it can be controlled by the government.

The informal economy has different names ranging from shadow economy, black economy, grey economy or lack economy, to cash economy. However, in this chapter, we use these terms synonymously. The informal economy includes all activities that are hidden from the purview of the relevant government authorities. It can also be referred to as all economic activities that are not within the control of official authorities for regulatory, monetary, and institutional reasons. These reasons could be to avoid government taxes and other regulatory charges, including administrative burdens, while institutional reasons may include corruption, the quality of institutions, and poor implementation of the rule of law. The informal entrepreneurial sectors also play very important roles in the process of industrialisation and sustainable economic growth. According to a CBN report, the informal sector is based on the enterprise's relationship to regulation by the state in that it either operates without binding official regulations or may operate under official regulations that do not compel the rendition of official returns on its productive processes.

Intra-regional trade in West Africa is low and mainly dominated by the informal sector, which is poorly documented, and believed to be dominated by informal entrepreneurial activities of individuals in the areas of staple food production, handcraft, and clothes-making.

However, the informal entrepreneurial sector has great potential to increase West Africa's intra-regional trade, growth and development if adequately harnessed and integrated, as the sector creates both regular and non-regular employment for over 70% of the population. It must be noted that the current food insecurity that the West Africa region is facing is largely due to the dwindling productivity of the informal agricultural production value chain entrepreneurs.

The informal entrepreneurial sector in West Africa faces several challenges, which include an unfavourable operating environment (multiplicity of official and unofficial duties, tariffs, levies and charges at national borders, lack of free movement and residence by ECOWAS citizens in all ECOWAS states, frequent harassment by state agents to the lack of government support. The West Africa region can fast-track her economic growth and development prospects by harnessing the potential of the informal entrepreneurial sector in line with the objectives of the ECOWAS regional integration programme; hence the need for this chapter, whose objective is to x-ray the potential and how it can be effectively harnessed. Although research on the informal economy has grown in recent years, this chapter focuses on the following issues:

- Analysis and review of the size of the informal economy in West Africa.

- Review the relationship between formal and informal entrepreneurship in West Africa.
- The potential of the informal sector in the West African region.
- Economic significance and welfare effects of the informal entrepreneurial sector.
- Challenges of entrepreneurship in West Africa and opportunities for informal activities in West Africa.

The Size Of Informal Economy In West Africa

An informal economy comprises economic activities and the income earned that circumvent regulations, different levels of taxes and observations. It includes monetary and non-monetary economic activities of legal nature. These activities may be deliberately concealed from the relevant authorities to avoid payment of income, value-added or other taxes and social security contributions or to avoid compliance with labour market standards, including safety standards, minimum wages, and maximum working hours. Activities in the informal economic sector would have normally been included in national accounts but remain underground due to regulatory or administrative burdens. The activities are legal but produced in illicit manners. Informal household economic transactions that are due to oneself and other neighbourly assistance are excluded from what is called the informal economy or shadow economy.

FIGURE 7.1: THE AVERAGE SIZE OF THE INFORMAL ECONOMY IN WEST AFRICA BASED ON THE MULTIPLE INDICATORS MULTIPLE CAUSES MODEL (MIMIC) APPROACH (% OF OFFICIAL GDP). (1996 – 2018).

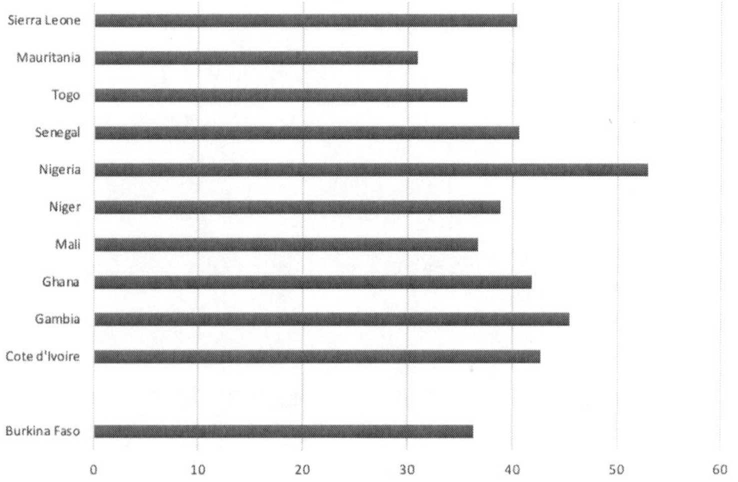

Source: *Author's computation using Tables 6.1 to 6.6*

Figure 7.1 shows that the trend of the size of the informal economy in West African nations is more than 36 percent of GDP. Even, Table 7.1 also reveals that Nigeria has the highest size of informal economy in the WAMZ members' countries between 2001 and 2018. This increased trend of the informal economic sector has been worrisome to policymakers, international agencies and governments at various levels because it distorts the economic planning and policies of the government, thereby creating non-inclusiveness in the implementation.

TABLE 7.1: TREND OF THE SIZE OF THE INFORMAL SECTOR IN WAMZ MEMBERS' STATE (2001-2018)

	2001-2006		2007-2012		2013-2018	
Country/Region	**MIMIC**	**DGE**	**MIMIC**	**DGE**	**MIMIC**	**DGE**
Gambia	44.9	44.8	45.5	40.8	48.3	40.0
Ghana	41.9	39.5	39.8	38.2	38.4	37.9
Guinea	39.4	43.5	39.4	38.9	38.3	33.2
Liberia	43.9	42.7	44.4	44.5	44.1	40.4
Nigeria	56.8	53.3	56.8	52.6	55.4	49.8
Sierra Leone	46.7	41.8	44.6	42.5	42.3	37.7
WAMZ	45.6	44.4	45.1	42.9	44.5	39.9

Source: *Computed by the author but data extracted from Elgin, Kose, Ohnsorge, and Yu. (2021). Dynamic general equilibrium model (DGE) (% of official GDP), Multiple indicators multiple causes model (MIMIC) approach (% of official GDP).*

The graphical analysis seen in Figure 7.1 displays that Nigeria has about 52.98 percent of GDP, followed by Gambia and Senegal with about 45 percent of GDP. The country that has the lowest size of the informal economic sector is Mauritania. Although the informal economy has some benefits, it creates loopholes for meaningful, sustainable economic development. It worsens economic and environmental policies due to the fact that underground activities are not monitored by the government.

Characteristics Of The Informal Entrepreneurial Sector In West Africa

Informal entrepreneurial activities may be classified as a set of legitimate and illegitimate activities carried out within an unofficial or shadow environment. The informal entrepreneurs recognise and exploit business opportunities within the shadow economic sector. This definition aligns informal entrepreneurial activities with the interaction between legality and legitimacy. The dualistic school of thought views the informal sector as the segment of the economy consisting of less-privileged people with unregulated economic activities for survival. In this case, informal entrepreneurship occurs due to the saturation of the formal economy. Therefore, being a worker in the informal economy is limited by choice, and most informal sectors are being evidenced with inefficiency. West African nations have extensive informal entrepreneurs who offer a diverse and vibrant range of entrepreneurial activities. The governments at different levels have encouraged citizens to embrace entrepreneurs who contribute more than 60 percent of employment in the West African economies and further lead to the development of small businesses with the potential to generate more income and reduce income disparities. The following constitute the features of informal enterprises in West Africa:

- It is important to note that most entrepreneurial activities in West African nations normally occur in the untaxed and unregulated informal economy. This is based on the fact that the rising number of employment seekers in the region are unable to find jobs in the formal economy, in which many of them turn back to the informal sector for survival.

- Some informal small businesses represent the

irregular, transitory means of survival for poor citizens, while others may pursue alternative opportunities to generate a sustainable livelihood. This kind of entrepreneurial system is called necessity-driven, which is anchored on the primitive aims of generating income to keep body and soul.

- Informal entrepreneurship may be generated from necessity and business opportunity, which is an enduring aspect of the West African business landscape. Therefore, the informal sector consists of non-registered and untaxed economic activities. Informal entrepreneurial businesses may be those of self-employed business owners without tax identification numbers.

- Most entrants in the informal sectoral business lives are being constrained by low capitalization and unskilled workers. Little capital is invested, and little income is generated below minimum income standards, while the sector lacks protections from the government due to the inability to estimate the size of relevant policy reforms.

- In the informal economy of West Africa, the two ways to acquire skills include traditional apprenticeship and on-the-job training. Traditional apprenticeship involves the informal sector of one-on-one contractual agreements between the parents and the master craftsman. They reach an agreement to provide practical training in the workplace for some agreed fee or reduced earnings while continuing learning. This arrangement takes about 41 percent of acquiring skills in the West African informal economy, while on-the-job training is common among the traders in the informal sector.

- The nature of informal entrepreneurial activities may be influenced by gender differences. The males, sometimes, through their attitudes, may prevent females from operating in the formal business sector because females may not be welcomed in the social clubs where only males meet for formal business deals.

- Most micro businesses in the informal economy employ a limited number of staff ranging from one to five, and most of them are family, friends, or relatives, while most female businesses are often self-employed. In some cases, one or two staff may be employed.

- Most small businesses owned by females in the informal economy have shorter business longevity compared to male counterparts due to discrimination in accessing physical and financial resources and difficulties in getting loans and other credit facilities.

- Another feature of the informal entrepreneurial sector is that females have some enterprising lines compared to males. For instance, most males involve in metal and wood products, while females involve in food selling, clothes, and crafts in some cases.

- In addition, informal entrepreneurs set up their businesses using skills gained based on working experiences and or based on special interest or hobby that has to do with outside formal employment.

- In some cases, informal entrepreneurs gain knowedge and skills from their families due to habitual activities or assistance to or from relatives and family members, and the operation size is small.
- On the legality of informal entrepreneurial activities, petty traders, market operators, and street sellers are classified as legal business operations but operate in the informal sector, while drug dealing and prostitution may be categorised as illegal ways of generating income.

Economic Significance And Welfare Impacts Of The Informal Entrepreneurial Sector In The West African Region

Informal entrepreneurship has much economic significance and welfare impacts in West African economies, as enumerated below:

(i) It serves as a seedbed for creating enterprises and industrial development. The informal entrepreneurial sector is a breeding ground for small and medium size business systems and a test bed for young, nascent, or inexperienced business owners. Most entrepreneurs in West African states do commence businesses as informal businesses, venturing into it with the sole aim of testing the viability.

(ii) According to Llanes and Barbour (*2007*), Williams (*2006*), Ajide (*2022*), it is believed that informal enterprises are very significant in reducing income inequality and poverty level because it provides a means of revenue sources to stay away from abject poverty.

(iii) Informal entrepreneurial sector is flexible in terms of when, where, and how to carry out duties, especially for women who are responsible for childcare at home.

(iv) It also reduces barriers to new business creation because it can be commenced with social capital and relations.

(v) It also affords the entrepreneurs not to undergo the process of corruption in the official economy. In other words, it is a means of escaping from corrupt officials.

(vi) It may serve as an exit strategy system where there are too many regulatory burdens that hamper business development in the formal economy.

(vii) In the informal entrepreneurial sector, some selected products can be produced at lower costs and are affordable to customers with no receipts after payment by cash.

(viii) Income generated from the informal entrepreneurship sector may be spent in the official economy. This means that informal enterprise assists in boosting aggregate demand for formal goods and services and contributes to economic development.

(ix) On-the-job training in informal entrepreneurial activities reduces pressure on the government and the relevant authorities during the time of a reduced spending agenda.

Furthermore, the informal economic sector creates more than 70% of employment opportunities in Ghana, Gambia, and Nigeria. Table 7.2 also shows that in West Africa, the informal sector generates employment for more than 75% in Liberia and Mali. In West Africa, over 79% of enterprises are informal, as shown in Table 7.3, which contributes more than 36.2% of GDP and more than 70% of employment (*Medina and Schneider, 2018; International Labour Organisation, ILO, 2018*).

TABLE 7.2: PROPORTION OF INFORMAL EMPLOYMENT TO TOTAL EMPLOYMENT

Reference area	Period	Total (%)	Agriculture (%)	Non-agriculture (%)
Côte d'Ivoire	2012	94.8	98.6	92.2
Côte d'Ivoire	2013	97.7	99.5	96.2
Côte d'Ivoire	2016	92.8	98.2	87.6
Côte d'Ivoire	2017	86.7	89.3	84.7
Gambia	2012	76.5	96.2	68.2
Gambia	2018	77.6	94.4	75.9
Ghana	2013	92.1	99.6	85.9
Ghana	2015	88.8	99.0	83.2
Liberia	2010	86.7	97.0	77.6
Liberia	2012	92.2	98.5	89.3
Liberia	2014	93.4	99.7	90.1
Mali	2013	89.9	92.4	82.9
Mali	2014	95.3	98.7	88.5
Mali	2015	96.1	99.1	91.2
Mali	2016	94.9	97.3	90.5
Mali	2017	94.7	97.1	90.6
Mali	2018	93.4	96.0	88.9
Niger	2011	95.4	98.1	86.4
Niger	2017	78.2	89.1	73.4
Togo	2014	95.1	99.8	91.8
Togo	2017	90.1	99.4	85.3

Source: *Compiled by the author from ILO (2020). ILOSTAT database. https://ilostat.ilo.org/data/. Accessed 6 Jan 2021*

TABLE 7.3: PERCENTAGE OF FIRMS COMPETING AGAINST UNREGISTERED OR INFORMAL FIRMS AND EMPLOYMENT IN WEST AFRICA

West African Nations	2016	2020
Ghana	108	118
Cabo Verde	129	137
Mali	141	148
Cote d'Ivoire	142	110
The Gambia	145	155
[illegible]	[illegible]	[illegible]

Source: *Computed by the author but data from World Bank Enterprise Surveys, International Labour Organization. n/a denotes not available.*

Studies also show that informality serves as the foundation for an entrepreneurial ecosystem in West Africa (ILO, 2018). By sector, informal entrepreneurial activities dominate up to 98.3% of agriculture, 91.5% of industry, and 85.4% of the services sector (*ILO, 2018*). These figures reveal how significant is informal entrepreneurship and employment in the West African sub-region. According to Grimm et al. (2012), there are three classes of informal firms: top performers, constrained gazelles, and survival entrepreneurs. The last two classifications occupy the informal sectors in West Africa with a large percentage. Informal entrepreneurs produce ordinary commodities or goods with little or no difference from what is being produced in the official economy.

Informal entrepreneurship provides a cushion effect for job loss during financial and other forms of crises because it provides sources of employment for the poor when the economy is experiencing a downturn. Scholars reveal that people resort to self-employment as a shock absorber in times of crisis (Rogan & Skinner, 2017). This implies that the establishment of entrepreneurial business assists in resolving unemployment issues and food crisis and increase the welfare of the populace. The informal entrepreneurial sector is also used to reduce the stringent and burdensome regulations in the official economy. It reduces bureaucratic procedures and transaction costs of firms' establishment and increases people's wealth.

Technology usage in informal entrepreneurial activities is affordable in accordance with business types. The use of local resources is common, which further supports the domestic economy.

Formalisation Of Informal Entrepreneurial Activities In West Africa

The formalisation of entrepreneurial activities involves bringing informal entrepreneurs into the official economy to get the recognition they deserve. The fact that formalising informal entrepreneurship is a good way to showcase its existence, it is also important to know the potential negative effects of pursuing the strategy and the main barriers of formalisation, which assist the policymakers in formulating the appropriate policy options.

One of the negative implications of formalisation is that informal entrepreneurs would not be able to test-run their businesses in an informal setting to gain understanding before moving to the formal economic sector. Another implication is that customers need to pay the standard prices of products or services due to VAT and other charges. Furthermore, there is no way entrepreneurs can escape government regulations. Table 7.4 shows the ranking for ease of doing business in West Africa, which has to do with the entrepreneurial environment, between 2016 and 2020. The Table shows that most of the countries are ranked low, which is below 100 on a total of 190 economies, implying the environment is relatively below international standards.

TABLE 7.4: EASE OF DOING BUSINESS WORLD RANKING FOR 2016 AND 2020

West African Nations	2016	2019
Ghana	83.73	84.29
Cabo Verde	83.45	83.39
Mali	66.05	84.05
Cote d'Ivoire	83.48	83.51
Gambia	67.32	69.91
Burkina Faso	86.69	88.19
Senegal	85.99	89.94
Sierra Leone	84.73	91.18
Niger	77.62	93.69
Togo	78.37	88.70
Benin	81.37	90.6
Mauritania	86.87	91.80
São Tomé and Príncipe	73.76	78.32
Guinea	77.40	83.90
Cameroon	74.80	86.26
Nigeria	77.64	82.97
Liberia	90.64	90.77

Source: *Extracted by the author from World Bank-Doing Business Platform (2020)*

FIGURE 7.2: EASE OF DOING BUSINESS BY DEVELOPING REGIONS

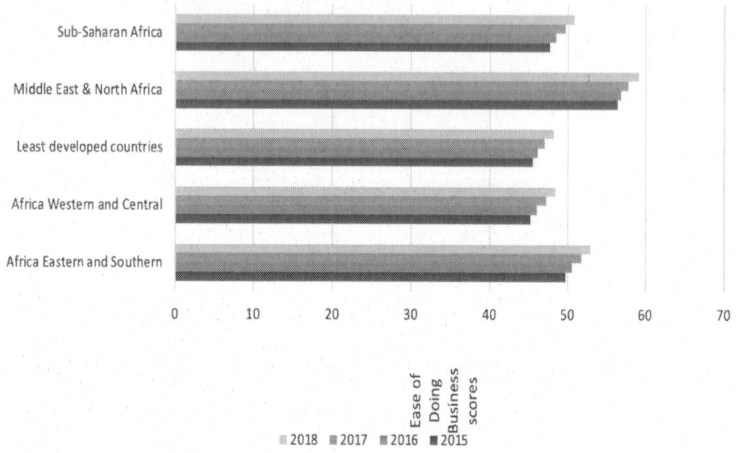

Source: *Computed by the author from the World Bank Doing Business database*

Figure 7.2 also reveals that the developing regions score below 50 points except for the Middle East and North Africa. It is important to note that African regions perform better in getting credit but underperform in getting electricity, cross-border transaction and registering property as documented in doing business in 2019. This implies that policymakers need to re-strategise appropriate policy options to make the business environment more friendly. This can potentially be overcome by adopting appropriate policies to reduce the bottlenecks in the process of formalisation and making it easy to access formal finances, including regular power supply and protection of intellectual property right in West Africa. In addition, entrepreneurs should be made to understand that the formalisation of informal entrepreneurial activities is a viable option for recognition with government subsiding support.

Table 7.5: Formalisation of entrepreneurial business (starting a business score) in West Africa

West African Nations	2016	2019
Ghana	83.73	84.29
Cabo Verde	83.45	83.39
Mali	66.05	84.05
Cote d'Ivoire	83.48	83.51
Gambia	67.32	69.91
Burkina Faso	86.69	88.19
Senegal	85.99	89.94
Sierra Leone	84.73	91.18
Niger	77.62	93.69
Togo	78.37	88.70
Benin	81.37	90.6
Mauritania	86.87	91.80
São Tomé and Príncipe	73.76	78.32
Guinea	77.40	83.90
Cameroon	74.80	86.26
Nigeria	77.64	82.97
Liberia	90.64	90.77

Source: *Extracted by the author from World Bank-Doing Business Platform (2020)*

Table 7.5 shows the easing of business formalisation based on the score of starting a business formalisation process. The score comprises the number of procedures to finish business formalisation, the time required to commence a new business in the official economy, the cost involved, and the minimum paid-up capital to commence business operations for men and women. The score is measured within the range of 0 (lowest) to 100 (highest) for selected West African nations. The Table reveals all the countries are doing well and scoring above 60 percent. The formalisation of informal entrepreneurs is made easier due to the abolition of requirements to notarise firms' documents which reduces costs as implemented in some countries and a reduction in time to get registration of informal firms.

Furthermore, some governments have launched service centres for pre-registration activities. This helps in reducing the time to formalise informal entrepreneurship to a maximum of 4 or 5 working days. African government implements about 32 reforms on the ease of getting credits to encourage formal entrepreneurial activities.

Economic Benefits of Formalising Informal Entrepreneurial Activities In West Africa

The formalisation of informal entrepreneurship is essential not only for policy relevance but also crucial for the achievement of sustainable development goals. The formalisation of informal economic activities serves as the route to economic prosperity, modernity, and advancement in West African nations. The economic benefits of formalising informal entrepreneurship are many; the following are summaries:

- Formalisation helps to eliminate or reduce the unhealthy competition in the informal sector and further assists entrepreneurial firms to pursue the road towards operational regulatory standards on economic and healthy conditions of staff and management.

- The formalisation of informal entrepreneurial firms helps to seek legal protections and escape the pressure of exploitation to comparable formal firms.

- It assists in securing formal property and intellectual rights on goods and services processes.

- It also helps to overcome barriers to accessing finances and seeking financial advice from formal financial institutions. Thereby reducing the financial constraints issue faced in the informal sector.

- Customers take advantage of formalisation by seeking product warranties and health and safety regulations.

- Formalisation also benefits the government at various levels by increasing the revenue base of the government, which can be used to provide public goods and services.

- Formalisation creates formal jobs and improves the employment participation of females in the formal economy.

- Formalisation assists in much control of job quality and services provided in the country and moves altitudes towards laws and regulatory compliance for greater welfare.

Generally, a formal entrepreneurial, operational framework helps in wealth creation and income sharing for the benefit of the whole economy by attracting much-needed capital from business stakeholders in addition to the owner's stake in the business. Through capital mobilisation, formal entrepreneurial activities create sustainable economic development in West Africa. The formalisation of informal entrepreneurship contributes towards balanced regional development. Formal entrepreneurship stands a chance to be the measure of economic prosperity that directly links to regional development. Entrepreneurs use economic resources to add value to the commodities, which increases the national product and income per capita. Unlike informal entrepreneurs, a formalised business enjoys advanced innovations and technologies for creating new products for the benefit of the citizens at large. This contributes towards increasing living standards for all and improving the quality of life in the nations.

Challenges And Policy Options In The Formalisation Of Informal Entrepreneurship

The transition from informal entrepreneurship to formal one has faced a new shape with the current declaration for the adoption of sustainable development goals (SDGs) in most West African countries. For instance, while respecting the fundamental rights of individual workers and entrepreneurs, there is a need to provide decent working conditions and a friendly business environment for entrepreneurial activities. This can only be achieved if entrepreneurs transition to operating in the official economy for proper capturing in the reforms and appropriate economic policies for social protection. The SDG 8 recognises the transition of informal entrepreneurs to a formal economy for possible inclusion in the development plans, promotion of inclusive growth, productive employment, and realisation of decent work for all by 2030.

One of the policy challenges in the process of formalisation of informal entrepreneurship is that it may be counterproductive to eliminate informal entrepreneurship in West Africa due to the current size of the informal economy and its possibility of furthering economic growth and development. Some scholars suggest that it is better to recognise informal entrepreneurial activities and accept it as a parcel of the socioeconomic phenomenon in society (*Adu-Amankwah, 2015; Williams & Nadin, 2012*). Several challenges and policy options have been identified in the process of seeking the formalisation of informal entrepreneurship. This includes:

- Lack of data or inadequate data to assess their

number for proper inclusion in the provision of public goods and services. This implies that we need to build a reliable database for this kind of economic activity, especially at the local government level. One major way is to build a database to encourage registration through the various associations organised by their local bodies in the formal economic sector.

- Recent policy agenda in SDG clamours for decent work for all. A formalisation policy will do well for informal workers. Shreds of evidence show that the institutions in charge of fresh registration of businesses are the beneficiaries of inherent problems in the cumbersome process. Therefore, West African governments need to check the inherent bottlenecks in bureaucratic procedures in the process of formalisation of businesses (*Adom, 2014; Adu-Amankwah, 2015*).

- The establishment of support programmes for individuals in the informal economy may facilitate the formalisation of informal entrepreneurial activities by supporting the youth population with a view to increasing productivity. This also includes the support for training needed for formal entrepreneurship.

- Formulation of laws to promote business incubators aiming at sharing culture and guidelines for start-up entrepreneurial activities in West Africa and strengthening the capacity to operate in formal settings.

- The use of social dialogue may also assist in the

transition of informal enterprises to formal ones through trade unionism and associations. This will help to understand their needs and provide reasons to integrate them into the formal economy.

- The use of the stick and carrots technique may facilitate the formalisation of some selected enterprises' firms. The formulation of laws to allow only formal enterprise firms to engage in some economic activities may help. In addition, the carrots technique may follow the relaxation of business regulations and a special tax system for small classes of business.

- Facilitating access to finances for employees either through self-employment supports in the official economy or by providing microcredit programmes to target some classes of employment or jobs in the informal entrepreneurial sector.

Conclusion

In conclusion, the informal economic sector provokes economic agents in West Africa for many reasons similar to other developing regions. Some of the reasons include economic crisis and weak institutional framework leading to unemployment in the formal sector and the tendency to avoid bureaucratic bottlenecks in formal business venturing. Due to economic downturns, citizens undertake informal entrepreneurial activities as a survival strategy to make up for income losses in formal economic settings. People with low education or skills prefer to operate in the informal economy because they have low chances of running enterprises in the formal economic sector. They join the informal sector to avoid living in poverty and generate unregulated incomes. Poor institutional quality and subsequent non-payment of taxes and low-wage costs have further encouraged the operations of the informal entrepreneurial sector. Given the features of the informal sector, with ease of entry and little or no regulations by the government, there is no adequate statistical data on the operations of informal entrepreneurs in West Africa because it is easier to operate anytime and anywhere.

However, as discussed in the chapter, most informal entrepreneurs face many constraints, including limited access to information, advanced skills and technologies, limited access to different sources of finances, limited access to business infrastructures, and low productivity with little or no legal protections. The formalisation of the informal entrepreneurial sector has been proposed to further open up opportunities for entrepreneurs, which reduces unfair competition and brings them to the legal protection of the government. This chapter also proposes different policy options to facilitate formalisation due to the huge contribution of the informal sector to the growth and development of West African nations. It is expected that formalisation will facilitate the degree of economic integration agenda of the WAMZ and increase the international opportunities for entrepreneurs in the region.

CHAPTER 7

Financial Sector Development And Financial Integration In WAMZ

One of the fundamental goals of the West African Monetary Zone (WAMZ) is financial integration, which is a requisite component for achieving a full monetary union. As stated in the WAMZ programme, the core objective is "to work towards financial market integration while undertaking the technical preparations for the introduction of the single currency". To achieve financial integration, a number of programmes and activities are initiated; these include:

- Full capital account liberalisation.
- Cross-listing of stocks.
- Regional currency convertibility or quoting and trading in WAMZ currencies.

- Harmonisation of banking supervision practices.
- And cross-border payments systems.

These programmes on financial integration are extracted from the Banjul Action Plan of 2007 and restated as Abuja Roadmap in 2009. Due to the level of differences among the WAMZ members, the level of financial inclusiveness must improve, and harmonisation of laws and other regulations is essential to facilitate the achievement of the stated objective. Furthermore, financial system development is an important component that will enhance smooth financial integration among members. Thus, a well-developed financial system would do well for the purpose of monetary policy effectiveness.

Although much has been done through the West African Monetary Institute to smoothen the process of capital and money market integration among WAMZ members, unfortunately, the insurance sector is lagging behind. The case of insurance is so because it is primitively localised in most WAMZ countries, creating a systemic problem towards the cross-border insurance market. A lot of efforts are still needed to further enhance deeper financial integration among members. This can come by a renowned monetary union arrangement to ensure a smooth monetary transmission mechanism through a convergence interest rate spread and evenly distributive liquidity policy.

This chapter examines the concept of financial integration

and the extent of financial integration in WAMZ. Since the level of financial development is very important in the process of integration, the financial system of WAMZ members is reviewed, and coin out the challenges of the integration and the way forward among the states' members.

The Concept Of Financial Integration

Financial integration can be described as the process by which the financial markets of different economies are more closely integrated. This integration could be regional or worldwide. Financial integration has made cash flows, security prices, and returns on financial assets to be equalised (*De Brouwer, 2005*). Baele et al. (*2004*) further gives a practical definition of financial integration by assuming that financial markets for a set of financial assets or instruments are said to be integrated if the potential market participants have the following relevant features:

(i) The participants face the same package of rules when dealing with the same financial assets.

(ii) The participants have equal access opportunities to the same financial assets or instruments.

(iii) Each participant is treated equally, and they are active in the financial market.

Financial integration may start by enforcing a formal

treaty which has two elements: (1) the provision of collusive policy responses in case of financial crisis or disturbances and (2) the eradication of any form of restrictions on international financial transactions by member nations, including harmonisation of regulation policy for the operations of the financial system to enhance unification of financial market systems. The financial market integration policy is related to the law of one price. This law states that if a class of financial assets has similar features, such as risks and returns, then they can be priced identically irrespective of the geographical location of the financial markets. If this law does not hold, there would be an opportunity for an arbitrageur. Therefore, financial integrated markets should be independent of any national financial frictions, even within a region. It comprises financial intermediaries such as bank and non-bank financial institutions and how they interact with each other in relation to the flow of funds to individual households, firms, and governments. Financial frictions may be present but should be symmetric to ensure optimal flows of financial transactions in the markets.

Thinking beyond the economic principles, financial markets can be integrated due to efficiency in information sharing as the behaviour of the economic actors becomes rationally expected in relation to the future course of new policy and development. For example, financial transactions between participants in financial markets may be imperfect due to regulatory barriers. However, an expectation may be formed on the fact that the restrictions may not continue in the long run with anticipation that there would be a policy shift towards greater financial liberalisation after some time. This kind of expectation may influence rational behaviour. Financial integration may also take the following forms: information and best practice sharing between two or more financial institutions and markets, sharing of technologies through users' licensing within the financial markets, lending and borrowing via global market interactions, international financial assets' investments, and rapid adoption of new global financial services and products in the domestic markets.

Furthermore, financial integration may be horizontal if there are inter-linkages between two or more domestic markets. This implies that there are linkages in various segments or sections demonstrating diversification in portfolio management by financial participants, including investors, savers, and other intermediaries. Horizontal financial integration may also occur if the financial intermediaries trade simultaneously in different segments (i.e. savings and loan markets). From another perspective, regional financial integration may occur due to inter-regional treaties, especially where a central financial system is serving them and inter-linkages in network externalities. Global financial integration is the opening of domestic financial markets for the free movement of capital and other financial operations across borders. In this case, there is an absence of restrictions and artificial barriers, including withholding tax and capital controls. In the presence of a global integration policy, there is a free movement of investors, financial instruments, and technology across the border. This kind of integration is encouraged by the international harmonisation of laws and standards through collusive agreements.

Benefits Of Financial Integration

There are many benefits to be derived from financial market integration. In accordance with Stavárek, Řepková and Gajdošová (*2011*), Baele et al. (*2004*), and Economic Commission for Africa (*2008*), the potential and actual benefits of financial integration include firms' access to broader financial markets, quality or better governance, international inflows of investment and growth, risk-sharing, and efficient financial resources allocation.

In an economy with financial integration, firms, including small and medium-sized firms, would have access to broader financial markets. Levine (*2001*) empirically suggests that financial integration strengthens the local financial system, allows a more efficient financial resource allocation and mass investment inflows and opens growth opportunities for firms. Efficiency is assured in the presence of financial integration because it allows healthy competition in the financial markets leading to better corporate governance. Financial integration is one of the factors driving economic growth. It facilitates international capital inflows into the economy in which the developing nations have a better advantage. This further reduces capital costs and increases foreign direct investment, an engine of productivity and economic growth.

Financial integration helps developing economies diversify into various productive activities. This reduces over-dependence on extractive industries, including natural resources, thereby reducing macroeconomic volatility. Financial integration can be used to forecast volatility in consumption in a risk-averse environment where financial markets are taken as insurance for income smoothening in the case of temporary idiosyncratic shocks in consumption behaviour. It also benefits the economy during international risk-sharing (*Lewis, 1999; Obstfeld, 1994*) – in other words, during the "bad" times, like an economic recession, and it also allows nations to borrow and lend during the "good" times, like the boom period. Therefore, financial integration is a source of smoothening household consumption through borrowing.

Integration of the financial system encourages and widens the scope of good governance and regulatory independence. It also increases transparency in financial markets and encourages adherence to standardized valuation rules of financial instruments, thereby increasing the financial stability of economic development. Because financial integration allows nations to draw from an international pool of resources through financial openness, it is a source of financing for domestic investment and growth. In many developing regions with financial constraints, financial integration is a blessing because it allows free flows of foreign finances and immigrants' remittances. It also facilitates the transfer of managerial and technological skills across developing nations for developing new products. This implies that it increases the welfare of the populace.

Financial integration boosts competition in the financial market because businesses and consumers have access to a wide range of financial products being provided by different financial institutions. This encourages market forces to be at play and drives financial institutions to innovate to provide quality services to customers and increases productivity in the financial market. Financial integration encourages good macroeconomic policies and penalises the bad ones; the free inter-border capital flows induce the government to embrace good and effective macroeconomic policies to attract adequate inflows of financial resources into the economy. It also encourages monetary and fiscal disciplines to have good macroeconomic stability.

Requirements For Financial Integration

For financial integration to exist, certain fundamental requirements should be in place. First, it is important to note that in a fully integrated financial system, economic actors often face a set of similar rules and must have equal access and the same treatment in the financial markets. This implies that the law of one price would eventually hold. That is a situation whereby the same class of financial assets with similar features, including maturity, would have the same risk-adjusted returns.

Second, financial integration implies that there should be eliminations or reductions, to a large extent, any restrictions concerning cross-border financial transactions. This enables the financial markets and institutions to operate without any hindrances. This permits firms to raise funds in the multinational financial markets, whether through bonds or equity. Although in real-life scenarios, few restrictions are placed on the financial system; this is done to reduce some market imperfections that may hinder the free operational system of financial integration.

Third, due to the removal of restrictions, financial integration requires that there should be healthy competition among the participants. This, in turn, allows efficient allocation of resources among the financial intermediaries and financial market participants.

Fourth, there should be harmonisation of national regulations. This includes the promotion of international financial reporting standards, banking and other financial laws, the supervision role of the Security and Exchange Commission, and codes of corporate governance. This is to ensure the promotion of convergence among the participating nations towards best international practices.

Fifth, there should be transparency as much as possible, and the free flow of information should be enhanced to avoid unnecessary arbitrage practices.

Sixth, the supervisory arms of the government should ensure an effective governance system, and the promotion of the code of practice should be harmonised with international standards to enhance comparability. The integrity and stability of the financial system must be sustained. Finally, the use of adequate tools, including financial technologies (FINTECH), should be encouraged and deployed to strengthen the financial integration policy.

Other requirements include interest parity, which is also important for an effective financial integration policy. A solid co-movement of financial asset returns among the nations will do well for a smooth financial system integration. The mechanism for risk-sharing and decoupling of domestic investment and savings should be entrenched.

Assessment of Financial Development in WAMZ CountriesThe financial sector consists of financial institutions, instruments, markets, and a set of legal systems for smooth financial transactions by extending credit and mobilisation of savings between surplus and deficit units. Financial development can be better understood as the process of financial innovation and institutional improvement of the financial system in an economy (*Hartmann et al. 2007*). This process has the effect of reducing transaction costs and asymmetric information and enhances the process of market completeness for possible contract enforcement with healthy competition. The main functions of any financial system include efficient allocation of financial resources, risk diversification and reduction, liquidity function, and pooling and mobilisation of savings.

The financial sector in WAMZ countries consists of formal and informal sectors. The banking industry accounts for 75 percent of the total assets in WAMZ's financial sector. This sector comprises commercial banks, microfinance banks, development banks, investment banks, non-interest-based banks, and merchant banks. The non-bank institutions include life and non-life insurance firms, pension firms, mortgage firms, stock exchange, stock broking firms, and investment houses, among others. Although money markets have been fully developed in many of WAMZ members' economies, the capital market, especially stock markets, remains underdeveloped, with the exception of Nigeria and Ghana. The following are the common features of the financial sector of members:

(i) The industry is dominated by banks; specifically, commercial banks' operations account for more than 50 percent.

(ii) Financial inclusion in these countries is very low.

(iii) Financial instruments have not been fully developed.

(iv) There is a higher level of fragmented financial regulation and supervision.

(v) There is a higher level of cross-border operations and the presence of foreign ownership of financial institutions.

(vi) And high-cost transactions.

According to individual members' monetary authorities, the number of foreign ownership in the banking sector in 2017 is as follows: The Gambia (8), Ghana (17), Guinea (16), Liberia (8), Nigeria (5), and Sierra Leone (10). In total, there are 64 foreign ownerships in WAMZ. The capital adequacy of members has improved over the years, and it is more than the minimum requirement of ten percent (10%). It is important to note that financial sector development means the extent of improvements in all components of financial intermediation in terms of depth, access, and efficiency. Tables 8.1 to 8.4 show the depth, access, and efficiency of financial development in WAMZ economies. The Tables also reveal the comparative figures for Africa, emerging economies, low-income economies, and the average of all countries in the World.

In Table 8.1, the IMF index of overall financial development is further broken down into the financial market and financial institutions between 2001 and 2019.

The average figures are further subdivided to enhance the flow of trends among the countries.

TABLE 8.1: AVERAGE OVERALL FINANCIAL DEVELOPMENT (FD) AND FINANCIAL INSTITUTIONS DEVELOPMENT (FI)

	2001-2005		2006-2010		2011-2015		2016-2019	
Country/Region	**FD**	**FI**	**FD**	**FI**	**FD**	**FI**	**FD**	**FI**
Gambia	0.085	0.166	0.089	0.170	0.103	0.195	0.105	0.196
Ghana	0.108	0.167	0.102	0.157	0.130	0.198	0.150	0.221
Guinea	0.068	0.130	0.069	0.131	0.077	0.150	0.088	0.150
Liberia	0.142	0.190	0.168	0.241	0.140	0.214	0.145	0.210
Nigeria	0.178	0.157	0.231	0.201	0.220	0.218	0.223	0.240
Sierra Leone	0.077	0.151	0.061	0.115	0.063	0.118	0.062	0.116
WAMZ	0.225	0.160	0.120	0.169	0.122	0.182	0.129	0.188
Africa	0.118	0.193	0.133	0.216	0.147	0.239	0.160	0.248
Asia and Pacific	0.290	0.344	0.318	0.380	0.333	0.413	0.350	0.442
Emerging economies	0.260	0.324	0.304	0.380	0.311	0.408	0.326	0.440
Middle East and Central Asia	0.221	0.259	0.254	0.289	0.246	0.316	0.260	0.337
Low-income countries	0.108	0.193	0.120	0.216	0.130	0.234	0.134	0.235
All countries	0.225	0.349	0.310	0.390	0.311	0.411	0.320	0.422

Source: *Computed by the author but data extracted from the IMF database*

TABLE 8.2: AVERAGE FINANCIAL MARKET DEVELOPMENT INDEX (FM) AND DEPTH OF FINANCIAL INSTITUTIONS (FID)

	2001-2005		2006-2010		2011-2015		2016-2019	
Country/Region	**FD**	**FI**	**FD**	**FI**	**FD**	**FI**	**FD**	**FI**
Gambia	0.085	0.166	0.089	0.170	0.103	0.195	0.105	0.196
Ghana	0.108	0.167	0.102	0.157	0.130	0.198	0.150	0.221
Guinea	0.068	0.130	0.069	0.131	0.077	0.150	0.088	0.150
Liberia	0.142	0.190	0.168	0.241	0.140	0.214	0.145	0.210
Nigeria	0.178	0.157	0.231	0.201	0.220	0.218	0.223	0.240
Sierra Leone	0.077	0.151	0.061	0.115	0.063	0.118	0.062	0.116
WAMZ	0.225	0.160	0.120	0.169	0.122	0.182	0.129	0.188
Africa	0.118	0.193	0.133	0.216	0.147	0.239	0.160	0.248
Asia and Pacific	0.290	0.344	0.318	0.380	0.333	0.413	0.350	0.442
Emerging economies	0.260	0.324	0.304	0.380	0.311	0.408	0.326	0.440
Middle East and Central Asia	0.221	0.259	0.254	0.289	0.246	0.316	0.260	0.337
Low-income countries	0.108	0.193	0.120	0.216	0.130	0.234	0.134	0.235
All countries	0.225	0.349	0.310	0.390	0.311	0.411	0.320	0.422

Source: *Computed by the author but data extracted from the IMF database*

TABLE 8.3: AVERAGE FINANCIAL INSTITUTION ACCESS (FIA) AND FINANCIAL INSTITUTION EFFICIENCY (FIE)

	2001-2005		2006-2010		2011-2015		2016-2019	
Country/Region	**FIA**	**FIE**	**FIA**	**FIE**	**FIA**	**FIE**	**FIA**	**FIE**
Gambia	0.066	0.441	0.78	0.450	0.147	0.414	0.160	0.407
Ghana	0.42	0.533	0.067	0.417	0.097	0.512	0.140	0.541
Guinea	0.009	0.248	0.015	0.478	0.031	0.508	0.042	0.502
Liberia	0.012	0.352	0.028	0.502	0.047	0.363	0.047	0.343
Nigeria	0.050	0.460	0.096	0.533	0.125	0.549	0.124	0.611
Sierra Leone	0.012	0.544	0.023	0.373	0.031	0.365	0.031	0.349
WAMZ	0.090	0.430	0.168	0.459	0.080	0.452	0.091	0.459
Africa	0.062	0.489	0.091	0.515	0.129	0.520	0.139	0.534
Asia and Pacific	0.233	0.602	0.275	0.631	0.328	0.640	0.362	0.643
Emerging economies	0.243	0.566	0.323	0.608	0.395	0.609	0.416	0.635
Middle East and Central Asia	0.164	0.587	0.206	0.609	0.264	0.609	0.292	0.622
Low-income countries	0.091	0.493	0.115	0.521	0.151	0.525	0.164	0.537
All countries	0.269	0.557	0.325	0.585	0.325	0.585	0.367	0.601

Source: *Computed by the author but data extracted from the IMF database*

TABLE 8.4: AVERAGE DEPTH OF THE FINANCIAL MARKET (FMD) AND FINANCIAL MARKET ACCESS (FMA)

	2001-2005		2006-2010		2011-2015		2016-2019	
Country/Region	**FMD**	**FMA**	**FMD**	**FMA**	**FMD**	**FMA**	**FMD**	**FMA**
Gambia	0.003	n/a	0.012	n/a	0.022	n/a	0.032	n/a
Ghana	0.039	0.003	0.055	0.004	0.065	0.004	0.087	0.010
Guinea	0.019	n/a	0.010	n/a	0.005	n/a	0.049	n/a
Liberia	0.238	n/a	0.238	n/a	0.162	n/a	0.202	n/a
Nigeria	0.028	0.502	0.064	0.502	0.053	0.406	0.064	0.504
Sierra Leone	0.003	n/a	0.015	n/a	0.016	n/a	0.013	n/a
WAMZ	0.055	0.084	0.066	0.084	0.054	0.068	0.075	0.086
Africa	0.054	0.047	0.061	0.044	0.065	0.042	0.080	0.051
Asia and Pacific	0.196	0.225	0.239	0.225	0.264	0.226	0.278	0.233
Emerging economies	0.157	0.207	0.202	0.226	0.180	0.210	0.204	0.232
Middle East and Central Asia	0.175	0.169	0.214	0.196	0.176	0.184	0.188	0.219
Low-income countries	0.033	0.012	0.037	0.013	0.043	0.014	0.050	0.014
All countries	0.184	0.199	0.221	0.209	0.215	0.200	0.224	0.219

Source: *Computed by the author but data extracted from the IMF database*

Among the WAMZ, the Nigerian financial sector is the most developed financial system, as revealed in Table 8.1, followed by Liberia and Ghana. This applies to the depth of bank and non-bank financial institutions. Table 8.1 shows that there is an improvement among the countries between 2001 – 2005 and 2016 – 2019. In terms of depth of financial market and institutional development, Table 8.2 reveals that in the period 2001 – 2005, Liberia performed better. However, between 2011 – 2015 and 2016 – 2019, Nigeria was better off compared to other countries in WAMZ. But the average performance of the WAMZ countries is still low when compared to countries in Asia and the Pacific and the average performance of all countries. In terms of access to financial institutions and markets, Tables 8.3 and 8.4 show that Ghana and Nigeria take up leading roles. However, the average performance of WAMZ is still very low compared to the emerging economies and the world, which is between 26% and 60%. Overall, this reveals that the level of financial inclusion is still low in WAMZ countries. In this case, efforts are still needed to improve the depth and access of financial development. This is necessary because to enjoy the benefit of financial integration policy, efficient and effective financial system development is a prerequisite. Trichet (*2005*) explains that an improved financial system fosters financial integration and reduces the level of the financial crisis, which in turn increases the level of economic development and sustainable growth. Financial integration enhances the economies of scale and increases the level of supply of funds from the surplus units of the economy for effective utilization in the real sector.

TABLE 8.5: RISK (Z-SCORE), BANKING CONCENTRATION (BC), AND DEPOSIT TO TOTAL ASSET RATIO (DMB/TA)

	2004-2011		2011-2017		2004-2011		2012-2017	
Country/Region	DMB/TA	BC	DMB/TA	BC	Z-score	Interest margin	Z-score	Interest margin
Gambia	9.428	96.773	7.485	100	9.724	9.802	9.400	8.933
Ghana	8.480	69.798	11.172	35.810	7.072	11.979	8.166	10.711
Guinea	4.108	100	6.186	80.866	6.517	9.4833	6.267	7.413
Liberia	1.611	n/a	3.94	n/a	6.307	10.482	7.847	8.096
Nigeria	12.455	56.809	17.820	40.404	12.630	7.644	15.667	7.578
Sierra Leone	5.339	74.455	11.322	84.492	12.227	5.354	10.759	4.209
WAMZ	6.904	66.306	9.654	56.929	9.080	9.124	9.684	7.823
Africa	21.181	75.345	20.556	70.526	10.625	8.306	13.877	6.509
BRICS economies	37.909	34.447	44.584	51.640	14.053	4.281	14.624	3.650
MENA economies	60.005	68.266	46.230	63.173	22.253	3.269	25.341	2.900

Source: *Computed by the author but data extracted from the IMF database*

One of the stances of the finance literature is that competition enhances financial stability. Table 8.5 presents the concentration ratio and bank Z-score in the WAMZ banking sector. The Z-score is an indicator of the level of risk or variability of the financial sector. In other words, it is an indicator of bank stability in the financial system of an economy. It is a measure of the standard deviation of assets' returns. We use it to compare the buffer of WAMZ members' commercial banking system in terms of capitalisation and returns on assets with the volatility of the returns. The Z-scores of the WAMZ countries are below 20 percent for the average period of 2004 – 2011 and 2012 – 2017. This indicates that the volatility of the financial system is higher among the countries when compared with what is obtained in African nations, but it is not better than BRICS and MENA economies.

However, it has been suggested that competition is necessary for banking stability. Table 8.5 also presents the 3-bank concentration ratio of the WAMZ banking industry, which is a structural approach for analysing the extent of competition in the banking industry. The results show that the banking industries of Gambia and Guinea are highly concentrated, with almost a 100% concentration ratio for the Gambia and more than 80% for Guinea. However, the banking industry of Nigeria and Ghana is moderately competitive due to a low level of concentration. Meanwhile, the interest rate margin is relatively low in Sierra Leone when compared to the average of WAMZ countries. The ratio of deposits to total assets of the commercial bank is also relatively low. This indicates that the banking sector remains underdeveloped compared to other developing regions like MENA and BRICS countries.

Table 8.6: Insurance Market (Life & Non-Life)

	2004-2010		2011-2017	
Country/Region	**Life**	**Non-life**	**Life**	**Non-life**
Gambia	n/a	0.460	0.087	0.605
Ghana	0.281	0.593	0.494	0.620
Guinea	0.002	0.003	0.018	0.015
Liberia	n/a	n/a	n/a	n/a
Nigeria	0.100	0.456	0.094	0.219
Sierra Leone	0.0029	0.318	0.100	0.367
WAMZ	0.064	0.305	0.132	0.304
Africa	11.022	0.759	0.219	0.783
MENA economies	2.908	1.737	2.670	2.085

Source: *Computed by the author but data extracted from the IMF database*

The insurance market, which is not relatively efficient in terms of operation and depth, contains a number of small firms competing for insurance premiums. It is only Nigerian and Ghanaian insurance markets that have more than $100 million gross premium base. The insurance sector in the Gambia and Sierra Leone is very small in size due to an insufficiently trained labour force or experienced workforce to revitalise the sector as well as insurance regulators. However, Nigeria and Ghana have a robust regulatory and supervisory arm of the government, which is no wonder why the insurance sectors of the two nations are booming. In addition, each country in WAMZ has its insurance laws and regulations. For instance, the Nigerian insurance sector has a larger capital base requirement for setting up life and non-life insurance firms. This also serves as a barrier to new firm entry. Some countries within the WAMZ have a quasi-independent insurance regulator. For instance, Nigeria has a professional body called the Chartered Institute of Insurance of Nigeria (CIIN) and the National Insurance Commission (NAICOM), while some country uses a department within government parastatals to regulate and supervise the sector.

Also, it is only a few people that are willing to take up or purchase insurance contracts or products. Customers believe that they do not derive maximum satisfaction in the insurance sector of WAMZ countries. No wonder the insurance penetration in the group of countries is relatively low compared to MENA economies and the average of all African countries, as shown in Table 8.6. Overall, although the financial activities in WAMZ have grown over the years, the level of development is still low. The financial depth is limited compared to the average of all African nations.

The Extent Of Financial Integration In WAMZ

In order to provide a practical discussion on the extent of financial integration in WAMZ, it is necessary to define financial integration in the context of the law of one price. This law states that a market is said to be fully integrated if the class of financial assets with similar characteristics are priced the same in the financial markets, irrespective of the geographical location. Figure 8.1 shows the level of financial integration across the WAMZ members' countries measured by the interest rate spread. That is the level of dispersion between the deposit rate and the saving rate. Full integration should improve the level of convergence of prices and yields among the countries.

FIGURE 8.1: AVERAGE INTEREST RATE SPREAD IN WAMZ COUNTRIES

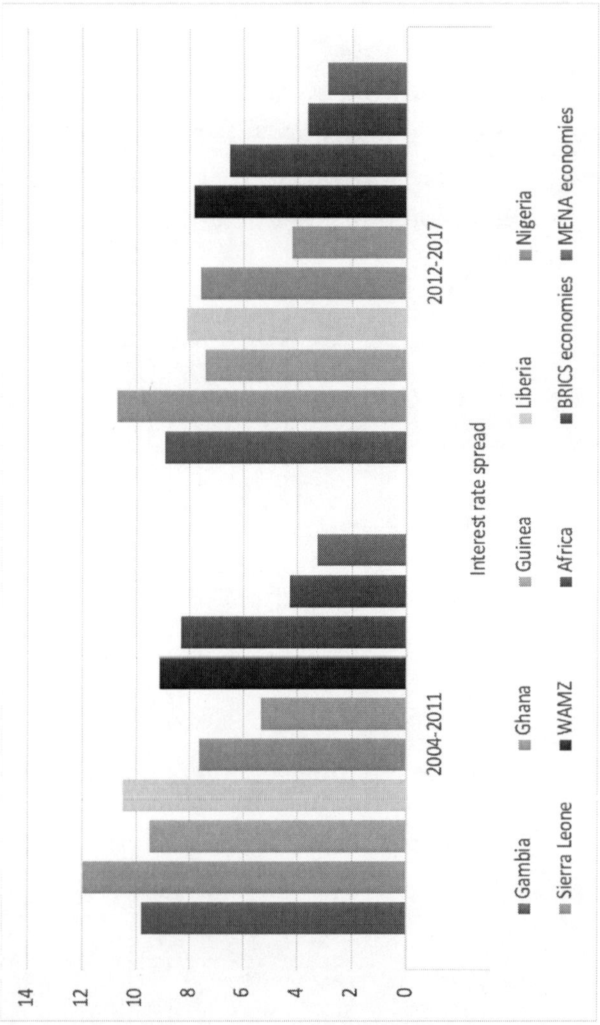

Source: *Computed by the author from the global financial structure database (World Bank)*

As demonstrated in Figure 8.1, there is evidence that WAMZ countries are moving towards convergence in the long run with the possibility of creating a single economic space. For instance, between 2004 – 2011 and 2012 – 2017, the interest rate spread of Nigeria, Gambia, and Guinea are approaching the average of WAMZ economies. The two countries with outliers are Ghana and Liberia. Also, between the average periods, there is evidence of a significant reduction in the interest rate spread across the countries.

TABLE 8.7: THE INDICATORS OF FINANCIAL INTEGRATION (FI)

	2001-2005		2006-2010		2011-2015		2016-2019	
Country/Region	KOF (FI)	Chinn-Ito	KOF (FI)	Chinn-Ito	KOF (FI)	Chinn-Ito	KOF (FI)	Chinn-Ito
Gambia	58.249	2.322	56.379	2.322	65.419	2.322	63.604	2.322
Ghana	49.681	-1.226	41.720	-1.226	43.668	-1.784	44.794	-1.924
Guinea	29.134	-1.505	36.782	-1.924	32.812	-1.924	23.244	-1.924
Liberia	65.181	2.322	58.577	2.322	58.773	2.322	60.102	1.119
Nigeria	53.473	-0.753	652.553	-0.651	49.792	-0.651	51.639	-0.65
Sierra Leone	32.247	-1.284	40.245	-1.265	43.166	-1.924	37.755	-1.226
WAMZ	47.994	-0.021	147.709	-0.070	48.938	-0.273	46.856	-0.381

Source: *Computed by the author from the global financial structure database (World Bank)*

Table 8.7 shows the extent of financial integration of WAMZ countries as reflected in the Chinn-Ito index and the KOF financial globalisation index. The Chinn-Ito index is a measure of capital controls or capital account restrictions in the economy. The table shows that most of the WAMZ countries have implemented some reforms that are gradually integrating the financial system into the globe. For instance, in 2001 – 2005, the averages of the two indices are low compared to what we have in 2006-2010 and 2011 – 2015. However, within 2016 – 2019, Gambia, Liberia, and Nigeria are leading in the financial openness of the economy. This is an indication that most of these countries are reforming their financial systems to have greater financial openness.

TABLE 8.8: DISAGGREGATION OF KOF FINANCIAL GLOBALIZATION INDEX

	2001-2005		2006-2010		2011-2015		2016-2019	
Country/Region	**De facto**	**De Jure**	**De facto**	**De Jure**	**De facto**	**De jure**	**De facto**	**De jure**
Gambia	53.733	62.766	48.037	64.751	64.550	70.287	55.961	71.244
Ghana	44.681	48.013	41.719	37.819	43.167	47930	44.794	52.568
Guinea	27.595	22.734	34.480	23.065	46.823	23.796	46.583	36.941
Liberia	79.713	50.649	77.967	54.054	62.700	56.114	62.092	57.299
Nigeria	45.977	60.970	47.655	57.452	42.719	56.870	44.915	58.363
Sierra Leone	34.216	32.278	42.381	38.108	55.633	34.700	46.265	29.263
WAMZ	47.653	46.235	48.706	45.874	52.599	48.282	50.102	50.946
Sub-Sharan Africa	49.721	47.652	48.943	41.408	51.758	47.800	54.385	41.861
Latin America and Caribbean	61.789	54.772	62.004	56.634	61.824	54.717	64.931	54.982
South Asia	31.741	38.639	35.344	40.728	36.740	38.092	36.600	34.563
Low-income countries	41.997	38.349	47.059	38.060	45.369	39.341	46.911	39.553
All countries	58.524	53.466	61.858	54.936	63.068	54.041	65.470	54.048

Source: *Computed by the author from data extracted in the KOF globalisation index database*

Table 8.8 distinguishes between de facto and de jure elements of the financial globalisation or integration index. The de facto reflects the actual international financial flows and transactions across the financial system, while de jure indicates the financial openness policies of the nations that affect the international movements of flows. The index indicates the financial investment policy, portfolio investment, capital account openness, foreign debts, foreign investment agreements and foreign reserves and international income payment. As reflected in the de jour and de factor, Gambia, Liberia, and Nigeria remain the leading economies among WAMZ countries in terms of financial integration, while other countries are at different levels of financial integration. This confirms the position of the Chinn-Ito index.

FIGURE 2: NET INTERNATIONAL FINANCIAL FLOWS IN THE YEAR 2020

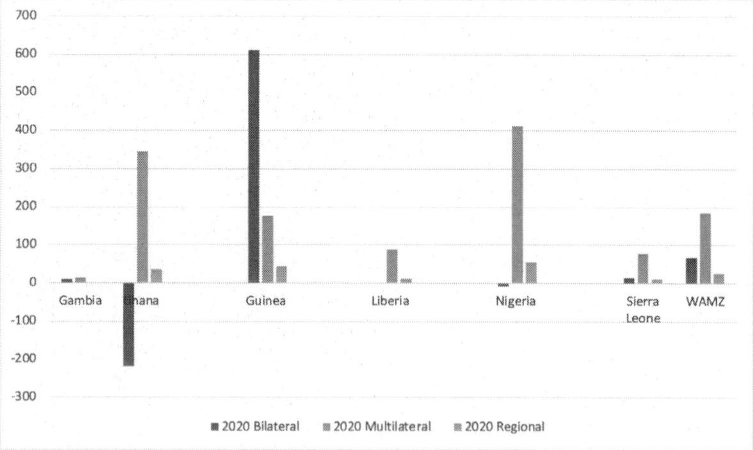

Source: *Computed by the author from the global financial structure database (World Bank)*

Figure 8.2 shows the extent of net financial flows in WAMZ countries. By net financial flows, we mean the difference between financial inflows and financial outflows from bilateral, multilateral, and regional sources in millions of US dollars. The figure shows that positive net financial flow was experienced in Guinea, Nigeria, and Sierra Leone in terms of multilateral sources. The larger positive financial flow is experienced by Guinea. This further shows that most countries in WAMZ have their financial openness improved.

Challenges And Way Forward For Financial Integration In WAMZ

For many years, there have been financial reforms in WAMZ countries, probably to revamp the sector from the financial crisis or undercapitalisation. This development has brought stability into the system and further ensures the integrity and moderate liquidity of the sector. The reform has also increased the integration of the financial sector, increased the presence of foreign banks, and promoted innovations and competition. From the review of the extent of financial integration in WAMZ, it has been discovered that most of the countries have reformed their financial sector and moving towards full financial openness, with the Gambia having the leading steps towards the mission of full liberalisation while others are at various level of integration. However, there are still challenges in the processes, and we offer these possible ways forward to resolve them:

- First, there is a weak process of gathering information on inter-border financial transactions among the WAMZ members, most especially the volume of insurance products acquired by customers. This has led to the underdevelopment of the insurance sector. Policymakers need to work with quality data and information so as to ascertain the effectiveness of policy or amend it if necessary.

- Due to the first systemic problem identified above, the cost of operating in the financial market is very high. In addition, tax systems and other regulatory differences hinder WAMZ's mission. Therefore, there is a need to harmonise the laws and other legal frameworks for operations among the WAMZ countries. This will not only enhance efficiency but also ensure smooth operations in inter-border transactions.

- There is a need to ensure cross-border monitoring and supervision policies. This will further deepen the cooperation and sustain integrity in cross-border transactions.

- Although Nigeria and Ghana have made some levels of progress in ensuring that there is a compatible infrastructural and financial system, more efforts are still needed to bring other WAMZ countries on board for effective financial integration in terms of payment and other settlement systems.

- The extent of capital market development varies among the members of WAMZ. The vibrant markets can be found in Nigeria and Ghana, while the operation of Sierra Leone is relatively low. Therefore, efforts to get an integrated capital market are very low in WAMZ and require a great effort to make it work effectively.

- Pension funds administrative organisation is at an early stage in most of the WAMZ member countries, with the exception of Nigeria. As demonstrated above, the level of insurance penetration is still very low. Appropriate policies should be implemented to ensure an efficient insurance market.

- In WAMZ countries, non-bank financial firms, including finance houses and investment portfolio managers, remain small players in the financial markets.

Among the possible solutions, it is recommended that bilateral and multilateral agreements should be reached, and planning for resolution should be scheduled for key divergent areas among the WAMZ members. Structural and efficient supervision of members would serve well in the integration policy. Regulation and rules, among others, should be well articulated and unified to reduce the transaction costs among members. There is a need to further streamline the integration of insurance markets among members to increase penetration. Financial infrastructure should be well coordinated, and members with deficit infrastructure should be encouraged to fix it.

Conclusion

The chapter clarifies the concept of financial integration and reviews the extent of financial development and integration among the WAMZ members. Financial integration in WAMZ is considered the policy tool for the unification of monetary policy and boosting resilience to external shocks via risk sharing. It is also considered a process that can increase the level of inclusive finance, reduce operational costs among the participants, and enhance competition and innovations. It is also discovered that due to the low level of financial development of most WAMZ members, the level of financial integration is still at the developing stage. Therefore, it can be suggested that appropriate financial reforms should be put in place to encourage a vibrant financial system to facilitate an effective introduction of a single currency and harmonise the laws and regulations among members for an effective financial integration policy.

Chapter 8

Assessment Of Trade Integration In WAMZ

Sequel to the successful launching of the Euro as the single currency of the European Economic and Monetary Union (EMU), there has been a quest globally to emulate the initiative of the European Union by other trading blocs. Such development led to the formation of the West African Zone in the form of the West African Monetary Zone (WAMZ). The WAMZ, composed of six countries, was formed in 2000 as a second monetary zone in addition to an already existing West African Economic and Monetary Union (WAEMU). The WAMZ member countries are Ghana, The Gambia, Guinea, Liberia, Nigeria, and Sierra Leone. "The formation of the WAMZ was accompanied by Maastricht-type convergence criteria, whose achievements by the six member states are decisive for the prospective monetary union" (*See Oshikoya, 2010*). The project is aimed to fast track and facilitate the deepening of economic integration in the Economic Community of West African States (ECOWAS). In April 2000, the ECOWAS launched the "Eco" initiative but later handed it over to the West African Monetary Institute (WAMI) to complete integration in the WAMZ. "A special function of such institution would be to offer advice and guidance to the whole region on monetary matters on the basis of the study of the special conditions and needs of the community" (*Ofori-Abebrese, 2006*). In January 2001, the West African Monetary Institute (WAMI) was established in Ghana as a specialized agency instituted by the ECOWAS. The WAMI is to commence technical preparations for the establishment of a single West African Central Bank and the initiation of a common currency called "Eco" in the West African Monetary Zone. The main objective of the WAMZ is to enhance the speedy integration of the six member states with a view to ultimately integrating with the WAEMU. Therefore, the WAMZ is set to achieve the greater objective of integrating ECOWAS into a monetary union.

Trade Profile Of WAMZ Countries

Trade profiles of the six countries in WAMZ are presented in this chapter. The trade profiles of the Gambia, Ghana, Guinea, Liberia, Nigeria, and Sierra Leone are presented in the sub-sections below respectively.

The Gambia Trade Profile

The Gambia trade profile covering 2005, 2010, 2015, and 2020 is presented in Figure 9.1 below:

FIGURE 9.1: TRADE PROFILE OF GAMBIA

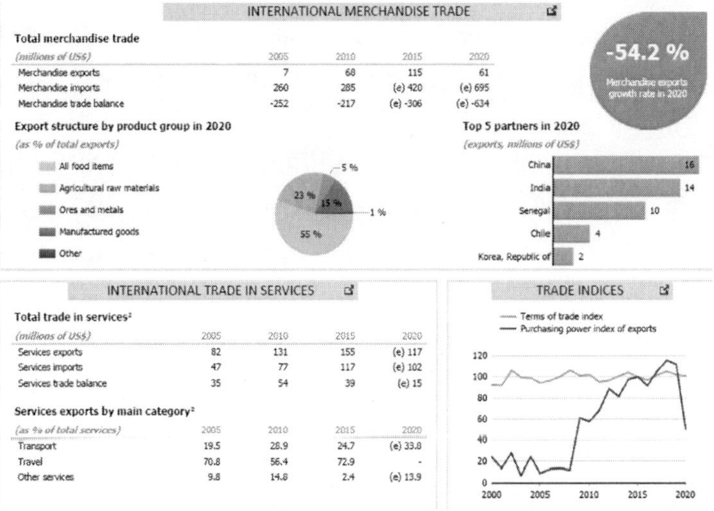

Total merchandise trade

(millions of US$)	2005	2010	2015	2020
Merchandise exports	7	68	115	61
Merchandise imports	260	285	(e) 420	(e) 695
Merchandise trade balance	-252	-217	(e) -306	(e) -634

Total trade in services[2]

(millions of US$)	2005	2010	2015	2020
Services exports	82	131	155	(e) 117
Services imports	47	77	117	(e) 102
Services trade balance	35	54	39	(e) 15

Services exports by main category[2]

(as % of total services)	2005	2010	2015	2020
Transport	19.5	28.9	24.7	(e) 33.8
Travel	70.8	56.4	72.9	-
Other services	9.8	14.8	2.4	(e) 13.9

Source: *Computed by the author*

The Gambia's total merchandise exports measured in millions of USD are shown in Figure 9.1. The merchandise exports range from 7 million, 68 million, 115 million, and 61 million in 2005, 2010, 2015, and 2020 respectively, while the merchandise imports are 260 million, 285 million, an estimated 420 million, and 695 million in 2005, 2010, 2015, and 2020, respectively. Also, the negative merchandise trade balance was recorded to be 252 million in 2005, 217 million in 2010, an estimated

306 million was recorded in 2015, and 634 million in 2020. The country's trade profile shows a negative merchandise export growth (-54.2%) in 2020. However, the export growth structure by product group in 2020 is shown as the percentage of total export.

The total trade in services, also measured in millions of USD, data revealed that Gambia services exports were 82 million in 2005, 131 million in 2010, 155 million in 2015, and an estimated 117 million in 2020. However, Gambia's services exports were 47 million in 2005, 77 million in 2010, 117 million in 2015, and an estimated 102 million in 2020. The positive services trade balance is recorded in the period under review. The top five trading partners in 2020 are China, India, Senegal, Chile, and the Korean Republic, respectively (*UNCTAD, 2020*).

Ghana Trade Profile

The Ghana trade profile covering 2005, 2010, 2015, and 2020 is presented in Figure 9.2 below:

FIGURE 9.2: TRADE PROFILE OF GHANA

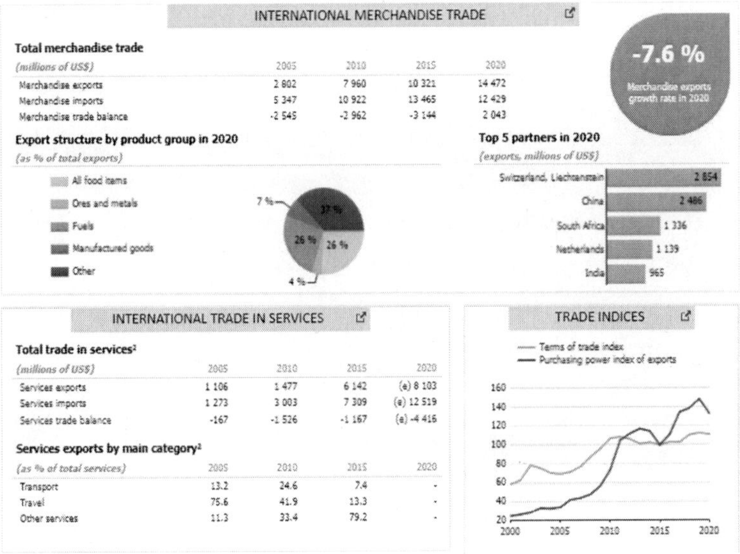

Total merchandise trade

(millions of US$)	2005	2010	2015	2020
Merchandise exports	2 802	7 960	10 321	14 472
Merchandise imports	5 347	10 922	13 465	12 429
Merchandise trade balance	-2 545	-2 962	-3 144	2 043

Total trade in services[2]

(millions of US$)	2005	2010	2015	2020
Services exports	1 106	1 477	6 142	(e) 8 103
Services imports	1 273	3 003	7 309	(e) 12 519
Services trade balance	-167	-1 526	-1 167	(e) -4 416

Services exports by main category[2]

(as % of total services)	2005	2010	2015	2020
Transport	13.2	24.6	7.4	-
Travel	75.6	41.9	13.3	-
Other services	11.3	33.4	79.2	-

Source: *Computed by the author*

Ghana's total merchandise exports measured in millions of USD were 2,802 billion in 2005, 7,960 billion in 2010, 10,321 billion in 2015, and 14,472 billion in 2020. In contrast, the import was 5,347 billion in 2010, 10,922 billion in 2010, 13,465 billion in 2015 and 12,429 billion in 2020. Moreover, merchandise negative trade balance was 2,545, 2,962, 3,144, and 2,043 billion in 2005, 2010, 2015, and 2020, respectively. The negative merchandise export growth rate (-7.6%) was recorded in 2020. However, the export growth structure by product group in 2020 is shown as the percentage of total export. Ores and metal recorded 7 percent, all food items 26 percent, fuel 26 percent, and manufacturing 26 percent, while other sectors recorded a higher percent of 37.

The country's services exports in 2005, 2010, 2015, and 2020 are 1106, 1477, 6142, and an estimated 8,103 billion, respectively. While the services imports of the same 2005, 2010, 2015, and 2020 are 1273, 3003, 7,309, and 12,519 billion, respectively. The country also recorded negative services trade balance in the period under review. The five top export destinations in 2020 are Switzerland, China, South Africa, Netherlands, and India, respectively (*UNCTAD, 2020*).

Guinea Trade Profile

The Guinea trade profile covering 2005, 2010, 2015 and 2020 is presented in Figure 9.3 below:
Guinea's total merchandise exports measured in millions of USD ranges from 853 million to about 5.6 billion,

FIGURE 9.3: TRADE PROFILE OF GUINEA

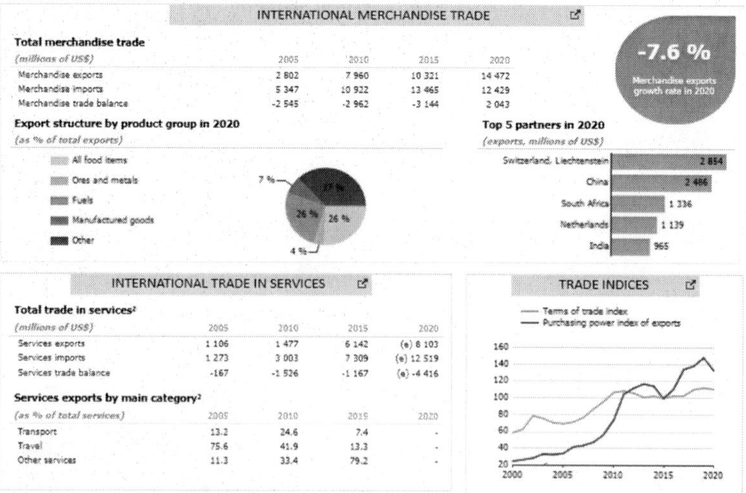
INTERNATIONAL MERCHANDISE TRADE

Total merchandise trade (millions of US$)	2005	2010	2015	2020
Merchandise exports	2 802	7 960	10 321	14 472
Merchandise imports	5 347	10 922	13 465	12 429
Merchandise trade balance	-2 545	-2 962	-3 144	2 043

INTERNATIONAL TRADE IN SERVICES

Total trade in services[2] (millions of US$)	2005	2010	2015	2020
Services exports	1 106	1 477	6 142	(e) 8 103
Services imports	1 273	3 003	7 309	(e) 12 519
Services trade balance	-167	-1 526	-1 167	(e) -4 416

Services exports by main category[2] (as % of total services)	2005	2010	2015	2020
Transport	13.2	24.6	7.4	-
Travel	75.6	41.9	13.3	-
Other services	11.3	33.4	79.2	-

Source: *Computed by the author*

while the imports are estimated to be 853 million, 1.4 billion, 20.2 billion, and about 3.4 billion estimated in 2005, 2010, 2015, and 2020, respectively. Moreover, the merchandise trade balance was estimated to be 33 million in 2005 and double (66 million) in 2010, while a negative trade balance of 411 million was recorded in 2015. But the trade profile also shows about 41.8 percent growth in merchandise exports in 2020. However, the export growth structure by product group in 2020 is shown as the percentage of total export. Ores and metal recorded 41 percent (41%), fuel four percent (4%), and manufacturing four percent (4%), while other sectors recorded a higher percent of 51.

The total trade in services measured in millions of USD is also shown in the table. The services exports range from 83 million, 62 million, 78 million, and an estimated 40 million in 2005, 2010, 2015, and 2020, respectively. While services imports of 288 million, 402 million, 503 million, and an estimated 1,011 billion were recorded in 2005, 2010, 2015, and 2020, respectively. Furthermore, a negative services trade balance was recorded throughout the period under review. The major five top export destinations of Guinea in 2020 are United Arab Emirates, China, India, Spain, and Ghana, respectively.

Liberia Trade Profile

The Liberia trade profile covering 2005, 2010, 2015

and 2020 is presented in Figure 9.4 below:

Figure 9.4: Trade Profile of Liberia

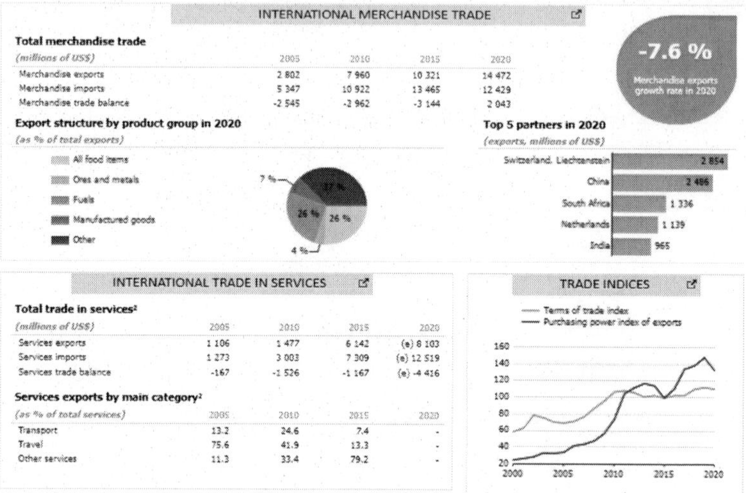

Source: *Computed by the author*

The Liberian total merchandise exports measured in millions of USD ranged from 131 million to 608 million, while the imports were 310 million, 730 million, 1,687 billion, and 1,102 billion in 2005, 2010, 2015, and 2020, respectively. Moreover, the negative merchandise trade balance is 179 million, 488 million, 1,404 billion, and 495 million in 2005, 2010, 2015, and 2020, respectively. But the trade profile also shows about 11.9 percent growth in merchandise exports in 2020. However, the export growth structure by product group in 2020 is shown as the percentage of total export. Ores and metal recorded 17 percent, agricultural raw materials 13 percent, and manufacturing 40 percent, while other sectors recorded 24 percent.

Furthermore, services exports of 213 million was recorded in 2005, while estimated services exports of 139, 203, and 11 million were recorded in 2010, 2015, and 2020, respectively. But the services imports of 855 million, 353 million, and 295 million were recorded in 2005, 2010, and 2015, respectively, while an estimated 309 million was recorded in 2020. The negative services trade balance was also recorded in all the years. The five major top exports destination of Liberia in 2020 are France, Germany, Switzerland, Turkey, and China, respectively.

Nigeria Trade Profile

The Nigeria trade profile covering 2005, 2010, 2015 and 2020 is presented in Figure 9.5 below:

FIGURE 9.5: TRADE PROFILE OF NIGERIA

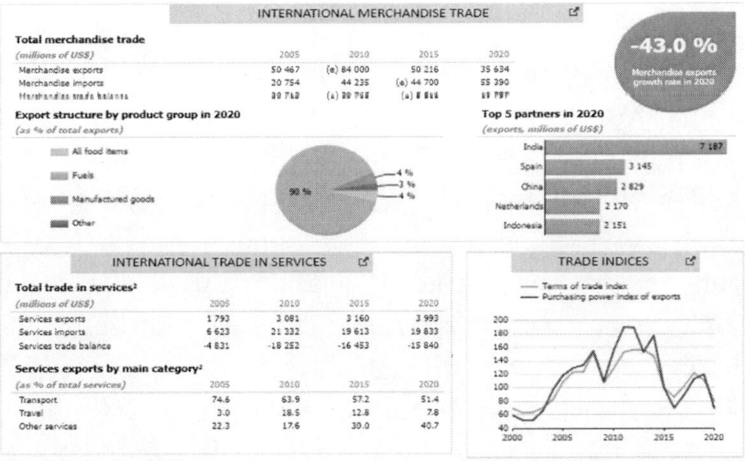

Source: *Computed by the author*

Nigeria's total merchandise exports measured in billions of USD were 50,467 billion in 2005, an estimated 84,000 billion in 2010, 50,216 billion in 2015, and 35,634 billion in 2020. While the import was 20,754 billion in 2005, 44,235 billion in 2010, 44,700 billion in 2015, and 55,390 billion in 2020. Moreover, the merchandise positive trade balance was 2,545 billion in 2005, an estimated 39,765 billion, and 5,516 billion in 2010 and 2015, respectively. The country recorded a negative merchandise trade balance of 19,757 in 2020 as a result of Covid-19 pandemic. The negative merchandise export growth rate (-43,0%) was recorded in 2020. However, the export growth structure by product group in 2020 is shown as the percentage of total export. Manufactured goods recorded four percent, all food items four percent, and others three percent, while fuel recorded a higher percent of 90 (*UNCTAD, 2020*).

The total trade in services measured in billions of USD is also shown in the table. The services exports range from 1,793 billion, 3,081 billion, 3,160 billion, and 3,993 billion in 2005, 2010, 2015, and 2020, respectively. While services imports of 6,623 billion, 21,332, 19613, and 19,833 were recorded in 2005, 2010, 2015, and 2020, respectively. Furthermore, a negative services trade balance was recorded throughout the period under review. The five major top export destinations of Nigeria in 2020 are India, Spain, China, Netherlands, and Indonesia, respectively.

Sierra Leone Trade Profile

The Sierra Leone trade profile covering 2005, 2010, 2015 and 2020 is presented in Figure 9.6 below:

FIGURE 9.6: TRADE PROFILE OF SIERRA LEONE

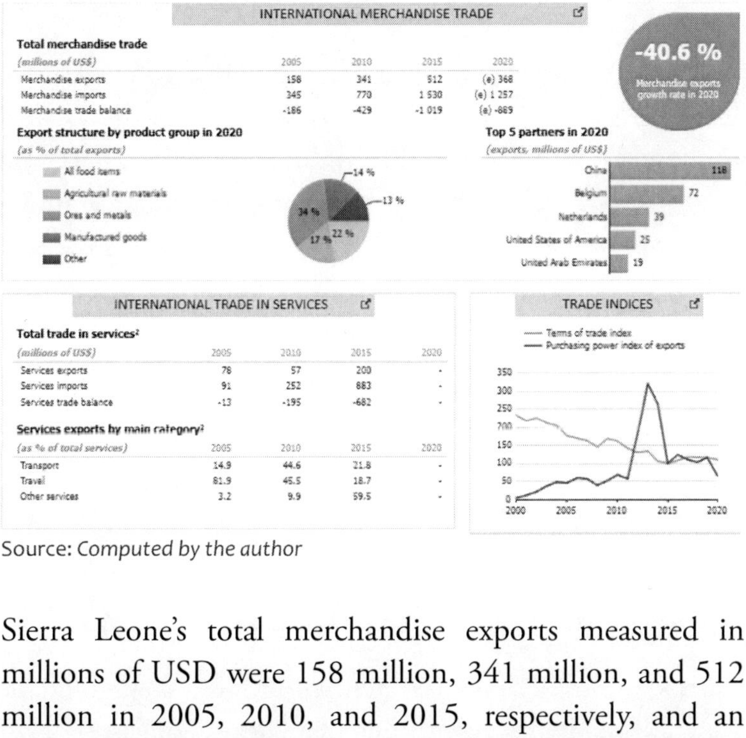

Total merchandise trade (millions of US$)	2005	2010	2015	2020
Merchandise exports	158	341	512	(e) 368
Merchandise imports	345	770	1 530	(e) 1 257
Merchandise trade balance	-186	-429	-1 019	(e) -889

Total trade in services[2] (millions of US$)	2005	2010	2015	2020
Services exports	78	57	200	-
Services imports	91	252	883	-
Services trade balance	-13	-195	-682	-

Services exports by main category[2] (as % of total services)	2005	2010	2015	2020
Transport	14.9	44.6	21.8	-
Travel	81.9	45.5	18.7	-
Other services	3.2	9.9	59.5	-

Source: *Computed by the author*

Sierra Leone's total merchandise exports measured in millions of USD were 158 million, 341 million, and 512 million in 2005, 2010, and 2015, respectively, and an estimated 368 million was recorded in 2020. While the import was 345 million in 2005, 770 million in 2010, 1,530 million in 2015, and an estimated 368 million in 2020. Moreover, merchandise negative trade balance was recorded during the period under investigation. The negative merchandise export growth rate (-40,6%) was recorded in 2020. However, the export growth structure by product group in 2020 is shown as the percentage of total export. Manufactured goods recorded 14 percent, all food items 22 percent, others 13 percent, and agricultural raw materials 17 percent, while ores and metals recorded a higher percent of 34.

The total trade in services is also measured in millions of USD, as shown in the table. The service exports were 78 million, 57 million, and 200 million in 2005, 2010, and 2015, respectively. While services imports of 91 million, 252 million, and 883 million were recorded in 2005, 2010, and 2015, respectively. Furthermore, a negative services trade balance was recorded throughout the period under review. The five major top export destinations of Sierra Leone in 2020 are China, Belgium, the Netherlands, the United States of America, and the United Arabs Emirates, respectively.

Assessing Trade Barriers In WAMZ

Barriers to trade have different meanings; they could be generally defined as government regulations, practices, laws, or policies that safeguard domestic products from external competition, encourage exports of domestic products, or fail to provide suitable and effective protection of intellectual property rights. Barriers to trade or other trade restriction policies affect export trade to another country of WAMZ since it can effectively impose costs on such exports that are not imposed on goods produced in the importing country.

The following are the main trade barriers in WAMZ countries:

Firstly, in the trade sector of the WAMZ, capital capability requirements differ significantly and would apparently create a regulatory arbitrage that serves as a barrier to entry into, for example, the Ghanaian or Nigerian trade and or from the other member countries.

Secondly, there are great dissimilarities in the regulatory and supervisory arrangements across the member countries. Even with the prepared uniform trade statute by WAMI, domestication in-country laws would be necessary to implement, and this has remained a challenge.

Thirdly, a recent study by the World Bank and WAMI (forthcoming) reveals that although quite a number of the WAMZ member countries were at various stages of improving the flow of credit information through private credit bureau or central bank-based credit risk management systems, no legislation exists that sanctions cross border sharing of credit information across the border. One of the most obvious barriers to capital market integration in the West African region is the imposition of outright restrictions on foreign ownership of domestic equities. Capital mobility controls also constitute a significant barrier to achieving the potential that a common capital market would have on catalysing economic growth and development in WAMZ. Lastly, an important obstacle to the cross-border trade in insurance services is the existence of a fragmented legal framework for the practice of insurance. Getting at harmonisation is becoming increasingly elusive, given the significant differences in capital adequacy requirements for the establishment of insurance companies.

Trade Promoting Policies In WAMZ

This section reviews trade-promoting policies in WAMZ, which enable intra-countries trade and economic development of the member states. The most important framework in literature to assess the appropriateness of a currency union is the Optimum Currency Area (OCA) model, propounded by Mundell (1961) and McKinnon (1963), with elaborations of Kenen (1969) and Krugman (1990). The OCA model compares the costs and benefits of states partaking in a currency union. Some of the advantages of currency unions include – lowered transaction costs, price stabilisations, improved efficiency of resource allocations, and access to products, factors, and financial markets, while the main cost is the country's loss of sovereignty to maintain its national monetary and exchange rate policies.

Trade Policy and Trade Promotion

Trade policy is the science of identifying the effective point of export and import policies in a spectrum whose extremes are total "government intervention" and total "free trade." Finding this efficient point, needless to say, is a complex task. In any event, some countries might devise trade policies characterised by a high degree of government intervention and a restriction of global trade, while other countries might consider that the opposite approach is better for macroeconomic purposes. The trade-promoting policies in WAMZ can be grouped into the following headings:

1. Customs Clearance and Documentation Procedures

ECOWAS Customs Code has been adopted by the WAMZ member countries, and they are making efforts to incorporate them in a bid to implement the ECOWAS Customs Union. The member states shall apply a harmonised code to trade in goods among themselves and with third states. In Ghana, customs clearance and documentation procedures remain harmonised with the World Trade Organisation (WTO) and ECOWAS standards. Integrated Customs Management System (ICUMS) is used for the processing of documents for the clearance of goods. ICUMS, commonly identified as UNIPASS, replaced the Ghana Customs Management Systems (GCMS), which was mutually operated by the West Blue Consult and Ghana Community Network (GCNet) services, in June 2020.

The Pre-Arrival Assessment and Report System (PAARS) and the single window clearing process ensure speedy clearance at the ports, allows prior processing of information on imports before arrival, and enables a safe trade platform that eases the exchange of information between the logistics community and Government of Ghana. The Integrated Custom Information System (NICIS) is used in Nigeria to monitor trade, with an abridged version called NICIS II. Documentations and customs clearance procedures harmonisation among the WAMZ countries reduces trade barriers and also encourages free trade and eases the movement of factors of production.

2. Free Movement of Individuals, Right to Reside and Establish

The establishment of the protocol on the right to reside and establish, and free movement of individuals, has been adopted by all WAMZ counties. The following are the development made in the implementation of the protocol over the years: the creation of information centres and surveillance units at some borders to ensure speed collection of data on cross-border trade and curtail harassment; abolishment of the residence permit and the use of biometric national ID cards for intra-regional mobility. These trade-enhancing policies facilitate trade among the member states.

3. African Continental Free Trade Area Agreement

All the WAMZ member states have signed and ratified African Continental Free Trade Area Agreement (AfCFTA). Nevertheless, the institutional, legal, and infrastructure readiness for the actual execution of the mega trade deal lags behind. Among the WAMZ countries, Ghana is the only country that has put in place customs and port infrastructure and "fit for purpose" systems, institutions and procedures that are consistent with the AfCFTA regulations.

The AfCFTA is projected to enhance industrialisation in Africa, diversify the economy and development, achieve an effective fiscal base, and promote African trade policy coherence to ensure that bilateral agreements between the member states do not unravel the objectives and benefits of continental integration.

4. Inter-State Road Transit of Goods Agreement

WAMZ Member States adopted the Inter-State Road Transit of Goods (ISRT) and the formation of the National Road Transport and Transit Trade Facilitation Committees, but the execution of the agreement remained a problem across the Zone due to the continued presence of roadblocks, lack of weighbridges as well as unpleasant activities by some uniformed personnel along some transit routes.

5. Harmonisation of Indirect Taxes

In an attempt to modify the provisions in the harmonisation of the ECOWAS member states' Legislations on Value Added Tax (VAT), draft legislation was revised and authorized. Member countries' Ministers for Finance also approved a draft Supplementary Act adopting community rules for the removal of double taxation with respect to taxes on capital, income, and inheritance, as well as the prevention of tax avoidance and evasion among member states. The Supplementary Act Complements Article 40 of the Revised Treaty and provides a regulatory basis for member states to cooperate in monitoring and imposition of taxes on individuals who have businesses or residences in several member countries (*West African Monetary Zone Trade Integration Report, 2020*).

Challenges And The Way Forward

The key challenges are how to ensure sustainable fiscal policies under a single currency region and promote a sound and stable financial system. This line of argument was supported by John Kitcher, Acting Director General of the West African Monetary Institute (WAMI), who concluded that "in the previous assessment period, the inflation and fiscal deficit criteria were the most challenging for the member states. On the secondary convergence criteria, four countries (The Gambia,

Guinea, Nigeria, and Sierra Leone) complied with two out of the six criteria, while Ghana satisfied one criterion, and Liberia met none of these criteria". Kitcher (*2012*) identified the major challenges as follows:

(i) Lack of a clearly defined regulatory framework and institution.

(ii) Lack of settlement arrangement.

(iii) Unstable exchange rate.

(iv) Weak regional payment and transfer systems.

(v) Existence of trade barriers.

(vi) Absence of a publicly agreed unit of accountability mechanism.

(vii) The large informal sector and limited formal intra-regional trade.

(viii) Money and capital flow problems.

(ix) Money lending problems

The WAMZ member states have numerous other challenges, which include the following:

- WAMZ countries are signatories to several multilateral trade agreements.

- Inadequate productive supply capacities and the lack of compliance with technical trade barriers (technical regulations and standards) pose hindrances for the WAMZ countries to accomplish their trade obligations and avert them from efficiently gaining the opportunities of international markets.

- WAMZ countries lack the capacity to produce goods that could compete favourably in terms of price, quality, and quantity in export markets.

- Although some member states may have a competitive advantage in agricultural products, only a small proportion of the produce is processed.

- In addition to the need to improve their productive capacities so as to have an adequate volume and wider range of goods to sell, they also have to compete in a demanding rules-based trading system.

Finally, among the several challenges that constrained intra-WAMZ trade, infrastructure deficiency stood out, particularly with regard to connectivity across transport modes. Infrastructure deficiency raises production and distribution costs. The infrastructure gap negatively affected the potential for existing businesses to expand and establish new ones. Transportation cost was high across the Zone as a result of the lower per capita density of rail, marine, road, and air connectivity.

The Way Forward

This section, therefore, recommends that the feasibility of achieving WAMZ should be anchored on strengthening the monetary, fiscal, and exchange rate policies performances by all the integrating WAMZ states and implementation of the many regional treaties such as the ECOWAS trade liberalisation scheme. The major stakeholders should implement a genuine, practical, and gradual tactic towards conducting the monetary and financial integration process. Upgrading and maintenance of existing infrastructure as well as bridging the infrastructure gap by constructing new infrastructural facilities to increase production and distribution, enhance competitiveness, and eventually boost trade between the WAMZ countries.

WAMZ member states should initiate an Institutional Support Project for Trade Facilitation, which includes trade negotiations, trade policy analysis, regional integration, settling investment disputes, the political economy of international trade or strengthening in the areas of trade law, capacity building, etc. Such tailored support to each WAMZ country will improve the capacity of the member states to better conduct trade negotiations and improve their trade competitiveness. Finally, the WAMZ states should undoubtedly meet Mundell's conditionality for an optimum currency area. Therefore, every effort should be made by the authorities to bring the WAMZ project to a successful conclusion.

Conclusion

There are numerous chances for all states to achieve

growth and development if they realise their obligation to adopt trade-promoting policies, minimize trade barriers, and be more flexible with the country's sovereignty. WAMZ common trade policy has the capacity to provide an exchange of goods and services, create jobs, and improve the means of production and distribution to benefit the masses. It also promotes the integration of all sectors of the economies of the member countries and establishes a common market for better business growth. This will be achieved through the following:

- The introduction of a common trade policy and a common external tariff.
- Free movement of persons, services, goods, and capital.
- The harmonisation of legislation in the areas necessary for the decent and suitable functioning of the common market.
- The adoption of common financial, economic, and social policies.
- And the creation of a common currency.

Chapter 9

Implications Of Insecurity On The Integration Agenda In The West African Monetary Zone

The West African Monetary Zone (WAMZ) is constituted by six West African countries, Ghana, The Gambia, Guinea, Liberia, Nigeria, and Sierra Leon, to enhance regional economic cooperation and integration, among other things. Regional economic integration involves the gradual removal of barriers to enhance free trade and the movement of factors of production across countries within a region (Bawa, 2018). Insecurity is the general sense of absence of safety of lives and property in society. Thus, insecurity in any member state within the region would inevitably create direct and indirect constraints or lead to policy reactions that would limit the free movement of people and goods, which would have some implications on the overall integration agenda. Insecurity can be grouped into two:

(i) **Interstate Insecurity** – this is conflicts that involve two or more nation states.

(ii) **Intrastate Insecurity** – this is conflicts that involve different groups within a country.

Though both have implications for regional integration, interstate insecurity is not common in the zone. What is common is intrastate at different degrees in almost all the countries in the zone. In recent times, there has been an upsurge in cases of intrastate security challenges in the forms of ethnic and religious conflicts, terrorism, banditry, kidnapping, maritime piracy, and other violent crimes in some West African states resulting in the loss of hundreds of lives and property, displacements of people and a general sense of panic among the people in the region. This is even as member countries such as Sierra Leone and Liberia are yet to recover completely from the colossal damages caused by decades of political violence and civil wars in the past. This chapter provides an overview of the security situation in WAMZ, discusses factors responsible for insecurity in the zone, and draws some implications for the Zone's integration agenda.

Overview Of The Security Situation In WAMZ

The security situation in WAMZ though not the worst in

Sub-Saharan Africa, has been an issue of recurrent concern. This is particularly serious over the past decade given the renaissance of military coups in Guinea and neighbouring Mali and Burkina Faso, political crises in The Gambia, Boko Haram attacks, and inter-ethnic conflicts in Nigeria. The political crises and conflicts indeed are obvious threats to the realisation of the economic integration agenda of the monetary zone. Historical trends have shown that member countries were relatively peaceful during the struggle for and attainment of their independence from colonial rule in the late 1950s and early 60s. However, the immediate years of post-colonial rule were dominated by ethnic-regional struggles for political power, mainly between the major ethnic groups in the northern and southern regions of the various states. These struggles have metamorphosed into violent political conflicts and, in some cases, military coups, counter-coups, and civil wars in some states. Examples of such civil wars include the Biafra war, which was fought between the Igbo ethnic group in the southeast and the Federal Republic of Nigeria between 1967 and 1970, the civil wars in Liberia (First between 1989 and 1996, and second 1999 and 2003) and Sierra Leone, 1991 and 2002. These wars altogether have caused hundreds of thousands of fatalities, humanitarian crises, instability, and sagged productivity and trade in the sub-region.

With the end of these wars and the democratisation of governance in most of the countries in the 1990s through 2000s, an atmosphere of tranquillity and political stability was felt in the zone. Unfortunately, this could not be sustained as many incumbents democratically elected leaders demonstrated an unwillingness to relinquish power by frustrating peaceful and popular transition processes. Most often, they use the parliaments to introduce changes to the Constitution that would suppress opposition and political competition to elongate their stay in office. They also manipulate the electoral processes and or rig elections to win. In consequence, these actions have, in some countries, resulted in violent uprisings, conflicts and political instability, and a general sense of insecurity. However, over the last one and half decades, different waves of armed conflicts, mainly internal, caused by ethnic and religious tensions, have emerged in the region. These conflicts have resulted in a rise in the number of internally displaced people, humanitarian crises, growing food insecurity, and sagged foreign direct investment. The conflicts are particularly predominant in Nigeria, which is a dominant player in the monetary zone (*see Table 10.1*). Nigeria accounts for over 80 percent of the total GDP and about 76 percent of the population of the zone.

Table 10.1 shows the trends of internal and external conflicts for the six WAMZ member states, Ghana, the Gambia, Guinea, Liberia, Nigeria, and Sierra Leon, for the period of 2001 – 2018. The external conflict index covers and assesses the occurrence of war, cross-border conflicts, and the intensity of foreign pressures on individual nations, while the internal conflict index covers civil war, coup threats, terrorism, political violence, and civil disorder. For both internal and external conflict indexes, a lower score indicates high risk, while a higher score suggests low risk. The indexes range from 0 (highest risk) to 12 points (lowest risk). Thus, with scores ranging between 6.07 and 11.48, Table 10.1 shows that the WAMZ member countries have been facing various degrees of risks of both internal and external conflicts. And among the six member states, Nigeria recorded the lowest scores during the periods reviewed, 6.34 in 2001 – 2006, 6.17 in 2007 – 2012, and 6.07 in 2013 – 2018 periods, which suggests that it is facing the highest incidence of internal conflicts, followed by Guinea with scores ranging between 7.65 and 8.07 (*See Table 10.1*). Although the government of Nigeria has done much to curtail the spread to the southern parts of the country and the scale of attacks by the Boko Haram insurgents, the recent surge in cases of kidnapping and activities of bandits in many parts of the country over the last decade has decimated the achievement. Hence, this might have been responsible for the fall in the country's score from 6.17 in 2007 – 2012 to 6.07 in 2013 – 2018. Meanwhile, Ghana, Sierra Leone, and the Gambia, which have relatively higher scores appear to be facing lesser incidences of internal conflicts. The pattern in Table 10.1 suggests that the incidence of conflicts has some relationship with the degree of ethno-religious diversity in member states. Countries like Nigeria, with multi-ethnic groups and religious diversity, have more ethnic and religious tensions in Table 10.2 and incidence of conflicts as shown in Table 10.1.

TABLE 10.1: TREND OF INTERNAL AND EXTERNAL CONFLICTS IN WAMZ MEMBERS' STATE (2001-2018)

Country/Region	2001-2006		2007-2012		2013-2018	
	Internal conflict	External conflict	Internal conflict	External conflict	Internal conflict	External conflict
Gambia	9.82	11.20	10.27	11.03	9.71	10.51
Ghana	9.19	11.63	9.42	11.48	8.97	11.00
Guinea	7.65	7.88	7.88	8.20	8.07	8.29
Liberia	7.98	6.26	8.69	9.38	7.94	9.66
Nigeria	6.34	10.40	6.17	9.48	6.07	9.18
Sierra Leone	9.71	9.69	9.92	10.13	9.30	10.50
WAMZ	8.45	9.51	8.72	9.95	8.30	9.86

Source: *Computed by the author using data from International Country Risk Guide (Published by The PRS Group). The score ranges from 12 points (Very Low Risk) to 0 points (Very High Risk).*

Aside from internal and external conflicts, terrorism has become a major source of security threat to many countries all over the world. Figure 10.1 shows the trend of the average Global Terrorism Index for countries in the WAMZ between 2011 and 2022. On a general note, Figure 10.1 shows that there has been an increase in the incidences of terrorism in WAMZ since 2017. Thus, indicating the risk of terrorism in WAMZ remains a serious threat in WAMZ. Not less than 48 percent of total deaths in the zones are accounted for by terrorism, and again, Nigeria is the major affected country.

FIGURE 10.1: AVERAGE WAMZ GLOBAL TERRORISM INDEX RANKING

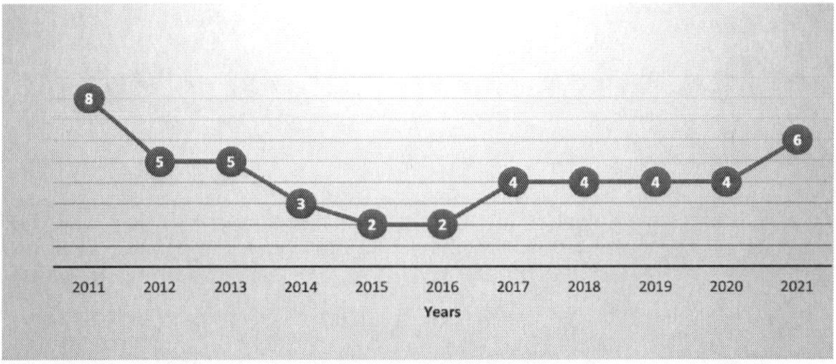

Source: *Computed by author using data from Global Terrorism Index (2011 – 2022).*

These conflicts have inflicted immeasurable human suffering and high economic and social costs to member countries and growing external pressures of different magnitudes. For instance, Figure 10.2 reveals that Nigeria recorded the highest homicide rate per 100,000 people among the WAMZ states between 2013 and 2018. Conflicts in WAMZ accounted for about 825,000 homicides between 2000 and 2018 (WDI 2019). The general sense of insecurity has increased pressure on governments of member states to raise military spending and firms to increase investment in security.

FIGURE 10.2: INTENTIONAL HOMICIDES (PER 100,000 PEOPLE)

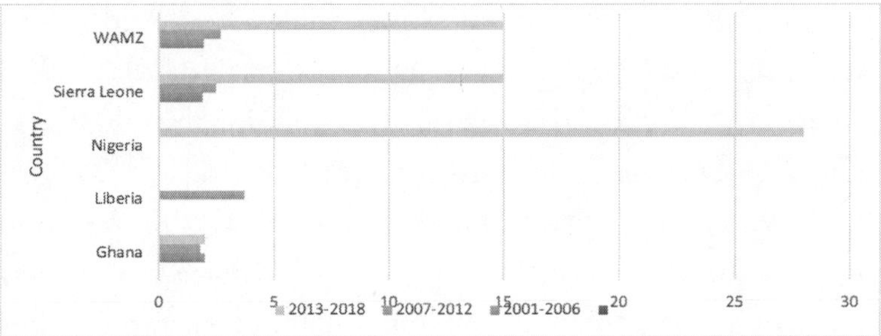

Source: *computed by the author using data from World Development Indicators*

Factors Responsible For Insecurity In The West African Monetary Zone (WAMZ)

The persistent conflicts and insecurity in the zone are caused by a combination of factors which include the scramble for political power among different ethnic groups and regions, religious extremism and intolerance, weak political institutions, scuffling for control of natural resources, particularly land, and socioeconomic inequalities and marginalisation (*Maze, 2015*). This sub-section discusses some of these factors.

The scramble for control of political power, natural resources (land), and consequent agitations by socially marginalised ethnic or religious groups have been directly or indirectly responsible for most violent conflicts in WAMZ member states, those with heterogeneous groups divided across different religions and ethnic tribes. In almost all violent conflicts in the states, ethnicity or religion are the root causes. For example, Charles Taylor's rebellious invasion, the repressive rule of Samuel Doe, Krahn and Mandingo in Liberia, and the Biafra war in Nigeria all have some link to ethnicity. The relationship between ethnic and religious diversity and conflicts in the zone can be appreciated when the ranking of countries in the zone based on internal conflict scores in Table 10.1 is juxtaposed with their ranking based on religious and ethnic tension scores in Table 10.2. For instance, Nigeria, which scored very low in the periods in the area of internal conflicts, also has the least scores on the religious tensions index, followed by Guinea and Liberia, while Ghana, with 6 points on a scale of 0 to 6 seemed to have the lowest rate of religious tensions. Table 10.2 reveals the rating of WAMZ countries in terms of religious and ethnic tensions based on scores on a scale of 0 and 6 points. Lower scores are given to nations where racial and national tensions are high and vice versa. The same applies to religious tensions. The religious tensions are social unrest arising from one religious group seeking to replace civil law with religious laws or having an undue influence in society, usually against the interests of other religious groups. Meanwhile, ethnicity also is part and parcel of the WAMZ political system used as an instrument for gaining employment and mobilising for ethnic identity with the aim of gaining ethnic group cooperation and national sympathy. In most cases, internal conflicts in member countries are rooted in ethnicity.

Tables 10.2: Trend of religious and ethnic tensions in WAMZ members' state (2001-2018)

	2001-2006		2007-2012		2013-2018	
Country/Region	**Religious tensions**	**Ethnic tensions**	**Religious tensions**	**Ethnic tensions**	**Religious tensions**	**Ethnic tensions**
Gambia	5.00	5.00	4.81	5.00	4.36	5.00
Ghana	6.00	2.34	6.00	3.50	6.00	3.50
Guinea	3.00	2.00	3.00	2.00	3.00	2.00
Liberia	3.56	3.00	3.76	3.00	3.50	3.00
Nigeria	1.47	1.72	1.66	2.00	1.50	2.00
Sierra Leone	4.42	3.25	5.00	4.58	5.00	3.93
WAMZ	3.91	2.89	4.04	3.35	3.89	3.24

Source: *computed by the author using data from International Country Risk Guide (Published by the PRS Group 2019). The scale is 6 (low tensions) and 0 (higher tensions).*

The use of ethnic and religious militias and violent agitations by groups to protect their common interest, intimidate and create threats in the society to press home their demands or get attention from the government, most often when felt marginalised over a long time, is another cause of conflicts and insecurity in some member states. This is common in WAMZ. In Nigeria, examples of ethnic and religious groups include armed militancy against the government by Niger Delta groups due to the government's irresponsible activity of environmental degradation emerging from oil exploration. These militant groups have always been involved in bombings, shootings, kidnappings, arson, and suicide bombing. Other examples include Boko Haram in the northeastern part of Nigeria. These activities have sped up the level of insecurity in the region.

Weak institutions and poor governance are among the factors contributing to the high rate of insecurity in WAMZ members' countries. Marginalisation, favouritism, and corruption weaken institutions and are more pronounced in countries where the institutions are already weak. Post-colonial rule in WAMZ countries has brought several challenges, which include bad governance, marginalisation, corruption, and weakening of institutions. After independence, a number of regimes in WAMZ nations mismanaged natural resources and further degenerated the governance system for selfish interest resulting in economic downturns, political apprehension, and socio-political instability. Social unrest in Nigeria, Guinea, Sierra Leone, and Liberia is majorly underpinned by weak institutions and mismanagement of the governance system. For instance, greed and lack of sincerity are the major causes of the Liberian civil war. Public corruption in Nigeria has been highlighted as one of the main factors of conflicts in the Niger Delta region of the country. For instance, the region is rich in oil, but it is one of the poorest regions in the country, leading to militant groups.

Violations of fundamental human rights also contribute to the insecurity in WAMZ. The incidence of human rights abuse is common in most of the states and forms the basis of the renewal of violent conflicts and civil war in the region. Sexual and gender-based violence is common, including reprisal killings and impunity, social injustice, and a repressive and brutal leadership system. These violations trigger war in the region. For instance, there are cases of human rights violations in the Niger Delta region of Nigeria emerging from economic marginalisation and environmental pollution. In Gambia, there are increasing cases of brutal leadership and an unequal and undemocratic governance system.

Another issue that triggers insecurity in WAMZ is the socioeconomic condition of the citizens. For instance, poverty constitutes one of the major setbacks in WAMZ. The UNDP Human Development Report has consistently suggested that there is a need to improve the socioeconomic conditions of West African states because almost half of the citizens are poor, which may increase the level of theft and other elements of insecurity in the West African region. Agitation to improve the economic conditions of the citizens also increase the level of insecurity in the region due to its correlation with civil war, as seen in Liberia and Nigeria (*Voz di Paz & Interpeace 2010; Annan, 2014*). Food insecurity and infrastructural issues, including lack of access to basic social needs, contribute to hunger and starvation, which increase violent conflict and civil strife.

Implications Of Insecurity For The Integration Agenda In WAMZ

Insecurity has direct and indirect implications for integration. The direct effects of insecurity on trade comes in the form of a rise in costs of international exchange, including transportation cost and the additional cost of investment in security measures. The increase in transaction costs of trade would directly lead to a reduction in trade. Insecurity may also lead to the loss of lives and damage to property, including transport infrastructure such as road networks, seaports, and other trade infrastructure. Also, if there is insecurity in society, shipments or goods moving across borders may be hijacked. Thus, extra costs will be incurred to ensure the safe delivery of goods and services. For instance, the costs of terrorism, internal conflicts, and external conflicts were estimated to be equivalent to a 30% tariff (*Bloomberg & Hess, 2006*). This, in turn, will lead to an increase in the prices of traded goods and a decrease in demand for such goods.

The effects of insecurity on trade may also be through the channel of productive activities. The volume of trade depends on production by exporting countries. Persistent conflicts do not only disrupt production activities but also lead to increased costs of production as firms take additional measures to guarantee the safety of the goods and workers. For instance, the production of agricultural products in Nigeria has been adversely affected by the insecurity in the north, where the bulk of farming takes place. Farmer-herder conflicts in the Middle Belt region, activities of bandits in the Northwest, and Boko haram insurgents in the northeastern parts of the country have made thousands of farmers abandon their farmlands for the safety of their lives. The bushes have become "death traps" as they are overtaken by bandits and Boko haram extremists. Analysed data from the West Africa Monetary Institute (WAMI) shows additional costs related to investment in security and losses due to insecurity incurred by firms in the Zone averaged over 5 percent of their annual sales between 2013 and 2018. Firms in Sierra Leone led the chart, followed by Nigeria and Liberia, while firms in Ghana and the Gambia incurred relatively lower costs (*Egbuna, Mohammed, Abubakari, Sambolah, & Adam, 2020*). These would have serious implications for the domestic output of goods and exports to other countries in the sub-region.

Marano, Cuervo-Cazurra, and Kwok (*2013*) argued that the location of insecurity matters because insecurity in the exporting country has a greater destructive impact on trade than insecurity in the importing country because the former destroys the tangible and intangible assets that support production. Since production is key to trading, conflicts that destroy production would, in turn, affect trading activities. They argued further that the effects of insecurity go beyond the borders of the countries that directly experience it, as trades are also negatively influenced by insecurity in neighbouring countries, which also destroys the tangible and intangible assets that support trade.

The persistence of political instability would affect the political and economic priorities of countries in the zone. Most often, leading to frequent changes in migration and trade policies of member countries. For instance, the free movement of labour within member countries would be hindered by a lack of trust occasioned by the influx of religious terrorists from neighbouring countries in the Sahel and due to growing waves of different forms of armed conflicts. Also, internal conflicts such as kidnapping by bandits, particularly in Nigeria, have created a general atmosphere of insecurity for foreign investors. Most of the WAMZ countries are reliant on the export of agricultural products and natural resources. Overall, insecurity would affect the integration Agenda through many channels.

Conclusion

This chapter examined the implications of insecurity on the integration Agenda of the WAMZ. The chapter concludes that the growing trend of conflicts and a general sense of insecurity in the zone, particularly Nigeria, which is the dominant country calls for serious concern and urgent measures. The extent to which the integration agenda will be achieved will largely depend on the level of progress made in ensuring peace, security, and relative political and economic stability in the zone.

Section Three
International And Insider Perspectives

Chapter 10

The AfCFTA: Opportunities And Challenges For West Africa Monetary Zone

Since the 1960s, several efforts have been made to achieve integration in the African continent. The pioneering effort was the establishment of the Organisation of African Unity (OAU) in 1963, with 32 members. The OAU was later transformed into African Union (AU) in 2002, with all 55 countries on the continent as members to foster cohesion and solidarity among African countries within the global governance and trading system (*Albert, 2019*). Further efforts by the regional body to promote cooperation between African States and minimize reliance on the West by promoting intra-African trade led to the signing of an African Continental Free Trade Agreement (AfCFTA) that will become the largest free-trade agreement in the world after the World Trade Organization (WTO). At the 2018 AU Summit, Heads of State and Government adopted a decision to establish a Free Trade Area for the continent and initiated a plan to boost Intra-Africa Trade in seven key areas of cooperation, namely: trade policy, trade facilitation, productive capacity, trade-related infrastructure, trade finance, trade information, and factor market integration. The agreement sets out to create a single market for goods and services facilitated by the movement of persons. This is aimed at strengthening the economic integration of the African continent, and it follows the Pan-African Vision of "an integrated, prosperous, and peaceful Africa" enshrined in Agenda 2063.

Given that all the countries in WAMZ and ECOWAS at large are signatories to the African Continental Free Trade Agreement (AfCFTA), the full implementation of AfCFTA will have monumental implications for the sub-region integration arrangements. Therefore, this chapter examines the opportunities and challenges of the African Continental Free Trade Agreement (AfCFTA) on the integration agenda in WAMZ. The remaining parts of this paper are organised into: Evolution and structure of AfCFTA, Opportunities and potential positive impacts of AfCFTA, potential challenges of AfCFTA implementation for the integration agenda in WAMZ, Differential treatments and impacts of the AfCFTA agreement, and then Conclusion.

Evolution and Structure of AfCFTA

The efforts aimed at developing the African continent led to the meeting of the First Congress of Independent African States, held in Accra, Ghana, in April 1958, which eventually culminated in the formation of the then Organisation of African Unity (OAU) in 1963 and later the African Union (AU) in 2001. This was aimed at promoting the unity and solidarity of the member states to intensify their cooperation and efforts to achieve a better life for the peoples of Africa and to defend the sovereignty of the newly independent nations. The union also struggled for the independence of the countries under the control of colonial rule. The organisation later adopted the Lagos Plan for Action in 1980, which aims at fostering the integration of the continent based on the "self-reliance, endogenous development and industrialization" of Africa. Subsequently, in July 1991, the OAU adopted the Abuja Treaty that promoted the implementation of a progressive approach to regional integration in the continent. This led to the creation of Regional Economic Communities (RECs) and a proposal for the formation of an African Economic Community by 2028. Part of the provisions of the Abuja Treaty, which was aimed at promoting cooperation between African States and minimizing reliance on the West by promoting intra-African trade, was to establish Free Trade Areas (FTAs) in each region, then customs unions, and finally, the establishment of a common market that will use a uniform currency.

There are a number of regional and sub-regional economic integration arrangements across the continent. These include:

(i) The Southern African Development Community (SADC), made up of sixteen countries.

(ii) The Eastern African Community (EAC), composed of five countries.

(iii) Common Market East and South Africa (COMESA), composed of twenty-one countries.

(iv) The Economic Community of West African States (ECOWAS), composed of fifteen countries.

(v) The Economic Community of Central African States (ECCAS), composed of eleven countries.

(vi) The Intergovernmental Authority on Development (IGAD), composed of seven countries.

(vii) The Arab Maghreb Union (AMU), composed of five countries.

(viii) Community of Sahel-Saharan States (CENSAD), composed of six countries.

These RECs were established as a stepping stone to regional unification; however, the fact that some countries had overlapping membership of more than one Economic community posed a hindrance to the actualisation of the planned integration. This led to the merging of SADC,

EAC, and COMESA in June 2011 and the launch of the Tri-Partite Free Trade Agreement (TFTA) negotiations in Johannesburg, South Africa. Based on this, a strong case for a continental-wide free trade area was made in January 2012 by the Economic Commission for Africa, and this initiated the negotiation process for the establishment of a free trade area agreement in Africa. Part of the discussion by the leaders of the African Union summit of 2012 in Addis Ababa was the creation of a new Continental Free Trade Area by 2017. The negotiations for the agreement were first discussed at the AU summit of 2015 in Johannesburg but eventually commenced in February 2016, and in February 2017, the technical issues were deliberated and implemented in the draft. In March 2018, the African Union Ministers of Trade approved the draft (Tralac, 2020) at the 10th Extraordinary Session of the AU on AfCFTA, and a total of 44 out of the 55 member states signed the agreement on that day. Two other agreements were also signed – the Kigali Declaration and the Protocol on Free Movement of Persons. The latter seeks to establish a visa-free zone with the AfCFTA countries and support the African Union Passport (Gwatiwa & Sam, 2019). During the 2018 summit in Kigali, the two largest economies of Africa, Nigeria and South Africa, withheld from signing the agreement; however, subsequently, more signatures were added to the agreement, with South Africa alongside four other nations at the African Union summit in Nouakchott, Mauritania on 1 July 2018. The agreement required that at least 22 member nations ratify it for it to come into effect, and this was achieved on 29th April 2019; the agreement consequently came into force on 30th May 2020, even though Nigeria, Benin, and Eritrea were yet to sign it at that point. However, on 7th July 2019, during the 12th extraordinary session of the assembly of the union on AfCFTA, Nigeria and Benin signed the AfCFTA leaving out Eritrea as the only country in the continent to sign the agreement (Mayeni, 2019) and Accra (Ghana) was selected by the Assembly of Heads of State and Government of the AU as the host country for the Secretariat of the AfCFTA.

The African Continental Free Trade Agreement (AfCFTA) is set to be implemented in phases which are still ongoing. The areas of agreement based on discussions from the Kigali summit were trade protocol, dispute settlement procedures, customs cooperation, trade facilitation, and rules of origin, which were part of Phase 1 (one) agreement. The AfCFTA implementation is in two phases. The first phase provides for the liberalisation of trade in goods and services and an instrument for dispute settlement. For trade in goods, the agreement provides the basis for eliminating tariffs on 90 percent of product categories. Countries can implement tariff reductions over a longer period in the case of sensitive goods or maintain existing tariffs — where the products are excluded for the remaining 10 percent of product categories (tariff lines). The protocol on trade in goods includes annexes on tariff concessions, rules of origin, customs cooperation, trade facilitation, non-tariff barriers, technical barriers to trade, sanitary and phytosanitary measures, and transit and trade remedies. This phase also provides for reporting and monitoring tools, institutional structures for the progressive elimination of non-tariff barriers (NTBs), and the facilitation of resolution of identified NTBs. On the liberalisation of trade in services, Member countries have also agreed to a request-and-offer approach based on seven identified priority sectors: logistics and transport, financial services, tourism, professional services, energy services, construction, and communications.

Phase II of the AfCFTA will focus on competition policy, investment, and intellectual property rights. Negotiations for Phase II were scheduled to begin after the Niamey Extraordinary meeting held on the 7th of July 2020, with an expected completion date of December 2020 scheduled for an extraordinary summit on the AfCFTA. Presently, 54 countries have signed the agreement while 34 countries have deposited their instrument of ratification, and 41 countries or customs unions have submitted their tariff offers, including EAC and ECOWAS. The start date of trading under the AfCFTA agreement was set at January 1, 2021.

FIGURE 11:1: THE STATUS OF THE AFCFTA PROTOCOLS AND ANNEXES

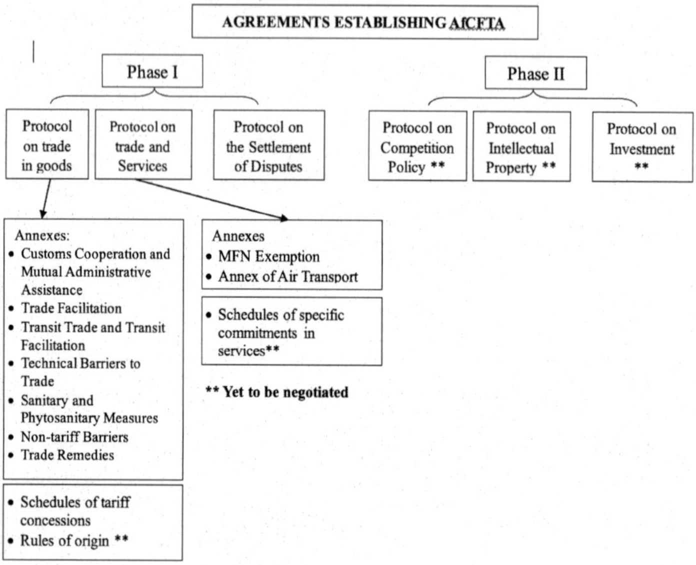

Source: *Signé L. & Van der Ven, C. (2019), Keys to Success for the AfCFTA Negotiations Policy BRIEF.*

Opportunities And Potential Positive Impacts For The West African Monetary Zone

The implementation of AfCFTA is expected to significantly reduce or eliminate both tariff and non-tariff barriers, as well as improve both hard and soft trade infrastructure. Thus, AfCFTA would yield freer intra-African trade, which further brings about increased production, output, income, decent employment opportunities, and by extension lower gender wage gap. More specifically, the World Bank in 2020 has simulated the various gains that would be derived from the implementation of AfCFTA to the African continent at large and to the sub-regions as well as to individual countries. The study forecasts the economic and distribution effects of AfCFTA in African countries till 2035. The study shows that trade in the continent will increase substantially. By 2035 it is expected that intracontinental exports will increase by over 81 percent, while export to non-African countries will increase by 19 percent. In monetary terms, intracontinental trade will grow from $294 billion (US Dollars) to $532 billion (US Dollars) with the implementation of AfCFTA by 2035. The study also shows that under the AfCFTA scenario, manufacturing exports will gain the most; it is expected that overall manufacturing exports will increase by 62 percent, with intra-Africa manufacturing trade increasing by 110 percent and exports to the rest of the world by 46 percent. In terms of volume, manufacturing exports will dominate the export picture for Africa, which is expected to increase to about $823 billion (US Dollars) by 2035.

After trade gains, the highest expected gain goes to employment, particularly employment related to public services, with a 15.2 percent rise. While employment in the business, recreational, and communication services are expected to increase by 3.2 percent, 2.5 percent, and 2.2 percent, respectively. Under the AfCFTA scenario, real income is expected to increase by 7 percent by 2035. This increment is equivalent to $445 billion (US Dollars) in monetary terms. The gains are, however, not even across countries; Côte d'Ivoire is expected to have the largest income gain. In terms of output gains, AfCFTA is expected to boost regional output by $211 billion (US Dollars) by 2035. The impacts on output are highly varied across sectors, with natural resources services expected to have the highest output gains. According to the study, the implementation of the agreement will take about 30 million persons out of extreme poverty while raising the incomes of over 68 million others who live on less than $5.50 a day. The document further suggests that the implementation of AfCFTA will cushion some of the adverse economic effects of the COVID-19 pandemic by supporting regional trade and value chains in the short term and providing a framework for increased cooperation, integration, and policy reform in the long term.

According to a study by the Economic Commission for Africa in 2018, which evaluated the implication of the AfCFTA on the good of African economies, the result showed that both the GDP and exports of these countries would increase even though the increase won't be as expected, mostly because a significant portion of West Africa's export is targeted outside the region. However, intra-regional trade will receive a major boost as certain restrictions such as tariffs and cost of trade will be eliminated or reduced and incentives granted. Some of the specific gains of the AfCFTA treaty are in the area of reduction of tariff and cost of trade, reduced import prices, trade liberalisation, and elimination of the intra-regional bottleneck in the trade as well as the increase in foreign investors in the region. There will be a significant reduction in import prices, thereby increasing the purchasing power of consumers, who will then have access to a wider range of products in the market. There will be more exports since it will become cheaper to engage in cross-border trade. The cost of raw materials and other factors of production will also reduce, thereby encouraging healthy competition among producers in the region.

There will be an increase in efficiency as firms will engage in more cost maximisation methods, improved technology resulting from a greater focus on R&D, and innovation will be commonplace in the regional market. The nature of the market at this point will attract multinational partners and encourage the spread of global best practices and the transfer of the latest technologies in the region. The influx of foreign investment will attract more capital to the continent and help solve most of its endemic economic problems, such as reducing the poverty rate, boosting incomes, accelerating growth, and diversifying exports, among others.

The UN Economic Commission for Africa (UNECA) projected significant growth of about 52.3% in the value of intra-regional exports and imports by 2022, when tariffs have been cut by 90% and trading rules harmonised. The study also suggests that the implementation of AfCFTA will boost trading of industrial products, agriculture and food products, and energy and mining products within the region by 25 – 30%, 20 – 30% and 5 – 11%, respectively, subject to the degree of liberalisation (*Albert, 2019*).

Assessing The Potential Challenges Of AfCFTA Implementation For WAMZ

The full implementation of AfCFTA is expected to bring a number of benefits, as discussed above; however, there are certain systemic issues that may delay or frustrate the realisation of these potential benefits. The integration agenda in WAMZ and ECOWAS at large is supposed to be a good stepping stone for the implementation of AfCFTA. According to Uche (2019), there are concerns that the institutional weaknesses in the region could be exploited by non-member nations to bring in goods from outside the continent and repackage them as goods made in Africa, thereby frustrating the achievement of the goal of the AfCFTA and stifling integration in the WAMZ sub-region. The introduction of an effective customs union will be a major step in tackling this challenge to enforce the agreement and ensure proper checks on goods tagged as "Made in Africa".

Given that the objective of WAMZ to attain full economic integration with a common currency and single currency in the Zone and ECOWAS at large could not be achieved after more than two decades of pursuing this, with the increasing focus on a continental-wide integration, members of WAMZ and ECOWAS may tend to abandon the sub-region agenda and the various ongoing negotiations in the Sub-region. Furthermore, the issue of a common currency has been a major concern for the sub-region since the wake of the new millennium with the establishment of the West African Monetary Zone and Institute. Part of the issue lies in the conflicting interest of the Anglophone and Francophone countries of the region. For instance, France has been able to retain the loyalty of its ex-African colonies by guaranteeing the stability and convertibility of the CFA Franc, making it difficult for regional integration to be possible. This issue was not holistically addressed under the AfCFTA agreement and, as a result, will affect the objective of regional integration for the region. Meanwhile, if a common currency is eventually introduced in WAMZ and ECOWAS, then currency convertibility issues will arise between countries in the sub-region and region with the other countries in the continent.

The idea of trade liberalisation is easier said than done as, in practice, there are other factors that can affect its implementation. The trade liberalisation and common external tariff scheme signed by WAMZ and ECOWAS member states have been poorly implemented, and this situation is likely to arise in the case of AfCFTA. In August 2019, the Nigerian government, in violation of the commercial and freedom of movement treaties signed under the ECOWAS FTA agreement, closed all land borders in the country, citing illegal importation and smuggling of goods through neighbouring countries as reasons for the action. With the full implementation of the AfCFTA, these institutional lapses may arise and will be a major clog in the wheel of economic integration for the West African region.

Equally, the effects of AfCFTA will not be evenly distributed across all the countries. For instance, Nigeria, with the largest economy, will have a different impact from a country like the Gambia, with the smallest economy in the region. Hence, the level of commitment will vary across the countries. Similarly, the expectation of fragile states will also differ; hence there is the possibility of a differential schedule of liberalisation in order to protect the more fragile economies.

TABLE 11.1: SCHEDULE OF LIBERALIZATION ENVISAGED UNDER THE AFCFTA REFORM.

		Tariff reduction		
		For non-sensitive products	For sensitive products	For excluded products
Country classification	Non-least developed countries	Fully liberalized over 5 years (linear cut)	Fully liberalized over 10 years (linear cut)	No cut
	least developed countries	Fully liberalized over 10 years (linear cut)	Fully liberalized over 13 years (linear cut)	No cut
	Group of seven**	85% fully liberalized over 10 years (linear cut); an additional 5% fully liberalized over 15 years (linear cut)	Fully liberalized over 13 years (linear cut)	No cut

** Djibouti, Ethiopia, Madagascar, Malawi, Sudan, Zambia, & Zimbabwe

Source: AfCFTA negotiation forums

Albert (*2019*) noted that the differential treatment might generate greater benefits for smaller economies such as Niger or the Gambia. The arrangement will ensure that the least-developed countries would experience the largest growth in intra-regional trade; hence it is a win-win situation which every country will benefit from. The World Bank's report on African Continental Free Trade Area: Economic and Distributional Effects further buttress the differential significance of the AfCFTA on different countries using the figures below:

FIGURE 11.2: REAL INCOME GAINS BY COUNTRY AND POLICY REFORM

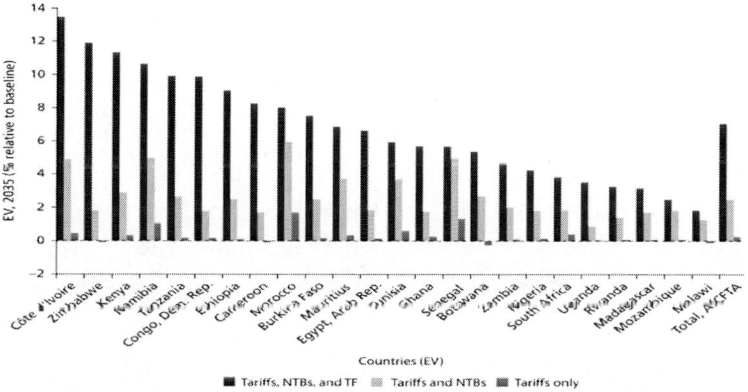

Source: World Bank (2020), The AfCFTA: Economic and Distributional Effects.

Figure 11.2 shows that the highest income gains for West African countries will occur in Cote d'Ivoire, followed by Burkina Faso, Ghana, and Senegal, before Zambia and Nigeria, who will have income gains of about 5% and above each by 2035. According to the report, these gains are related to the level of trade barriers and costs that exists among the countries.

FIGURE 11.3: EFFECTS OF AFCFTA ON WAGES BY SKILL LEVEL

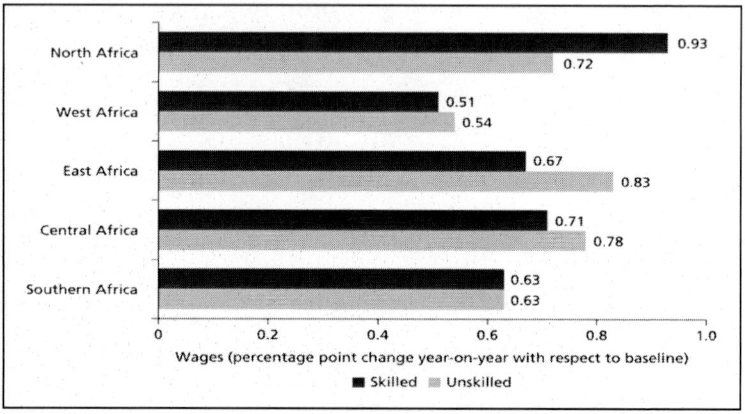

Source: World Bank (2020), The AfCFTA: Economic and Distributional Effects.

There will be more to benefit from improved market access by those with fewer barriers to trade but less benefit from their own liberalisation. On the other hand, countries with heavily protected trade will face increased import competition, although they will have more benefits from lower imported input prices.

Furthermore, according to the World Bank report, as depicted in Figure 11.3, the full implementation of AfCFTA is expected to have a significant positive effect on wages. However, the West African region is expected to have the least gains in wages, largely resulting from changes in the composition of output, towards more labour-intensive industries in some regions and more capital-intensive industries in others due to the implementation of the agreement.

FIGURE 11.4: EFFECTS OF AFCFTA ON WAGES BY GENDER

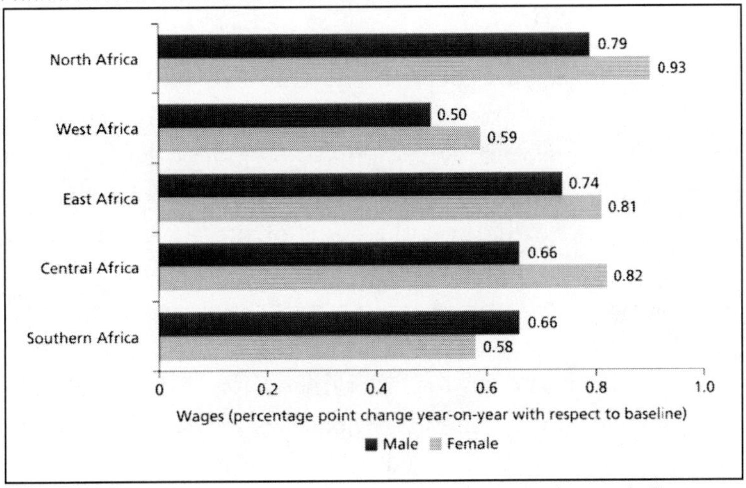

Source: World Bank (2020), The AfCFTA: Economic and Distributional Effects

The agreement, when fully implemented, is projected as seen in Figure 11.4 above, showing a grouping by region and gender that the West African region with all of the other regions except Southern Africa will have higher wage gains for women than men due to the potential of the agreement to expand out in female labour-intensive industries.

Conclusion

The AfCFTA officially entered into force on May 30th, 2019, even though its implementation is not fully negotiated and is fraught with various difficulties and bottlenecks. It represents a major landmark to further deepen WAMZ integration. Further reducing the cost of cross-border trade within the sub-region and the entire continent is expected to promote economic development and poverty reduction.

To ensure a seamless implementation of the agreement, policymakers must sit to address the challenges squarely. According to a PwC report on AfCFTA, the real issue is with the implementation of AfCFTA by actually converting the negotiations and agreements into practical realities for regional integration. The recommended solutions to these problems, and to harness the gains of the agreement, is for all the member nations to get involved and work together to review and harmonise existing trade and macroeconomic policies. Also, the areas of competitive advantage among the members should be identified, develop, and build institutional and human capacities across trade and investments, policies, and dispute resolution; address non-tariff barriers to trade such as policies relating to industries, agriculture, fiscal, banking, investment competition, ICT and telecommunication, transport, standards, labour markets, and government procurement. Then develop preferential policies and anti-benefit abuse clauses to protect infant industries, engage key stakeholders to reach a consensus, and finally build and establish a robust infrastructure among the member nations.

Furthermore, as the implementation of the agreement commences, there may be a need to undertake rigorous impact assessments to better enlighten stakeholders on the expectations and options as well as necessary adjustments. Regular review should be taken to direct future negotiations, and the various parties involved must express an active commitment to ensure the agreement is fine-tuned continuously to fully appreciate the gains of an FTA as is obtainable globally.

CHAPTER II

Africa Export And Import Bank (Afreximbank) Influence On Trade Promotion In WAMZ

Africa Export and Import Bank (AFREXIMBANK) has been recognised as a key regional integration bank due to its role in trade promotion across the continent. Its success in enhancing development and growth resilience across the continent has been well noted. The bank supports multinational trade rooted in African nations with a wide range of trade financing services that assist in the management of cross-national settlements and its associated risks, including the provision of working capital.

It is important to note that trade financing activities are diverse services of the bank or bank products that are peculiar to trade facilitation. It may be export or import-related transactions. Trade financing services may be for the short or medium term, but sometime, it may be for the long term, especially when it involves capital goods supported by long-term credits. AFREXIMBANK sometimes assists in working capital needs by providing trade finance credits or loans to African exporters or importers. Under this arrangement, loan documentation may be linked to either letter of credit or to other documents relating to international trade transactions. The bank has brought several innovations to trade financing activities in African financial markets. This can be evidenced by the recently launched payment system solutions, namely: the Pan African Payments Settlement System (PAPSS) and other levels of security showcased by the bank in the settlement aspects of international trade finance in Africa. However, the bank still has some challenges, which include differences in preferences in terms of sovereignty in specific areas for regional and trade integration, lack of harmonisation of country-specific policies in relation to capital controls, poor transport infrastructure and institutional framework across the continents. The objective of this chapter is to x-ray how the activities of AFREXIMBANK influence trade promotion in WAMZ.

Overview of Trade Financing Structure and Programme

The African Export-Import Bank (AFREXIMBANK) was set up in 1993 to improve and promote intra-and extra-African trade. The bank has been involved in activities to ensure the smooth growth of cross-border trade in Africa, trade facilitation, trade infrastructure enabler, and other activities to develop trade-technological ecosystems. The Article II of AFREXIMBANK's charter lists the main function of the bank as follows:

- Extension of direct credit to eligible African exporters by providing shipment finance.
- Extension of short-term indirect credits and, in some cases, medium-term credit to exporters and importers in Africa via financial intermediation of banks and other financial institutions.
- The promotion and finance of intra-trade in Africa.
- Promotion of finance exports of non-traditional African goods and services.
- Provision of finance to export-generating African imports.
- Promotion and finance of trade between Africa and other Global South nations.
- Acting as an intermediary between African exporters and non-African importers by issuing a letter of credit, guarantee, and other necessary trade documents.
- Promotion of trade with African nations and issuance of bankers' acceptance and other supporting documents.

- Provision of insurance and guarantee services for commercial and non-commercial risks in relation to African exports.
- Provision of support for payment arrangements towards expanding multinational trades among African nations.
- The bank may also involve in research leading to the development of African trade.
- Provision and support of other services that may boost African exporting activities.

One of the main functions of AFREXIMBANK is the trade finance programme. Trade finance includes credit extended to firms or bilaterally between firms or nations in a supply chain or between different organisations of different lines of business. The bank also plays an important role in trade facilitation via the establishment of the payment system for multinational trade. There are many trade finance programmes operated by the bank, ranging from structured and unstructured activities to support and enable African cross-border trade. The bank trade financing programmes include:

Structured Trade Finance

This consists of programmes and facilities focusing on addressing markets and product diversification issues that many African nations may face. It covers exports and imports activities and intends to remove any bottlenecks to trading of services and products near production or already produced. These trade finance facilities are self-secured and self-liquidating style facilities. In addition, most facilities in this scheme are normally classified under two forms of programmes: Dual Recourse and Non-Dual Recourse Programmes.

The dual recourse category programmes are the ones in which the bank lends to a corporate against the guarantee of another corporate creditworthy or acceptable bank. This implies that AFREXIMBANK will rely on the proximity of the domestic banks in the residential area of the borrowers in the process of monitoring and supervising the loans. This helps in reducing the bank's risk of lending to new exporters. However, the Non-Dual Recourse programmes and facilities can be discussed under the following headings:

- **Line of Credit Programme:** The bank provides credits via funded and unfunded credit lines to creditworthy banks. These banks can be African or non-African banks but should be actively involved in African trading activities. This programme is an instrument in which the bank provides loan facilities and empowers intermediary banks like a local bank to offer credits to small and medium-sized trading firms whose statement of financial position (balance sheet) and the size of trade turnover would not usually qualify for the bank's direct lending. The kind of facilities normally provided under this programme include Export-Import financing Facilities, Pre- and Post-Export Financing, Letters of confirmation of credit, and refinancing facilities. Sometimes, the bank issues Reimbursement Guarantee Facility.

- **Direct Financing Programme:** In this programme, AFREXIMBANK provides pre- and post-export financing directly to firms whose statement of financial position size is not less than $2 million (US Dollars) with an annual trading volume of not less than $10 million (US Dollars).

- **Syndications Programme:** This is a risk-sharing programme leveraged on support rate and project activities across the African continent. The bank arranges a club of reputable multinational and or African banks to finance entities in Africa.

- **Special Risks Programme:** The programme is conceived as a risk-bearing programme through which the bank's objective is to:

- Provide opportunities to restructure trade financing deals.
- Provide opportunities for African banks to take payment responsibilities and risks of their African counterparties.
- Provide opportunities for multinational banks to lend over a longer period to Africa.
- Strengthening African exporters' position in gaining access to new markets by covering the

exporters against the economic and political risks.

Other Financing Programmes Of AFREXIMBANK Include:

Note Purchase Programme: In this programme, the bank gives financing to corporates through the acquisition of promissory notes or other similar instruments accepted by the bank or guaranteed by the acceptable bank or corporates.

Receivables Purchase Programme: This is also known as Discounting Programme consisting of facilities by a family that engages in the acquisition of a particular class of receivables from the sale of goods and services to domestic or foreign buyers, with or without recourse to the sellers. Those facilities in this programme are Invoice and Receivables Discounting, Forfaiting, Factoring and Receivables Management, and Joint Bill Discounting and Refinancing.

Asset-Backed Lending Program: This is a programme that assists entrepreneurs in Africa to meet the growing demand for financing, especially the acquisition of physical assets with the framework of privatisation, with the aim of promoting local-content opportunities. One benefit is that the assets may serve as collateral.

Country Programmes: This programme is a platform

used by the bank to help the nation under peculiar cases which are not within the solution menu offered by the bank's regular programme.

Factoring: Factoring involves the acquisition of trade receivables due to suppliers and exporters (sellers) by a financial institution called a Factor, and the Factor assumes full credit and responsibilities to collect. This is being done at a discount in exchange for immediate cash for the purpose of financing business continuation. Factor performs some important functions, such as credit protection, prepaid function against account receivables, collection responsibility, and credit management. AFREXIMBANK uses the factoring function to expand and facilitate trade in Africa and particularly to support SMEs.

Trade Finance Intermediaries: AFREXIMBANK uses Trade Finance Intermediaries to serve its clients. It is being used by the bank to serve numerous and diverse classes of eligible exporters to act as Local Administrative arms or agents of the AFREXIMBANK.

Food Emergency Contingent Financing Facility (FECONTRAF): This is a substitution of physical food (e.g. grains) reserves for a standby facility and allows vulnerable nations to finance their commercial imports of grains or other staple food of choice. This programme is normally deployed where there is a food emergency.

The benefits of the programme include saving the cost of storage, reducing the level of hunger during a crisis in African nations, helps budgeting and other fiscal challenges. Among the tools normally used for these services include a standby letter of credit and a food emergency reserve account.

The Payment System Solution By AFREXIMBANK: PAPSS

Pan African Payments Settlement System (PAPSS) was launched in Ghana in January 2022 by AFREXIMBANK in conjunction with African Union, WAMZ countries, and African Continental Free Trade Area (AfCFTA). This move follows the successful pilot period in WAMZ countries, which enhances instant cross-border settlement in local currencies between African markets. The essence of the pilot phase is to facilitate a smooth implementation of AfCFTA among African nations. PAPSS is a payment platform that intends to transform and boost intra-African trade with the opportunities to connect African markets and trading partners to each other at a reduced cost.

Before the introduction of PAPSS, intra-African trade was saddled with much reliance on US Dollars and non-African correspondent banks for clearing systems with huge transitionary costs. This places limitations and often discourages smooth transaction deals in the intra-African trade system to the extent that originating a fund transfer between trade partners in Africa was more complex than fund transfers between an African trade partner and a European partner. Another limitation is that transfer of funds between African trade partners is often faced on a person-to-person basis, different countries' laws, among others. However, the advent of PAPSS has provided a solution to this hurdle.

The Framework For The Operation Of PAPSS

PAPSS is a payment system with a centralised settlement infrastructure for intra-African transactions. The deployment of PAPSS technology has made it easier to connect different African countries for the utilization of real-time payment systems with financial intermediaries as the participants. The PAPSS operates in such a way that every payment transaction is done instantaneously or almost instantaneously between the originating country and the receiving country. On the receipt of transaction instructions in domestic currency, the originating financial intermediaries circulate the transaction instruction to PAPSS for validation and onward transfer to the designating bank from which the payment is cleared in favour of the beneficiaries. PAPSS operates in such a way that there is no need to source for the beneficiary's domestic currency or even the US dollars. For instance, a

Nigerian can originate a fund transfer to Ghana in Naira, and it will be remitted to Ghanaian trading partners in Cedi. To originate payment via PAPSS, it is necessary to note that there are legal frameworks to be followed. These include:

- The payment must be for the eligible imports and or exports, depending on the countries. Some countries, like Nigeria, state that the goods or services must be of African origin.

- The prevailing exchange rate at investors and exporters' Forex window may be used for the cross-rate conversion. Only eligible transactions and authorized dealers would be given approval. These conditions vary from country to country.

- Furthermore, the net settlement model of PAPSS relies on pre-funding by the participating financial intermediaries via the local Real Time Gross Settlement (RTGS) system. AFREXIMBANK is the settlement agent, while the individual country's monetary authority would maintain a US Dollar settlement account with AFREXIMBANK. This facilitates fast validation of eligible transactions on a net basis.

The Benefits Of Using PAPSS By African Countries

One such benefit is that PAPSS is a relief for most African countries where US dollars are relatively scarce for cross-border transactions. This reduces the pressure of demand for foreign currency in the domestic markets. Other benefits include:

- PAPSS will reduce the cost, time, and duration of cross-border payment settlement. It will also reduce the liquidity requirements of financial intermediaries for intra-trade payment in Africa and strengthen the monitoring system in cross-border payment by African central banks.

- PAPSS has the tendency to improve the value of the local currencies of the participating countries. This is because the new system does not require sourcing for foreign exchange for intra-African trade settlement.

- It can create jobs because third parties like financial institutions are needed for payment infrastructure. Even mobile money agents would be needed for the smooth operation of the platforms.

- The PAPSS may facilitate the WAMZ's single currency agenda because it brings different central and commercial banks in the continent together using a unified platform for payment settlements.

- The platform supports an instant payment system and facilitates retail and wholesale real-time payments. It enhances the instant and irrevocable credit system and is available 24/7, 365 days, thereby reducing the waiting period of the conventional system of payment.

- The PAPSS also increases the level of transparency in cross-border trade transactions. It brings an optimal level of monitoring and enhances the potential to generate revenue for the government.
- It increases the level of inclusive financial development, growth, and intra-trade activities in African regions.
- African entrepreneurs and SME owners get improvement in working capital through the payment certainty guaranteed by PAPSS due to the fast transaction and access to many payment facilities options with the growing networks of financial institutions.

The Trend Of Trade Financing By AFREXIMBANK

AFREXIMBANK was set up to perform, promote, and finance extra and intra-African trade. From its inception, the bank has championed this process and further encouraged the economic integration of African nations, directly involved in financing African trade growth, trade facilitation, and expanding the trade-enabling infrastructure and development of the technology ecosystem. As explained by Oramah (*2021*), the bank expanded its support for African trade by disbursing more than $40 billion (US Dollars) within five years. This is to facilitate inter-regional agreement and enhance its implementation.

Furthermore, the bank has been able to launch many programmes, as discussed above, to close the trade finance gap in intra-African trade caused by the withdrawal of multinational banks from African trade financing. In order to do this, AFREXIMBANK has been working with more than 350 banks in different parts of the world and over 120 lines, which amount to $2.2 million (US Dollars) spread across about 32 nations. The bank is trying to set up lines in all its member economies and to onboard about 550 African banks to the programme.

FIGURE 12.1: TRENDS OF MULTINATIONAL TRADE AS A PERCENTAGE OF TOTAL TRADE.

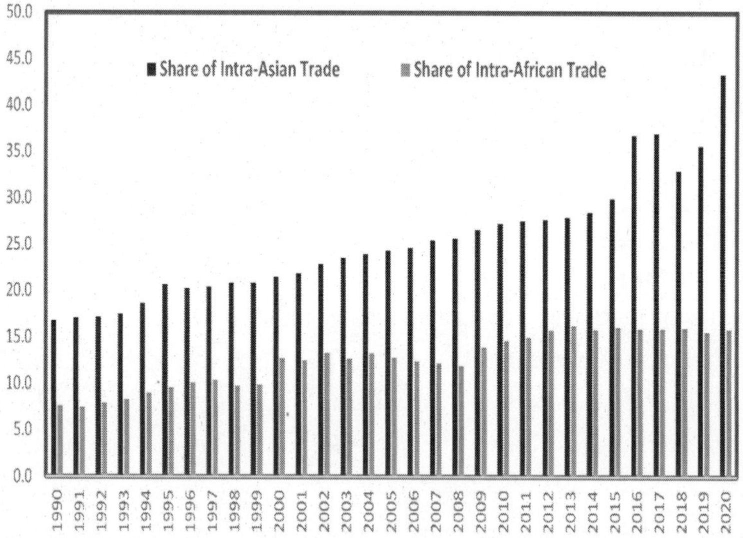

Source: Computed by the author from IMF Trade Statistics (2021)

Figure 12.1 shows the share of intra-trade in Africa compared with Asian trade. There is evidence that the intra-African trade is growing but not at the level of Asian regions. In order to increase the depth of intra-trade in Africa, AFREXIMBANK came up with a 5-year strategic plan to commence in 2017. In this plan, the bank brings some shifts in the composition of the trade finance portfolio by raising more funds for intra-trade to about 25 percent of the total trade finance in 2020 from 7.4 percent in 2015, thereby increasing the intra-trade financing to $20 billion (US Dollars) (*Oramah, 2021*).

Figure 12.2: Trend of Loan Disbursed by AFREXIMBANK Group.

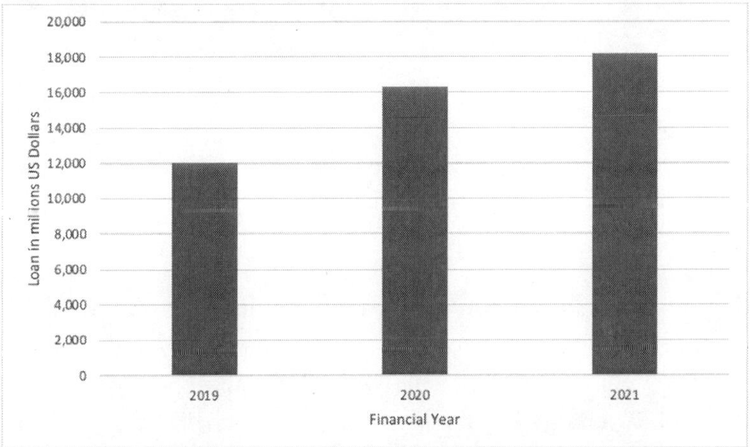

Source: Computed by the author from IMF Trade Statistics (2021)

Figure 12.2 shows that the trend of loans by the bank is growing from 2019 to 2021. Since 1993, it has been documented that the bank has approved more than $97.7 billion (US Dollars) in furtherance of its mandates for members. The bank experiences growth in total assets by 13.4 percent ($2.5 billion), which is due to the increase in net loans and advances on trade financing activities in 2021, growth in guarantees, and letters of credit, which is in line with bank's strategic plans to improve African trade through financing supports.

FIGURE 12.3: TREND OF LOAN BOOK OF AFREXIMBANK GROUP.

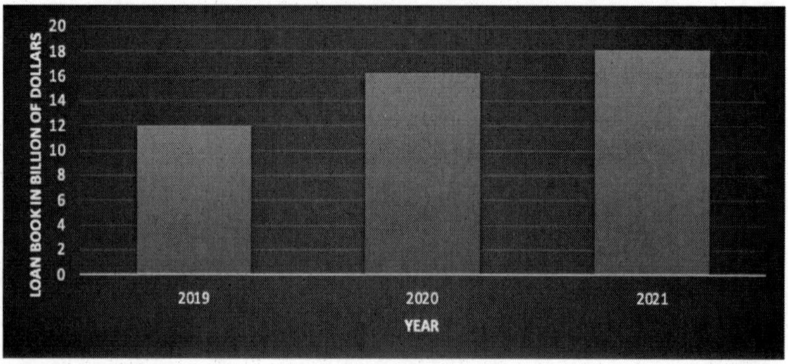

Source: Computed by the author from AFREXIMBANK Group's Annual Report (2022)

Figure 12.3 shows the growth of the loan book, which is consistent with the improved capital position of the Bank. Figure 12.4 shows that the West African region gets more than 35 percent of trade finance, which is the highest, followed by North Africa and Southern Africa. Therefore, it is expected that more trading activities would take place in West Africa compared to other sub-regions.

FIGURE 12.4: TREND OF TRADE FINANCE BY SUB-REGIONS.

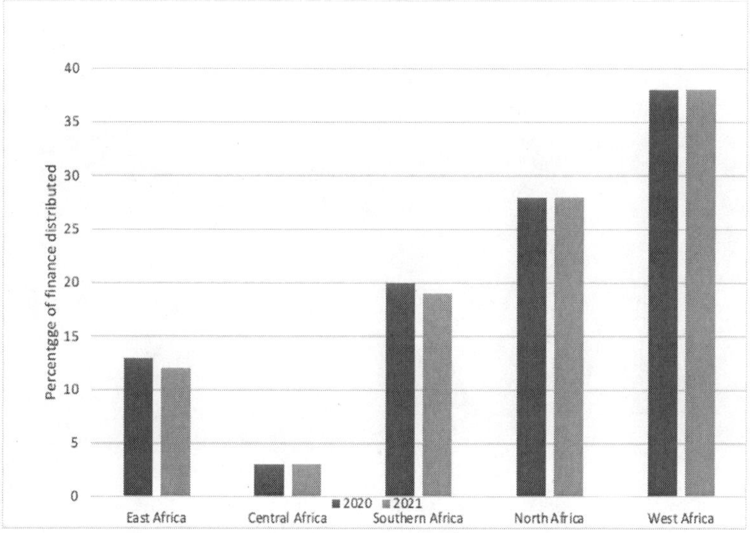

Source: Computed by the author from AFREXIMBANK Group's Annual Report (2022)

In Figure 12.5, the regional trade financing split remains stable during the period under review. The Financial sector accounted for 52 percent in 2021, which is below 55 percent in 2020. The Oil and Gas sector increased to 21.6 percent (2021) while it remained 14.4 percent in 2020.

FIGURE 12.5: TREND OF TRADE FINANCE BY SECTOR.

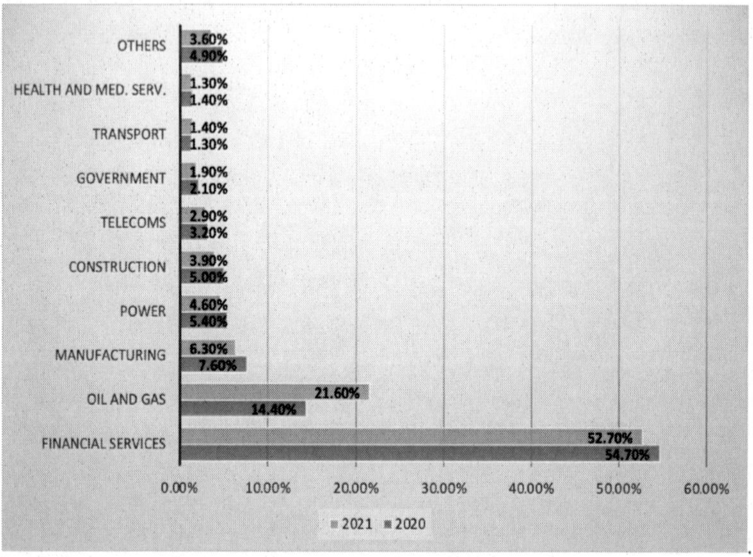

Source: Computed by the author from AFREXIMBANK Group's Annual Report (2022)

It is obvious that the bank supports trade in all the key sectors of African nations, including the telecomms, construction, and power sectors. Various interventions by the bank have helped to reduce the adverse impact of external shocks through its investment in growth diversification sources. For instance, the bank incorporated an insurance management company in 2021 to assist in retaining some sizable proportion of trade-related insurance premiums in the continent. The benefit of this arrangement is that trading partners would be protected against non-payment risk. For instance, export insurance reduces payment risks related to doing business globally by giving the exporter an assurance that payment will be made if the trading partners are unable to settle their obligations when due. It covers commercial risks like bankruptcy, protracted defaults, and certain political risks, like trade wars.

Also, AFREXIMBANK does organise trade fairs occasionally to promote intra-trade in Africa. For example, the bank collaborates with the African Union and the secretariat of the African Continental Free Trade Area (AfCFTA) to organise the trade fair between November 15 and 21, 2021, where more than $42 billion (US Dollars) worth of investment and trade deals was finalised. The programme allows every participant to share trade, market, and investment information, as well as opportunities available for trade facilitations and finance solutions for intra-African trade systems. The programme sets up business-government and business-to-business platforms for stakeholders, including advisory services.

Challenges Of Trade Financing And Opportunities Ahead

There are a number of factors limiting the availability of trade financing in WAMZ, ECOWAS, and Africa at large. The major challenges facing trade financing generally in Africa are discussed in this section. The opportunities available for trade financing are also discussed. Also highlighted in this section are the challenges facing trade financing, the solutions, as well as the opportunities.

Challenges of Trade Financing

There are many challenges facing the business of trade

financing in Africa. They are highlighted as follows:

- Capital requirements of assets on trade finance from Basel III, the anti-money laundering policy, including know-your-customer compliance, have consequently increased the cost of meeting due diligence costs. This makes the business of trade financing activities less profitable, which has reduced the number of financial institutions engaging in trade finance activities in Africa.

- Due to the high costs of compliance coupled with the high cost of doing business in Africa, small banks see trade financing activities as less profitable and, sometimes, unable to meet high overhead costs. This has also increased the rejection rates, especially for small-medium sized firms, and reduction in the supply of trade finance. Because most small firms are unable to meet the credit-worthiness assessment – this increases the rate of trade finance gaps in Africa.

- Another factor leading to trade finance gaps is the frequent changes in trade values and regulatory challenges, including declines in commodity prices exported by most nations in Africa.

- COVID-19 also created uncertainties and further contributed to the trade finance gap in African nations. Most nations are unable to meet up with their indebtedness due to border-close down and restrictions of movements.

- Even the future trajectory of trade finance may be difficult to predict due to uncertainties. For instance, the balance sheet of most African banks has deteriorated, which further creates several challenges for closing trade finance gaps in Africa due to their reluctance to lend or finance any potential trading activities.

- The non-availability of insurance schemes to adequately cover trade financing activities when needed is also a major challenge.

- Weak local banking system also contributes to the problem of trade financing. The weaknesses of the domestic banking system provide avenues for multinational banks to reduce trade credits extended to local firms or organisations.

- Low international ratings of a nation is another factor that may have a negative impact on trade financing.

Solutions And Opportunities Ahead

The regulatory system needs to be addressed, including the reclassification of some trade facilities as less risky assets. This may reduce the capital burden on small and correspondent banks, encourage more potential banks to be involved in trade finance activities and reduce the rejection rate of some classes of transactions. The regulators should set up an inter-operable credit system where banks can access and share the records of exporters and importers in real-time. This will reduce the burden of compliance costs in the long run. Opportunities were also presented in the recently signed African Continental Free Trade Agreement by 52 African nations in May 2019. Through the creation of a single continental market, there is a tendency that this action will further enhance the much-needed free movement of goods and services, investments, and businesspeople. Intra-African trade will expand, and better harmonisation and coordination of the trade facilitation process will be assured. This represents a distinguished opportunity to strengthen trade financing activities across African nations.

Implications Of AFREXIMBANK Trade Financing On Integration In WAMZ

There are several implications of AFREXIMBANK trade financing on regional integration in WAMZ, as highlighted below:

- The activities of the Bank through the organisation of seminars and trade financing have helped in deepening the harmonisation of rules and other administrative regulations for effective integration in WAMZ. There has been a reduction in the overreliance on Bretton Wood institutions for relief and regulation of trading activities. The prevailing complexities of the global financial market, the trend of trade regulation, and the burden of trade financing twist by the multinational banks have been reduced by AFREXIMBANK. This has broadened the regional integration in WAMZ.

- Factors like differences in structural features, the pursuit of import-substitution policies, and uneven distribution of cost when accessing trade facilities have been reduced due to the involvement of AFREXIMBANK in WAMZ. This has further enhanced the promotion of WAMZ integration.

- Another implication of AFREXIMBANK trade financing is that it has broadened the need for financial resource pooling and has harmonised the mind to have regional financial market initiatives, which help the WAMZ states overcome some limitations of a fragmented financial system.

- The trade financing functions of AFREXIMBANK have helped overcome divisions that may reduce the limitations on the free flow of goods and services, capital, people, and diffusion of technology among WAMZ members. The trade finance initiatives of AFREXIMBANK have helped to promote a common institutional framework and trade infrastructures. The divisions between countries in terms of trade infrastructure and geography may reduce the degree of regional integration. However, AFREXIMBANK initiatives have helped to overcome these challenges.

- The activities of AFREXIMBANK have enabled many countries to substantially gain from improved financial market efficiency, share the cost of physical and trade infrastructures, and take the decision for collective well-being.

- Finally, the recent African trade agreement reached also serves as a major booster for the role of AFREXIMBANK in the continent. Because the bank has designed some strategic policies, including financial backing, to encourage African trade integration – this happens through a policy for trade liberalisation, free movement of people, facilitation instruments and investment across borders. This is another unique opportunity to improve and strengthen the trade finance sector in WAMZ.

Conclusion

Trade constitutes one of the factors influencing inclusive growth and sustainable development because it facilitates the exchange of goods and services, the movement of capital, and fosters cultural and ethical linkages between citizens and other people in the world. Trade promotes economic integration, growth, and poverty reduction. Within the period of 2015 and 2019, UNCTAD estimates that African trade value is approximately $760 billion (US Dollars) per annum on average, which is about 29 percent of GDP. Intra-African trade has continued to facilitate regional development, including cross-border infrastructure, intra-regional investment, and a reduction in unfavourable boundaries of landlocked nations. Despite the importance of trade, there are still wider gaps in African trade finance. African nations are yet to capture the full potential benefits of cross-border trade.

AFREXIMBANK and other financial institutions have continued to assist in relieving nations of the trade finance constraint they face, but there is still much to be done to smoothen the cross-border trade in WAMZ members' nations. The bank promotes trade through its functions by providing critical fluidity and security settlement systems to encourage the movement of goods and services among nations in Africa. It also provides the mechanism by supporting two fundamental aspects of trade facilitation: liquidity and risk mitigation. In a cross-border trade environment, risks are intensified by factors like financial crisis and macroeconomic volatility, politically related risks, asymmetry information, and moral hazard.

Evidence shows that AFREXIMBANK has made a significant effort to reduce trade finance gaps in the last decade. The bank has made significant efforts to de-risk transactions for financial intermediaries through sound financial backing and different trade finance programmes.

For instance, the bank launched AFREXIMBANK's Mansa in July 2018. This is a platform for checking due diligence to facilitate intra-African trade. Technology and different innovations are being explored to facilitate smooth trade finance. Notwithstanding, much effort is still being deployed to ensure efficiency and effectiveness in cross-border trade activities in Africa.

Chapter 12

Financial Integration Experiences In EU And ASEAN: Lessons For WAMZ

Since 1994, cross-border capital flows (measured by gross capital inflows globally) have grown at a pace of 16 percent per year on average, far faster than global commerce or global GDP. With the number of cross-border capital movements increasing, so have cross-border ownership of financial assets. In principle, financial integration with the global economy may provide several benefits to a nation, ranging from cheaper capital costs and improved risk-sharing to more government, bank, and non-bank corporate discipline. In practice, however, the favourable impacts of financial integration on economic development have been difficult to find in statistics. For instance, after reviewing a large body of empirical research, Kose et al. (2003, 2010) found that financial integration had no substantial, robust, or causal influence on economic growth in a typical developing nation.

Previous financial crises have highlighted the hazards posed by unrestricted capital movements. For example, both the Asian financial crisis of 1997 – 1998 and the global financial crisis of 2008 – 2009 demonstrated that increasing financial interconnectedness has potential hazards as well as advantages. Economies with a high degree of financial openness tend to be more vulnerable to the impacts of financial contagion. Avoiding financial integration, on the other hand, is unrealistic. Since the early 1990s, a surge of financial deregulation, innovation, and liberalisation has driven cross-border financial integration. Several noticeable advances in financial innovation and globalisation, such as financial institutions' use of offshore special-purpose vehicles, the spread of securitisation, and the increase in institutional investors and hedge funds, have all enhanced the rise in cross-border financial integration (*Bakoup & Ndoye, 2016*).

Although there are slight distinctions between financial openness, financial integration, and financial liberalisation, given that financial openness and liberalisation are closely related and only represent the easy movement of financial assets across borders, they are just a step of financial integration, which is a broader concept that connotes a close link between the financial markets in neighbouring or regional economies (*Phutkaradze et al., 2019*). Therefore, financial openness and financial liberalisation seem to be the means to financial integration (Le, 2000). These terms are used interchangeably in this chapter due to the similarities of their concepts to capture the easy movement of cross-border financial assets with the aim of achieving improved economic activities among countries.

Given the aforementioned trend in financial integration across the globe, it is pertinent to briefly discuss the historical account of major experiences, such as those of the European Union (EU) and Association of Southeast Asian Nations (ASEAN), of financial integration, a single currency, and monetary union around the world, to take some lessons for the West African Monetary Zone (WAMZ). First of all, just like every other monetary union and single currency programme, the WAMZ was developed on the belief that monetary and economic integration brings about increased welfare and prosperity to the member states. Historical accounts seem to support this belief, albeit with some challenges which are inevitable due to some peculiar differences associated with the countries of the union.

First, from the European Union's viewpoint at the moment, the EU includes 27 member states and engages in both supranational and intergovernmental cooperation. The European Union (EU) sprang from the European Coal and Steel Community (ECSC), which was founded in

1951 by six European nations the Netherlands, Belgium, Luxembourg, Italy, France, and Germany). Since then, it has expanded in size with the admission of additional member states, as well as in authority with the addition of new policy areas to its jurisdiction. The publication of the report of the committee for the study of the Economic and Monetary Union in 1989 was a watershed moment in the history of European integration. A three-phase transition to monetary unification was recommended in the so-called Delors Report, named after the head of this group. The primary recommendations of the Delors Committee were integrated into the 1992 Treaty on the European Union, which eventually led to the establishment of the single currency and the European Central Bank (ECB). The European Commission's announcement of the Financial Services Action Plan (FSAP) in May 1999 was a significant milestone for financial integration. The FSAP's goal was to remove legal and market barriers that impede cross-border financial services supply and the free movement of money inside the EU, as well as to provide a fair playing field for market players.

As for the experience of the ASEAN, the bloc was founded on August 8, 1967, in Bangkok, Thailand, with the signing of the ASEAN Declaration (Bangkok Declaration) by the founding five (5) countries, namely, Thailand, Singapore, the Philippines, Malaysia, and Indonesia. Brunei Darussalam joined on 7 January 1984, followed by Vietnam on 28 July 1995, Lao People's Democratic Republic (PDR), Myanmar on 23 July 1997, and Cambodia on 30 April 1999, forming what is now ASEAN's ten (10) member states. Since the Asian financial crisis of 1997 – 1998, the ASEAN bloc has worked tirelessly to improve the framework of financial integration and ensure regional financial stability. Two ASEAN Economic Community (AEC) designs featuring financial integration and liberalisation aspects have been adopted to attain regional financial integration and complement financial stability and inclusion. Though the endeavour appears daunting, regional efforts in sustainable finance, financial resilience, financial stability, financial inclusion, taxation, payment and settlement systems, capital markets, capital accounts, insurance, and banking have been agreed upon and partially implemented.

The objective of this chapter is to examine the financial integration and single currency experiences in the EU and ASEAN and then draw lessons for WAMZ. It is relevant to reveal the experiences of both blocs in that the EU is characterised as a fully integrated monetary and economic region that can be used as a model for full financial integration, and the ASEAN is characterised by a partially integrated economic and trade region that can serve as a partial financial integration model.

The Concept Of Financial Integration

Financial integration is a process by which one country's financial markets become more tightly connected with the global financial markets or those of other economies. This indicates a rise in the flow of capital as well as a propensity for prices and returns on traded financial assets to equalize across countries (Brouwer, 2005). Financial integration might move further with the implementation of a formal international treaty. This refers to two separate parts. One example is the option for coordinated or cooperative policy responses to financial disruptions. The other is the abolition of cross-border financial transaction limitations by member nations and the harmonisation of financial system rules to achieve full unification of regional financial markets, taxes, and regulations between member economies.

There are various advantages to formalising financial system integration. The first is the use of economies of scale, which can assist enterprises, particularly small- and medium-sized ones with credit restrictions, to get greater access to larger financial or capital markets. Individual risks might also be reduced by integrating into a wider market while increasing portfolio diversity. Furthermore, regulatory independence might be strengthened through formal integration, broadening the possibility for financial system governance involvement. Financial institutions functioning under the effect of multiple countries' integration arrangements should follow a uniform valuation criterion, which enhances not only the transparency of specific financial sectors but also the overall stability of connected financial systems. Financial integration, on the other hand, might occur in the absence of explicit agreements. Thus, financial information sharing, foreign participation in local banking, insurance and pension fund industries, direct borrowing of domestic corporations in international financial markets, and so on are all possibilities.

It is difficult to define a uniform metric of financial integration. There are many different types of financial transactions, and some countries impose a complex array of price and quantity controls on a wide range of financial transactions, making measuring cross-country differences in the nature, intensity, and effectiveness of barriers to international capital flows extremely difficult (*Eichengreen, 2001*). Three types of empirical investigations are commonly used to assess the degree of financial integration or, simply, financial openness. Frankel and MacArthur (*1988*) measure the degree of capital mobility and capital account liberalisation using interest rate differentials and forward premiums and discounts. However, these measurements continue to be a compelling argument due to the difficulties in precisely estimating the scale and efficacy of government limitations and the relatively limited coverage of nations and periods.

The second kind is an on-and-off indication that indicates the presence of rules and restrictions that impede cross-border capital movements. Quinn (*1977*) examined the International Monetary Fund's (IMF) restriction measures by going through narrative descriptions of capital account limits and awarding ratings to the strength of capital restrictions. Other studies advocate stringent measures for a small number of nations, focusing solely on regulations on foreign equity sales and acquisitions. However, it may be argued that a variety of variables, rather than only direct administrative hurdles, may influence cross-border capital flows. For example, they might be a variety of policies and situations, such as the attitude of monetary or fiscal policy, the size of the local economy, and global conditions.

The last form of empirical study measures financial openness using actual foreign money, financial flow, or stock. The stock of international assets and liabilities as a proportion of GDP is a popular metric. A high percentage indicates that an economy is financially open to the rest of the globe. Unlike the second type of measure, this openness measure takes into account all other variables impacting the degree of capital flows, such as the characteristics of domestic financial markets.

Financial Integration And Single Currency Experience In European Union (EU)

From the EU's perspective, intending to put an end to the recurrent and violent battles that culminated in World War II, European officials began the process of establishing what is now known as the European Union. The European Coal and Steel Community, established in 1951 but came into being in 1952, was the first step towards achieving sustainable peace. Six nations signed a deal to operate their coal and steel sectors jointly under the Schuman plan. As a result, no one country may turn the weapons of war against others, as in the past. Belgium, France, Germany, Italy, Luxembourg, and the Netherlands are the six countries. The Treaty of Rome, signed in 1957, created the European Economic Community (EEC) and ushered in a new age of ever-closer collaboration in Europe. Relying on the achieved progress made in the Coal and Steel Treaty, the six founding countries broadened their collaboration to include other economic sectors. They formalise this by signing two treaties that establish the European Economic Community (EEC) and the European Atomic Energy Community (EAEC) (Euratom). During this time, however, the continent was divided by a Cold War that lasted more than 40 years. At the end of the 1960s, the condition of the world economy saw a shift. There arises a risk to the stability of the currencies of the then-member countries. As a result, suggestions for better coordination of member states' economic policies and closer collaboration in monetary affairs began to emerge. The leaders of state and government decided in December 1969 at a conference in The Hague that the formation of the Economic and Monetary Union (EMU) would become an official aim of European integration. From the three stages of the EMU establishment plan, according to the Warner Report of 1970, basic economic and monetary decisions were to be made at the Community level. The stages include the following:

(i) Reducing the fluctuation bands of member states' currencies, broader economic policy guidelines at the Community level, coordinated budget policies, and the preparation of changes;

(ii) Integration of financial markets to facilitate the free flow of capital, a progressive elimination of exchange rate fluctuations, closer coordination of short-term economic policies, and budgetary and fiscal measures;

(iii) Irrevocable fixing of conversion rates, the convergence of economic policies, and the establishment of a system of central banks at the community level.

Due to the suspension of the main monetary stability instrument, which was then, the US dollar's convertibility to gold, the US dollar conversion rates' fluctuation band became widened, and a wave of instability in the exchange rate ensued. This consequently led to a temporary abandonment of the EMU project. Thus, in a bid to restrict this exchange rate fluctuation, a "snake in the tunnel" was established in 1972, a special system designed to curb the fluctuations of the exchange rate between the six member states. Despite its success in limiting member-states currency fluctuations in relation to the US dollar, the oil crisis that started in the 1970s put pressure on the system and eventually caused its collapse.

The formation of the European Monetary System (EMS) in December 1978 at the European Council meeting in Brussels was the next stage in regulating exchange rate fluctuations of member states' currencies (then nine members, with the entrant of United Kingdom, Ireland, and Denmark). The EMS was based on the following principles:

(i) Exchange Rate Mechanism (ERM);
(ii) Single Currency Unit (ECU);
(iii) Credit Mechanisms.

The ERM was a fixed but flexible exchange rate system, with restricted member states' bilateral exchange rate fluctuation and accommodated the inclusion of all member states currencies, except that of the United Kingdom.

The Single European Act was signed in 1986 for the establishment of an area without internal borders to ensure a free flow of people, goods, services, and capital (an internal market), thereby eliminating trade barriers. In 1989, the Delors Report outlined a plan for the resurrection of the EMU, which was expected to be vital for the success of the Single European Act. The report proposed the creation of a monetary institution (the European System of Central Banks) that would be in charge of developing and executing monetary and exchange rate policies. The report was adopted during the European Council meeting in Madrid in June 1989, when it was decided that the first stage of EMU would commence on July 1, 1990.

The first stage of EMU, spanning between July 1990 and December 1993, paved the way for the full liberalisation of capital flows among member states and the removal of the free movement of capital barriers. In addition, increased coordination of member states' economic policies was encouraged, as well as strengthened cooperation between their respective central banks. The prohibition of public sector financing by the central bank and public sector privilege access to financial institutions was also obliged.

The second stage started in 1994 and ended in December 1998. The second stage was meant to establish the European Monetary Institute (EMI), the predecessor of the European Central Bank (ECB), which would later be established in June 1998. The EMI was mainly entrusted with improving collaboration among national central banks and coordinating member states' monetary policy. It was also in charge of the preparations for the launch of the new unified currency. Meeting the convergence criteria was also obligatory among member states, as well as the establishment of central bank independence. The European Council meeting in Madrid in December 1995 marked the confirmation of the Euro as the name of the new single currency and replaced the generic term ECU. Some basic elements about the changeover were also agreed upon, as well as its standard abbreviation and graphic symbol (EUR and €) till today.

To establish the stability and growth path of member states, the European Council meeting of Amsterdam was held to ensure fiscal policy discipline among member states and respect the medium-term goal of a budget surplus or a balanced budget. To further ensure the stability between the currencies of other member states that have not adopted the single currency, and the Euro, a new exchange rate mechanism (ERM II) was established. In 1998, it was decided that while the ECU should be replaced by the Euro on a 1:1 basis, an irrevocably fixed conversion rate was established for the currencies of member states that adopted the Euro.

The third stage of the EMU started in January 1999. This stage features the introduction of a new single currency, the euro, and monetary policy responsibility transfer to the national central banks of the member states and ECB, which make up the Eurosystem. The Euro was initially established as book money, pending the introduction of Euro banknotes and coins in January 2002. Given a transition period that spanned between January 1999 and December 2001, the use of the Euro was based on the principle of "no compulsion, no prohibition." Economic entities were allowed to use their discretion on whether to use the euro during this period and were not bound to use it. Even though the euro began full adoption in January 2002, a two-month period (although shorter in some countries) of "dual circulation" existed in the countries that adopted the Euro. During this period, both the banknotes and coins of member states and Euro banknotes and coins were permitted. Starting from March 2002, the only legal tender acceptable in the member states was the Euro banknotes and coins, and the banknotes and coins of the respective member states were only acceptable at the national central banks for exchange to Euro.

By 2004, new member states were not obligated to adopt the Euro simultaneously as they joined the EU; the adoption of the Euro was introduced as they met the conditions for doing so. But before the year ran out, a number of the new member states had their respective currencies included in ERM II. The inclusion of local currencies of new member states in the ERM II continued through the end of 2005, and the introduction of the euro was done in each of the countries as they met the conditions to do so.

Financial Integration and Single Currency Experience in the Association of South East Asian Nations (ASEAN)

The Association of Southeast Asian Nations (ASEAN) was founded in August 1967. It is undoubtedly the most effective and long-lasting regional organisation in the developing world. ASEAN has first and foremost built diplomatic cohesion among its almost 600 million population in a region ravaged by violence and separated by a varied colonial heritage. The 1967 Bangkok Declaration, drafted initially by the presidents of five member nations – Thailand, Singapore, Malaysia, the Philippines, and Indonesia), was comprehensive in its seven aims. Some of these aims are:

- To promote regional peace and stability.
- To accelerate economic growth, social progress, and cultural development in the region.
- To promote active collaboration and mutual assistance in the economic, social, cultural, technical, and administrative spheres.

The other five countries in the region subsequently joined the bloc as follows: Brunei Darussalam (1984); Viet Nam (1995); Lao PDR and Myanmar (1997); and Cambodia (1999).

Four phases characterised the evolution of ASEAN. The first phase began with its founding in 1967 in a highly unpredictable regional and global context dominated by war. At the height of the cold war, warfare was raging in Lao PDR, Cambodia, and Vietnam. Indonesia had only just renounced its ambition to "crush" Malaysia; Singapore and Malaysia had split after a brief union; the Philippines and Malaysia were at odds over Sabah, and all except Singapore had substantial communist insurgencies. Thailand was generally seen as the next "domino" to succumb to communist progress. Earlier attempts to form a regional organisation, such as the Association of Southeast Asian Nations (ASA), and a hypothetical three-nation "Malay" group, Maphilindo, had failed. As a result, the leaders' goal was largely focused on fostering regional cohesion. While they were all staunchly anti-communist, they expressly prioritized socioeconomic cooperation and growth over military and security. The ASEAN Foreign Ministers commissioned the United Nations to perform a study on ASEAN economic cooperation in 1969. The final report, the Kansu Report (named after its head, Professor G. Kansu), which was concluded in 1972, however, was not widely distributed and not properly published until 1974.

Its report's recommendations on economic cooperation mirrored both public opinions at the time as well as ASEAN member nations' preferences. It suggested trade liberalisation through selective tariff negotiations, package deal agreements for significant industrial projects, and financial cooperation. Meanwhile, many cooperative activities had commenced, including reports from several committees covering trade and industry, agriculture, tourism, transportation, and telecommunications. For Example, the Commerce and Industry committee investigated the potential of trade fairs and collaboration, trade liberalisation, trade data harmonisation, and industrial complementation initiatives as early as 1971. The spirit of the Kansu report was largely embraced, including the concepts of cooperative industrial initiatives and reciprocity among relevant parties in principle.

The second phase began in February 1976, with the Bali Summit of the five leaders. This was the first formal set of regional cooperation initiatives. The ASEAN Preferential Trading Agreement (APTA), ASEAN Industrial Projects (AIPs), ASEAN Industrial Complementation (AIC), and ASEAN Industrial Joint Ventures were among them (AIJVs). The most important of the four was APTA, which was the first attempt to increase intra-ASEAN trade through institutional integration and regional trade preferences. The AIPs, on the other hand, were intended to construct a large-scale, inter-governmental initiative in each member country. The AIJVs and AICs were established to encourage specialisation in complementary goods and to allow resource pooling.

With this development, ASEAN became a more active player in international affairs. It began to meet as a group, for example, at the United Nations and on topics of mutual importance, such as market access for its labour-intensive manufacturing and tropical cash crops. Dialogue-partner ties were created with diverse nations and areas, some of which served as the foundation for following regional architectural efforts. ASEAN also began to be diplomatically active, particularly in its desire to isolate Vietnam for its assistance in the demise of Cambodia's horrific Khmer Rouge dictatorship.

However, none of the four projects for economic cooperation had a substantial influence on regional economic connections (Imada & Naya, 1992). Indeed, they were purposefully engineered to have little impact. Despite initial excitement, the APTA had little influence on intra-regional commerce. Tariff decreases were imposed on a product-by-product basis rather than across the board; as a result, commodity coverage was limited, tariff decreases were insufficient to have any visible effect on trade, and execution was haphazard. Furthermore, APTA did not address non-tariff barriers (NTBs), which were a more substantial hindrance to trade than tariffs. The AIP, AIC, and AIJVs were likewise unsuccessful. In the instance of AIJVs, for example, the Philippines and Thailand were at odds over producing the same car parts (Ajanant, 1997). More broadly, the failure of these attempts reflected the members' unwillingness and inability to pursue trade liberalisation or regional integration at the time. Infant industry concepts were still prominent. During the 1980s, there was little more development. Brunei Darussalam gained independence in 1984 and joined the Commonwealth. The Philippines was mired in an economic and political crisis from 1984 to 1987 and essentially departed from ASEAN. The mid-1980s commodity price collapse pushed both Indonesia and Malaysia and, by extension, Singapore into recession, spurring fast and successful reforms but diminishing interest in the larger regional agenda.

What can be regarded as the third phase began in 1992 with the announcement of the ASEAN Free Trade Area (AFTA) during another leaders' summit – this was a distinct break from the past. For the first time, "free trade" was the regional goal, there was a specific timeframe for implementation, and a "negative list" strategy was chosen, in which all products commerce was to be included inside AFTA unless explicitly excluded. The six leaders committed to lowering Common Effective Preferential Tariff (CEPT) rates to 0% – 5% by 2008, with an intermediate objective of 20% by 1998 – 2000. This date was eventually pushed back to 2005 during the Fifth ASEAN Summit in 1995 and then to 2003. There was also a consensus among leaders that 85 percent of each country's tariff lines should be on the "Inclusion List" by 2000 and 90 percent by 2001.

The fourth stage of ASEAN's growth is dominated by two important elements. The return to growth (despite the immediate consequences of the GFC) and the effort to identify its logic against the backdrop of a rapidly changing regional and global environment, including a slew of initiatives altering commercial policy architecture, are examples of these.

Historically and from the discussion so far, the ASEAN has four (4) broad characteristics. First, it is an area with one of the most diverse groups on the planet. For example, its economic, political, cultural, and linguistic variety exceeds that of the European Union, and this diversity was made prominent by their colonial experiences. Singapore, Myanmar, Malaysia, and Brunei Darussalam had their colonial history traced to the British Empire; Vietnam, Cambodia, and Laos were colonised by France; Indonesia was colonised by the Netherlands; and Thailand was not formally colonised. The region also has states with diverse political structures. For instance, Brunei Darussalam has an all-powerful sultanate structure; Myanmar has an authoritarian government dominated by the military; Singapore and Malaysia have political structures best described as a heavily managed democracy with one party in continuous rule since independence; Thailand runs a constitutional democratic government with highly influential monarchy; Laos and Vietnam have communist political structures; and the Philippines, Indonesia, and Cambodia have freewheeling democratic structures (*Hill & Menon, 2010*).

These countries are equally diverse in terms of income level. One very wealthy country (Singapore), about 80 times richer than the poorest in the region, exists together with some of the world's poorest ones. In terms of population structure, unlike the EU, ASEAN is highly diverse, with Indonesia being the fourth most populous country in the world (about 277 million); Brunei being a tiny state with less than half a million population; Lao PDR and Singapore having just above seven million and five million people, respectively; Cambodia and Malaysia have about 17 and 33 million population, respectively; and Myanmar, Thailand, Vietnam, and the Philippines have between 55 and 111 million population.

The second characteristic of the ASEAN group is that most of the countries have achieved rapid economic development for more than three decades now, and longer in some cases. While some of them (Lao PDR, Cambodia, and Vietnam) have successfully transformed from planned to market economies, others, like Thailand, Singapore, Malaysia, and Indonesia, have been regarded by the World Bank as "miracle" economies (*Hill & Menon, 2010*).

As for the third characteristic, ASEAN maintained cooperation and diplomacy that can be regarded as a caution, pragmatism, and consensus-based decision-making. This is because of these nations' approach to non-interference in others' internal affairs and the deliberate avoidance of establishing a powerful regional institution like the EU type by creating an underpowered ASEAN secretariat that serves merely as a conference organizer and diplomatic facilitator. Although this characteristic is a strength of the bloc, in that, it explains its durability; it is also a weakness as it restricts the capacity and effectiveness for strong and decisive steps.

The fourth characteristic relates to the third. ASEAN is not and will probably not be an EU-type organisation in the foreseeable future. The bloc does not seem to adopt a common external trade regime, with completely free commerce among member states. Furthermore, ASEAN is not likely to come up with a formal mechanism for macroeconomic policy coordination, which may result in having a single central bank or currency.

Although some successes have been reported, there are several challenges facing the bloc. It is acknowledged that ASEAN is too small to solve some of the bigger post-crisis macroeconomic coordinating concerns. For instance, the bloc is considered much too tiny to opt for coordinated macroeconomic policy, such as a single currency rate system. In terms of emergency or crisis preventive measures, such as currency swaps and fiscal standby agreements, North Asia's massive foreign reserves require that these countries will be important players in any regional and international accords on emergency financing. Furthermore, ASEAN nations have varied interests and goals. Each member has distinct social, economic, and political difficulties. As a result, everyone appears to have little option but to concentrate on their internal matters. This concentration on home issues will undoubtedly have an impact on ASEAN's overall well-being. Corruption, demographic shifts, unequal social development, differences in economic development and technology adoption, environmental degradation, and other concerns relating to politics and the rise of authoritarianism also form part of the challenges facing ASEAN.

Lessons For The West African Monetary Zone

As seen from the discussions above, financial integration has some benefits which tend to accrue to the member states, ranging from a more stable macroeconomic environment to increased trade. The European Union (EU) has long been the most developed form of regional integration; however, it was badly rattled by past and current economic crises, creating rising questions about the integration process. The absence of a prompt and cohesive response to the Euro crisis brought the Eurozone's integrity into question, revealing structural and institutional fault lines highlighted by the financial crises. It was noted that the EU has developed and integrated swiftly without comparable development of its political and economic structures. Therefore, the growing gap between required coordination and institutional capability in the EU provides a lesson for other regional groups if and when they reach later phases of integration. As such, to achieve financial integration from the lessons learned from the EU's experience, there is no need for haste or rigid timelines; instead, efforts should be undertaken to build the political and economic institutions that will be in charge of implementing regional integration initiatives.

Furthermore, despite the obvious successes made by ASEAN in promoting integration, it remains distinct from any traditional concept of integration in that it only partially enables free trade in goods and services, does not address labour mobility, and has not sought to be a monetary union. As Africa prepares to expand its integration, ASEAN offers a pragmatic, market-oriented strategy with less emphasis on developing regional institutions, making it an alternative model with pertinent lessons.

Despite these, however, achieving financial integration in the region comes with potential risks and challenges. This includes the risks and challenges of non-convertibility of currencies, lack of independence of central banks, and weak financial management capacity. For instance, the absence of central bank independence has a negative influence on the legitimacy and efficacy of monetary policy, as well as its impact on the economy. The Central Bank Independence Index for West African Countries reveals that Nigeria had 0.44, Ghana had 0.50, and Guinea had 0.63, compared to an African average of 0.47 (*Bakoup & Ndoye, 2016*). Also, the non-convertibility of currencies may pose a challenge because the region's exchange rates are very volatile, and the majority of the eight currencies used in the region's 15 nations are not convertible. Convertibility is described as the ability to freely exchange a country's currency for foreign currencies, promoting greater integration into the global economy. To address this issue for effective financial integration, monetary integration is vital to unify the various currencies and fluctuating exchange rates.

Conclusion

Integrated financial markets continue to be an important component of the transmission mechanism and hence of the smooth conduct of monetary policy in the WAMZ's proposed single central bank setup. Financial integration also improves risk diversification and contributes to financial stability by increasing countries' ability to absorb shocks. On the other hand, highly linked financial markets allow shocks to spread more swiftly among market players and across borders, necessitating proper protections. A major lesson the WAMZ can learn from past regional integration, particularly from the EU and ASEAN experience, is that the swift integration of economies without comparable development of their political and economic structures may create a growing gap between required coordination and institutional capability. To avoid risks and maximize the advantages of financial integration, there should exist a political will among the different political and institutional settings in the countries. Improved collaboration among many stakeholders, including regulatory bodies, is also essential for effective integration. Financial integration, as a global experience, must be conducted intentionally and conscientiously, with clear and achievable deadlines defined for the various components of the integration activities. The WAMZ must develop urgent and realistic solutions to speed the financial sector's integration process in order to ease trade in products and services within the Zone.

Chapter 13

Integration In WAMZ: An Insider's Perspective

This chapter presents the perspectives of the author based on the experience gathered first as Director of the Financial Integration Department between 2011 to 2016 and later as Director General of the West African Monetary Institute between 2017 to 2021, in six areas that will propel economic integration efforts in WAMZ. The six areas are:

(i) The link between technological advancement and single currency agenda.

(ii) The need for a regional regulatory sandbox in WAMZ.

(iii) The need to transform WAMI into a commission.

(iv) The harmonisation of statistics among member countries.

(v) The need for women empowerment.

(vi) The need to estimate informal cross-border trade.

However, the WAMZ and ECOWAS region at large is already making highly welcome efforts on many fronts to coordinate policies and presents itself globally as a united group under the guidance of the ECOWAS commission with a single currency agenda.

It is clear that West African economies need each other because they have long recognised the value of working together. Improving and sustaining the pace of integration through intra-regional trade and policy coordination is the only panacea for the economies to build resilience and scale, as well as enhance the bargaining power on the African and global stage. The West African region has the potential to benefit from the AfCFTA and global trade arrangement. Integration of the region is fundamental for member countries to effectively compete favourably. Integration and collaboration in the region will also help overcome the limitations and vulnerabilities inherent in the relatively small size and underdevelopment of individual economies. Regional integration also offers great opportunities to learn from each other's experiences on common issues, such as education and fiscal and monetary policies.

The rest of the chapter is arranged as follows:

(i) Technological advancement and WAMZ single

currency agenda.

(ii) The need to establish a regional regulatory sandbox in WAMZ; the need to transform the West African Monetary Institute into a Commission.

(iii) The need for the harmonisation of statistics in WAMZ.

(iv) The need to empower women: uncovering barriers to financial inclusion in WAMZ.

(v) The Need for Estimating Informal Cross-border Trade (ICBT) in WAMZ.

(vi) The conclusion.

Technological Advancement And WAMZ Single Currency Agenda

There is rapid advancement in payment system technology that makes payments for cross-border trade easy, such that people are asking what the need for a single currency in WAMZ and ECOWAS is at large with the advances in technology. It is important to remark that technological advances and a single currency in an economic union are not substitutes for each other; rather, they can be a compliment. There is no denying that technology has transformed how we trade and do business and financial transactions. For instance, e-commerce has revolutionised the transparency of pricing within and across countries. These technological advances can affect how domestic inflation reacts to shocks, the pass-through of exchange rate movements into inflation, and the domestic impact of global developments and inflation. But these impacts are not as pronounced and effective as in using a single currency where prices are quoted in the same currency for several countries.

Technology can facilitate the operationalisation of the single currency agenda of countries striving to promote regional economic integration. Therefore, technology can only serve as a facilitator in achieving a single currency objective and not replace it. The idea of a single currency is not just about the currency itself but the economic integration that the use of a single currency amongst nation states can achieve. However, technological advances without a single currency cannot achieve all the expected benefits of a single currency. However, advances in technology would lead to a reduction in transaction cost, price transparency, and facilitate market transactions. This can be done by way of a well-developed cross-border payment and settlement system and e-commerce platforms (for example, Amazon, Alibaba, etc.). With the full implementation of the Pan African Payment and Settlement System (PAPSS), member states of the WAMZ union would begin to use the platform to trade in local currencies – a key functionality that makes the PAPSS an ideal platform for a multi-currency environment.

With the presence of the PAPSS and the advances in mobile money, payment gateways, and e-Commerce platforms in the Zone, cross-border transactions would be carried out in both high and low value. A buyer in The Gambia can buy goods on an e-Commerce platform in Ghana using her dalasi account with relative ease. Technology would therefore reduce transaction costs and make it more convenient. However, the advantages of a single currency area, that is, elimination of exchange rate fluctuation, a more stable currency, prevention of competitive devaluation of the currency, etc., would not be achieved by a mere advancement in technology.

As much as technology has revolutionised financial services and the world economy at large, the benefits of a single currency transcend technology. There are socio-economic and regional integration gains to be achieved when countries use the same currency, which technological advancement cannot achieve. A single currency is, therefore, still necessary amid technological advancement.

The Need To Establish A Regional Regulatory Sandbox In WAMZ

The speed of innovations in the financial sector in WAMZ requires a robust regional response in the form of a region-wide regulatory sandbox for the burgeoning financial space. The need for the regulatory sandbox is a response to the challenges posed by the advent of products and services using innovative techniques and infrastructures, specifically in what is known as financial technology (FinTech). The WAMZ is awash with new FinTech, which provides services that have a significant contribution to the integration agenda of the region. FinTech deserves the necessary support and guidance, and a regulatory sandbox is an ideal platform for understanding its processes and operations.

The proposed project is expected to benefit the central banks of member states of the West African Monetary Zone by providing an avenue for engagement with FinTech firms in the payment space. It is expected that the proposed sandbox project in WAMZ will increase the potential for advancing the financial inclusion of those who are hitherto excluded and the underserved customers through the promotion of innovative financial products and services. Also, the sandbox would reduce barriers and costs involved in financial transactions. The project will equally ensure adequate provisions in regulation to create an enabling environment for innovation without compromising the safety of customers and the entire payment system. Hence, the introduction of a regulatory sandbox in WAMZ will promote competitiveness in the financial market and eventually lead to economic growth.

The project would consist of three main components,

first, harmonisation of laws on regulatory sandboxes in WAMZ. The main activity under this component is to identify and assess the relevant legal and institutional framework in each country to propose and develop harmonised policies, laws, and regulations for the use of regulatory sandbox in the WAMZ. The cost of this component should cover the recruitment of consultant(s) to support WAMI, drafting of legislation, workshops, and seminars, as well as support for the development of the oversight framework. The second component is the implementation of a regulatory sandbox in member states.

Key activities involved in this component are initial policy and technical assessment, development of a sandbox implementation tool kit, and technology architecture and infrastructures. It may include the country's priorities, process, and requirements for the deployment of an integrated digital onboarding process, automated workflows, test environment, and transparent approval records. The technology will be consumable, reliable, robust, and scalable, with a long-term service level agreement (SLA) for sustainability. The third component is capacity building and sensitisation of stakeholders. This seeks to provide the needed training of stakeholders who are expected to participate in the operation of the system. It also involves the sensitisation of the public about the importance and benefits of the regulatory sandbox. Awareness may include educational symposiums, jingles, billboards, and promotions. The following activities are expected to be undertaken:

- Training of legal officers of WAMI, National Central Banks and Commercial Banks.
- Sensitisation of stakeholders on the regulatory sandbox.
- And study tour for staff on regulatory sandbox in the WAMZ region.

The implementation of the project would be in five phases:

Phase 1: Perform Initial Policy and Technical Assessment

- Assessment of existing framework and links to the financial market infrastructure of all stakeholders.
- Outline a strategy for system-wide process mapping and integration mode.
- Collaborate with stakeholders to gather key requirements, perspectives, and emphasis, as well as an implementation plan and milestones.
- Perform capacity building on best practices for sandbox integration and governance.

Phase 2: Develop Sandbox Implementation Tool Kit

- Develop sandbox strategy and related frameworks.

- Develop implementation steps based on strategy and framework.
- Facilitate capacity-building workshops with various stakeholders.

Phase 3: Develop Sandbox Technology Architecture and Infrastructure

- Evaluate existing infrastructure.
- Sandbox customisation and integration.
- Initial software installs and hosting infrastructure.
- Capacity building on technical design.

Phase 4: Develop Sandbox Technology Governance Structure

- Evaluate existing infrastructure and governance requirements.
- Support the development of governance frameworks and oversight.
- Capacity building on governance requirements, including KPI review and optimal technical operation model.

Phase 5: Execute Sandbox Strategy and Oversight

- Develop operational milestone.
- Conduct workshops.

The Need To Transform West African Monetary Institute Into A Commission

The West African Monetary Institute (WAMI) was established in 2001 with a mission to undertake technical preparations for full monetary integration with a common West African Central Bank and single currency. Thus, one of the key mandates of the Institute is to monitor the convergence criteria required for the introduction of a single currency. However, the mandate of the Institute has been expanded over the years to include taking measures that will facilitate trade integration, financial sector integration, payments system development, and statistical harmonisation.

The adoption of a Single-Track Approach to monetary integration in ECOWAS and the setting up of the ECOWAS Monetary Institute (EMI) implied the phasing out of the WAMZ and its institutions, loss of a forum to drive economic integration in the WAMZ and the truncation of the gains made so far. To this end, the WAMZ Convergence Council, at its 34th Meeting held in July 2014 in Abuja, Nigeria, directed WAMI to prepare a detailed position paper on the feasibility of establishing a Commission to provide a platform to make meaningful dialogue on issues of common interest among the member states of the WAMZ and to speed up the economic integration process in ECOWAS. The preparation of a Commission Project Document was preceded by a study Report, which was discussed at the WAMZ Statutory Meetings held in Conakry, Guinea, in August 2016. Upon the comprehensive review of the study Report, the WAMZ Convergence Council, at their 36th Meeting, directed WAMI to prepare cost estimates and outline a roadmap towards setting up a Commission.

Following the review of the cost implications of establishing the proposed Commission, the WAMZ Convergence Council, at its 37th Meeting held on February 10, 2017, in Freetown, Sierra Leone, approved the establishment of a Commission, a roadmap leading to its activation, the convening of a WAMZ Heads of State Summit and instructed WAMI to prepare a project document and proposals for a new WAMZ Agreement and a Commission. However, in 2018 at the Council meeting in Banjul, The Gambia, it was directed that WAMI suspend the process of establishing a Commission in view of the assessment of the ECOWAS 2020 Single Currency Programme. Also, WAMI should continue to implement its work programme as required by its current mandate.

My perspective is that WAMI should be transformed into a commission; hence the need to establish a commission as a separate organisation would be necessary, and all staff of WAMI, including seconded staff, shall be transferred to the Commission. However, staff shall be placed in Departments and Units according to their competence and experience. Member state central banks may replace their seconded staff as desired. Member states shall continue to advertise vacancies in the Commission and shortlist candidates for consideration and recruitment by the Commission. Also, the Staff Manual of Rules and Regulations, audit charter and code of business ethics of WAMI shall guide the operations of the Commission in so far as the provisions are not in conflict with the operationalisation of the Commission's mandate until such time that these instruments are amended.

The Need for The Harmonization of Statistics in WAMZ
The need for the timely production of high-quality and harmonised statistics to foster the implementation of regional integration initiatives and enhance the socio-economic development of countries in the West African Monetary Zone (WAMZ) cannot be overemphasised. Though WAMZ countries have made some progress over the past two decades to strengthen statistical systems towards improving the production and dissemination of comparable economic, financial, and social statistics, the supply of harmonised and comparable statistics from member states has been less than satisfactory to date. For instance, some of the member states are still using the System of National Accounts 1993 (*SNA 1993*) to compile national accounts, while others have adopted the SNA 2008. Equally, some countries are using International Standard Industrial Classification Revision four (ISIC Rev.4) in publishing the national

accounts while others are using ISIC Rev.1. The same token goes for Consumer Price Index (CPI) even though all member countries are implementing the Classification of Individual Consumption by Purpose (COICOP). There are differences among countries regarding the composition of the baskets of goods and services, and some countries are using 12 COICOP divisions or functions whilst others are using 13 COICOP divisions or functions. In addition, in terms of geographical coverage, some member states cover both rural and urban areas in the computation of the CPI basket of goods and services, while others concentrate only on the urban areas. Furthermore, the weights assigned to the commodities in the CPI basket of goods and services differ across countries in terms of the methodology used in compiling them and the age of the weights. In line with international best practices, the weight should not be more than five years old for the indices to reflect current households' expenditure patterns. On the same note, some countries are implementing Balance of Payments Manual 5(BPM5), whilst others have migrated to BPM6; the Fiscal Responsibility Laws or Framework in the zone are also different.

The key constraints limiting the statistics harmonisation process include differences between countries in terms of data collection instruments and methodologies used to produce core economic statistics, limited institutional capacity and financial resources to strengthen statistical systems, and lack of modern information technology and statistical infrastructure to facilitate data capture. These challenges call for more collaborative efforts to strengthen statistical systems across countries to help them to produce reliable and harmonised statistics to ensure the effective implementation of the integration initiatives of the Zone. Hence, the need to develop a project to support the efforts of National Statistics Offices to strengthen statistical systems for timely production, harmonisation, and dissemination of core economic and financial statistics across countries over time. Since the 44th Meeting of the Convergence Council of Ministers and Governors of the central banks of the member states held in September 2020, WAMI has been working assiduously towards making substantial contributions to the project through a collaborative programme that would strengthen statistical development and harmonisation.

Project's Activities, Tasks And Deliverables

To achieve the objectives of the project, WAMI has identified core activities to be pursued between 2021 to 2023 so as to improve the capacity of WAMZ countries to produce timely and harmonised statistics and disseminate comparable statistics to support the economic integration agenda of the region. More specifically, the project consists of five main components, and each of the components is subdivided into specific tasks and activities. Table 14.1 presents the components and the tasks.

For each of these activities, a proposal, detailed budget, and work plan (with timelines) will be prepared and approved by the Steering Committee and or a special team set up for that purpose before it will be executed. All procurement activities undertaken under the Project will be conducted in accordance with WAMI's procurement rules.

Execution of the tasks and activities listed in Table 14.1 will yield the following outputs:

(i) Common methodological manual for compiling CPI, GDP, and other macroeconomic indicators in WAMZ produced.

(ii) Harmonised CPI, GDP, and other macroeconomic indicators for member countries published.

(iii) Compilers of CPI, GDP, and other macroeconomic indicators in WAMZ countries trained.

(iv) Use of electronic devices in the compilation of CPI and GDP improved.

Implementation Strategy

A Steering Committee should be established to monitor the implementation of the project. The duties and

Table 14.1: Components and Tasks of Implementing Statistical Harmonisation Project

S/No	Components	Tasks/Activities
1	Training of compiler of CPI and national Accounts in NSOs	Develop Training Manuals; Organise Training of Trainers Workshop; Organise Training Workshops for CPI, GDP Compilers
2	Harmonisation of data collection instrument & methodology	Develop common compilation manuals for CPI and GDP, Organise Training Workshops for CPI and GDP, Organise Training in modern classification for CPI, GDP publication.
3	Improve use of electronic devices for CPI and GDP	Procure weighing scales and tablets for NSO CPI, GDP data collection.
4	Improving WAMI website for enhance dissemination of WAMZ regional data.	Hire consultant to upgrade WAMI website. Hire consultant to develop a secured database.
5	Improving Institutional collaboration within WAMZ	Visit to UEMOA, WAMA, and ECOWAS Commission; Undertake country assessments compilation of CPI, GDP and other core economic indicators; Meeting with Heads of National Statistics Offices and compilers of CPI and GDP.

Source: Computed by the author

responsibilities of the Committee will be clearly defined by members of this Committee before the implementation of the project. Some of the key functions of the Committee will include monitoring and assessing progress towards capacity building to enhance statistical development, harmonisation of instruments and methodologies to produce comparable data and development of a database platform to interface with the databases of National Statistics Offices and Central Banks to facilitate the timely dissemination of data to relevant stakeholders. WAMI will serve as the Secretariat, producing periodic reports to the Committee on the state of implementation of the project. The reports will provide information on the strides made towards achieving the objectives of the project. The Committee will undertake periodic reviews of the governance of the entire project to identify priority areas, the project's milestones, and the next steps for future collaborations.

To strengthen cooperation among national agencies and facilitate the implementation of the project, an Expert Working Group (EWG) should be set up for each identified statistical area to be headed by one member of the lead national institution. Each EWG will be made up of members comprising a specialist from the West African Economic and Monetary Union (WAEMU – UEMOA) region, specialists from the National Statistics Offices, Research and Statistics Departments of Central banks and Ministries of Finance in the six WAMZ Member countries, and Research and Statistics Department of WAMI. The Lead country for each statistical area will be determined by members of the EWG based on the capacity of the country to coordinate activities under each statistical area.

WAMI will establish a dedicated Unit within its Research and Statistics Department to drive the harmonisation process and dissemination of statistics to stakeholders. The staff deployed to the Unit will participate in the EWG meetings and will be sufficiently trained to enhance their capacity for database management and the use of relevant statistical infrastructure. Under this project, the Institute will begin to play an advocacy role to ensure that member states carry out their National Statistics Development Strategy (NSDS) and Sector Statistics Development Strategy (SSDS) to ensure the timely production and dissemination of harmonised statistics.

Challenges

The low level of governments' investments in statistical development and coordination of statistical activities is one of the major challenges confronting WAMZ countries in producing harmonised, reliable, and timely statistics to inform policymaking in the Zone. Inadequate funding has greatly limited the capacity of National Statistics Offices to support the statistical harmonisation process, as well as building the required capacity over time and deploying modern IT and statistical infrastructure to facilitate data capture. The associated institutional weaknesses and inadequate coordination of statistical activities have undoubtedly impeded the production of high-quality statistics across countries. Poor quality data is a critical obstacle to the promotion of evidence-based decision-making, which is so crucial in addressing the socio-economic development challenges in WAMZ countries.

The Need To Empower Women: Uncovering Barriers To Financial Inclusion In WAMZ

Women economic empowerment is about creating an environment and policies that encourage and support women to participate equally in production and benefit from this process. To empower a woman, therefore, involves giving her equal opportunity to access and control productive resources and to access education, healthcare, and decent jobs. It is nearly a global consensus that economically empowering women is a necessary step towards closing the gap in gender inequality, realising women's rights, and achieving wider developmental goals. Economically empowering women often yields a win-win result because it does not benefit only women but society at large benefit. Economic empowerment of women would lead to improvement in household education, health, productivity, income, and the general wellbeing of the household. Hence, women empowerment is critical to significantly reducing household poverty. In aggregate, women empowerment would lead to an increase in inclusive economic growth and development of a nation.

Women economic empowerment is fundamental to reducing the gender financial inclusion gap. More economic empowerment for women would mean more income to women and then more access to the financial sector. On the other hand, women financial inclusion is pivotal to women's economic empowerment. When more women can access and use financial services, their ability to invest and undertake productive activities increases. Therefore, providing low-income women with the right financial tools to save and borrow money, make, and receive payments, and manage risk is important for women's empowerment.

There is a significant improvement in women's financial inclusion across the globe, including countries in WAMZ. According to Global Findex Report (*2021*), the gender gap in account ownership across developing economies has fallen from the nine (9) percentile to the six (6) percentile points. However, despite this progress, the gaps in financial access for underserved adults, particularly women, the poor, and young people, are still imperative. For instance, the 2018 EFInA Access to Finance survey shows that 58.9% of women in Nigeria are financially included while 67.4% of men are, implying that the gender gap in financial inclusion is 8.5%. The report shows that the gap is higher in rural areas, where only 24% of women own formal accounts compared to 54% of men. It was observed that the financial exclusion of women is higher among the low-income group. Similarly, according to Findex 2017 report, 54% of women have formal financial accounts in Ghana as against 62% of men, meaning that there is an 8% gender gap.

Therefore, there is a need for both fiscal and monetary authorities in WAMZ countries to intensify efforts toward women's economic and financial empowerment. There is a need for WAMZ and ECOWAS at large to design programmes and policies that would yield greater educational attainment for girls and women in the ECOWAS region. This is because increasing women's and girls' educational attainment contributes to women's economic empowerment and more inclusive economic growth. Education, upskilling and re-skilling, especially to keep pace with rapid technological and digital transformations, are critical for women's and girls' health and wellbeing, as well as their income-generation opportunities and participation in the formal labour market.

Specifically, the following should be on the front burner of discussions:

- Highlight key challenges and constraints to women's economic empowerment in the WAMZ from a holistic perspective bringing in experiences from the policy side, the private sector and the cross-border.

- Identification of best practices from different types of stakeholders that address challenges and enhance women's economic empowerment and participation in the financial sector in the WAMZ and discuss how they can be scaled up and replicated.

- Country-level commitments should be highlighted and plans to enhance women's economic empowerment with a focus on clear monitoring and reporting mechanisms (progress to be reported preferably on a yearly basis).

- Launch the "WAMZ Gender Financing Facility" aimed at supporting member states in achieving their commitments towards enhancing women's economic empowerment.

In the end, the following outcomes would be delivered:

- A better understanding of key challenges and constraints to women's economic empowerment in the WAMZ.
- Identify best practices from different types of stakeholders that address challenges and enhance women's economic empowerment and participation in the financial sector in the WAMZ.
- Provide specific country-level commitments and plans to enhance women's economic empowerment.
- Propose clear monitoring and reporting mechanisms of which progress would be reported annually.
- Finally, launch the "WAMZ Gender Financing Facility" aimed at supporting member states in achieving their commitments.

The Need For Estimating Informal Cross-border Trade (ICBT) In WAMZ

In recognition of the importance of effective trade integration for an economic integration programme, WAMI in 2005, as contained in the "Banjul Declaration", was assigned an expanded work programme including the promotion of good trade governance, monitoring and reporting on member states' compliance with ECOWAS trade integration obligations as well as providing analytical, advisory services on trade matters, among other issues. In its efforts to effectively deliver on the above-mentioned expanded work programme, WAMI identified the need to assist each member state of the WAMZ to determine the magnitude (value and volume), the direction of flow, and the product basket of informal cross-border trade.

The Ministers of Trade of the member states of the WAMZ at their Seventh Meeting held in Banjul, The Gambia, on December 4, 2015, decided, among other issues, that WAMI should seek financial and technical support from development partners to conduct a survey on cross-border informal trade in each member state of the WAMZ. In view of the Decision of the Ministers alluded to in the paragraph above, WAMI sought financial and technical support from Afreximbank to support member states in formulating a framework for estimating informal cross-border trade for the purpose of augmenting balance of payments and national accounts statistics.

Putting it all in context, Intra-ECOWAS trade is estimated at an average of 10.0 percent (2011 – 2014), while intra-WAMZ trade is estimated at about 14.0 percent (WAMI, 2019). A substantial amount of cross-border trade in the region is informal and mostly unrecorded. The low intra-regional trade is in part attributed to significant unrecorded cross-border trade, among other issues. A significant share of intra-regional trade consists of informal cross-border trade, which is not captured in official trade statistics. A large proportion of products traded within the region are raw materials, agricultural products (mainly food and livestock) or semi-processed petroleum products, as well as manufactured items.

Meanwhile, data on informal cross-border trade is essential for the complete balance of payments and national accounts compilation. To this end, it is important to formulate a framework for estimating informal cross-border trade. A survey of literature has shown that the Bank of Uganda, in collaboration with relevant agencies such as the Uganda Bureau of Statistics, Uganda Revenue Authority, and Uganda Immigration Department, among others, in 2007, put in place a framework for estimating informal cross-border trade based on monthly surveys of trade at major border posts and markets. Other countries in Africa have conducted ICBT surveys: Rwanda in 2009; Kenya in 2011; Sierra Leone in 2015; Nigeria in 2016, among others.

All the WAMZ member states capture formal trade through Automated System of Customs Data (ASYCUDA) or any other platform, while informal cross-border trade is not captured. None of the WAMZ member states, except Nigeria, has ever conducted an ICBT survey. Non-recording of ICBT transactions results in the understating balance of payments, intra-regional trade flows and national accounts. ICBT survey is an economic survey covering transactions in goods between residents and non-residents of a country that are not recorded by customs clearance systems. Under the United Nations' general framework of compiling international merchandise trade statistics (IMTS 2010), all goods entering or leaving a country should be recorded, except goods in transit. The long-term objective of the ICBT survey is to build a robust institutionalised sustainable capacity framework for providing comprehensive and reliable external trade data and information for trade-related policy analysis. However, in the short term, the objective of the survey is to provide comparable and complete informal cross-border trade statistics necessary for the computation and compilation of a comprehensive balance of trade and national accounts, informal cross-border trade flows (in values and volumes), and determine commodities transacted.

Therefore, I strongly recommend that all member states of WAMZ should conduct an ICBT survey. It is expected that this will yield several outcomes, including the following:

- Publish monthly or quarterly ICBT bulletin in terms of product basket, trade flows (values and volumes) and direction of flow.
- Generate statistics on informal trade transactions to supplement balance of payments and national accounts statistics.
- Measure ICBT's contribution to the economy in terms of potential for revenue generation and income for traders.
- Form the basis to create policy, regulatory, institutional and business environment which will enhance the role of informal cross-border traders, legitimise their activities and gradually mainstream them into the formal economy.

Conclusion

Many efforts have been directed towards actualising full economic integration in WAMZ and ECOWAS at large with a common currency and single central bank. However, there is still the need to emphasize certain core areas that are critical to the attainment of a full monetary union. These include:

- The need to take advantage of technological advancement for the achievement of the single currency agenda.
- Establishment of a regional financial regulatory sandbox; transformation of WAMI into a commission.
- Harmonisation of statistics among member countries.
- Empowerment of women.
- And the need to estimate informal cross-border trade.

References

African Develoment Bank Group (2022). Guinea Economic Outlook. Retrieved from *https://www.afdb.org/en/countries/west-africa/guinea/guinea-economic-outlook.*

African development Bank Group (2022). Gambian Economic Outlook. Retrieved from *https://www.afdb.org/en/countries/west-africa/gambia/gambia-economic-outlook.*

African Development Bank Group (2022). Ghana Economic Outlook. Retrieved from *https://www.afdb.org/en/countries/west-africa/ghana/ghana-economic-outlook.*

African Development Bank Group (2022). Liberia Economic Outlook. Retrieved from *https://www.afdb.org/en/countries/west-africa/liberia/liberia-economic-outlook.*

African Development Bank Group (2022). Nigerian Economic Outlook. Retrieved from *https://www.afdb.org/en/countries-west-africa-nigeria/nigeria-economic-outlook.*

African Development Bank Group (2022). Sierra Leone Economic Outlook. Retrieved from *https://www.afdb.org*

/en/countries-west-africa-sierra-leone/sierra-leone-economic-outlook.

Annan, N (2014). Violent Conflicts and Civil Strife in West Africa: Causes, Challenges and Prospects. Stability: International Journal of Security & Development, 3(1), 1-16.

Adom, K. (2014). Beyond the marginalization thesis: An examination of the motivations of informal entrepreneurs in Sub-Saharan Africa: Insights from Ghana. International Journal of Entrepreneurship and Innovation, 15(2), 113–125.

Adebowale, H. A. (2018). Impact of logistics infrastructure on manufacturing sector performance in Africa: Lessons for Nigeria. The Nigerian Journal of Economic and Social Studies, 60(3), 1 - 19.

Adelakun, O. J. (2020). Does a Monetary Union Matter for the Degree of Inflation Persistence? The Case of the West Africa Monetary Zone (WAMZ). Studies in Economics and Econometrics. 44(1):1-34.

Adetiba, T. C. (2019). Dynamics of Ethnic Politics in Nigeria: An Impediment to its Political System. Journal of Economics and Behavioral Studies, 11(2 (J)), 132-144.

Adetula, V.A.O (2009) "ECOWAS and the Challenge of

Integration in West Africa" in U. Joy Ogwu & Warisu O. Alli (eds.) ECOWAS: Milestones in Regional Integration. Nigerian Institute of International Affairs (NIIA), pp. 15-58

Albert, T. (2019). The African Continental Free Trade Agreement: Opportunities and Challenges. Geneva: CUTS International, Geneva.

Alesina, A., Devleeschauwer, A., Easterly, W., Kurlat, S., & Wacziarg, R. (2003). Fractionalization. Journal of Economic growth, 8(2), 155-194.

Adom, K., & Williams, C. C. (2012). Evaluating the explanations for the informal economy in third world cities: Some evidence from Koforidua in the Eastern Region of Ghana. International Entrepreneurship and Management Journal, 8(3), 309–324.

Adu-Amankwah, K. (2015). Foreword. In J. Assens & E. Tabor (Eds.), Paving the way for formalisation of the informal economy. Copenhagen: LO/FTF Council.

Ajide, F.M. (2022). Economic complexity and entrepreneurship: Insights from Africa. International Journal of Development Issues, DOI 10.1108/IJDI-03-2022-0047

Afreximbank group (2022). Annual Reports and Accounts.

Ajanant, J. (1997). AFTA: An introduction. In Hourn, K. K., & Hunter, S. eds. ASEAN free trade agreement: Implications and future directions. London: ASEAN Academic Press. 13–24.

Asante, R.D. & Masson, P.R. (2001). Point/counterpoint: the pros and cons of expanded monetary union in West Africa. Finance and development. Quarterly Magazine. International Monetary Fund (IMF), 38 (1).

Bah, M. S. (2015). Real convergence in West African Economic and Monetary Union (WAEMU). Economics Letters volume 135, 19-23.

Balogun, E.D. (2009). Inflation Differential in the West African Monetary Zone (WAMZ) Area: Implications for Unionization MPRA Paper No. 13045. Online at *http://mpra.ub.uni-muenchen.de/13045/Google Scholar*

Bayoumi, T. & Ostry, J.D. (2010). Macroeconomic shocks and trade flows within Sub-Saharan Africa: implications for optimum currency arrangements. J. Afr. Econ., 6 (3): 412-444.

Boahen, A. A. (Ed.). (1985). Africa under colonial domination 1880-1935 (Vol. 7). Univ of California Press.

Bundu, A. (1997). ECOWAS and the future of regional integration in West Africa. Regional Integration and

Cooperation in West Africa, A Multidimensional Perspective.

Baele, L., Ferrando, A., Hördahl, P., Krylova, E., & Monnet, C. (2004). *Measuring Financial Integration in the Euro Area.* European Central Bank Occasional Paper Series No. 14.

Brouwer, G. (2005). Monetary and financial integration in Asia: empirical evidence and issues. In Asian Development Bank (Ed.), *Asian Economic Cooperation and Integration: Progress, Prospects, Challenges* (1 ed., pp. 269-293). Asian Development Bank.

Bawa, S (2018). Understanding regional economic integration: In Towards regional integration in the West African Monetary Zone: Achievements, issues and the way forward in Honour of Dr. Abwaku Englama; N. E., Egbuna ed. Pg 5-12.

Bakoup, F., & Ndoye, D. (2016). African Economic Brief. AEB Volume 7.

Brouwer, G. (2005). *Monetary and Financial Integration in Asia: Empirical Evidence and Issues.* Asia Economic Cooperation and Integration, Asia Development Bank, Manila, the Philippines, 269-293.

Cham, T. (2009). Is WAMZ An Optimum Currency

Area (OCA)? West African Journal of Monetary and Economic Integration 9(2), 96-120.

Chidozie, F., & Abiodun-Eniayekan, E. (2017). ECOWAS and the new Scramble for Africa: Interrogating the Francophone/Anglophone Dynamics. *Journal of International Politics and Development* (JIPAD), 15(1), 81-103.

Daya, P. (2014). Diversity and inclusion in an emerging market context. *Equality, Diversity, and Inclusion: An International Journal*, 33(3), 293-308.

Deng, F. M. (1997). Ethnicity: an African predicament. *The Brookings Review*, 15(3), 28-31.

Economic Commission for Africa (2008). *Assessing Regional Integration in Africa III. Towards Monetary and Financial Integration in Africa*, Addis Ababa: United Nations Economic Commission for Africa.

Egbuna, N. E., Jarju, I., Bawa, S., Diallo, I., Mendy, I., Haffner, O., & Adams, K. (2018). A composite index of economic integration in the West African Monetary Zone (WAMZ). WAMI occasional paper series NO. 15

Egbuna, E. N., John-Sowe, M., Mohammed, D., Abubakari, H., Sambolah, E., & Adams, K (2020). Optimizing the potential benefits from the African

Continental Free Trade Area Agreement (AFCFTA) in the West African Monetary Zone through enterprise development. WAMI Occasional Paper Series No. 21. The West African Monetary Institute, Accra, Ghana.

Eichengreen, B. (2001). *Hanging Together? On Monetary and Financial Cooperation in Asia*. Global Change and East Asian Policy Initiatives, World Bank, Washington, D.C.

Elgin, C., Kose, M. A., Ohnsorge, F., & Yu., S. (2021). *Understanding Informality*, C.E.P.R. Discussion Paper 16497, Centre for Economic Policy Research, London

Frankel, J. A., & MacArthur, A. T. (1988). Political vs. currency premia in international real interest differentials: A study of forward rates for 24 countries. European Economic Review, 32, 1083-1114.

Faujas, A. (2014). Why Francophones are lagging behind Anglophones. *Africa*.

Global Terrorism Index, 2011-2022

Grimm M, Knorringa P. & Lay J (2012) Constrained gazelles: High potentials in West Africa's informal economy. *World Development* 40(7): 1352–1368.

Gwatiwa, T. T. and Sam, M. N. (2020). "How the free

movement of people could benefit Africa". The Conversation. Retrieved December 28, 2020.

Hartmann, P., Heider, F., Papaioannou, E., & Lo Duca, M. (2007). *The role of financial markets and innovation in productivity and growth in Europe.* European Central Bank. Occasional Paper Series No. 72.

Huh, H.-S., & Park, C.-Y. (2017). Asia-Pacific Regional Integration Index: Construction, Interpretation and Comparison. *ADB Economic Working Paper Series No. 511.*

Hill, H., & Menon, J. (2010). ASEAN economic integration: Features, fulfillments, failures and the future. *The ADB Working Paper Series on Regional Economic Integration*, No. 69.

Imada, P. & Naya, S. (1992). AFTA: The Way Ahead. Singapore: Institute of Southeast Asian Studies.

International Labour Organisation (ILO, 2018) *Women and Men in the Informal Economy: A Statistical Picture*. 3rd edn. Geneva, Switzerland: ILO.

Jooji, Innocent (2011), ECOWAS Parliament and Regional Integration in West Africa (2001-2006), Makurdi: Selfers Academic Press Ltd.

Kenea, P. B. (1969). The theory of optimum currency

areas: An eclectic view. In A. R. Swoboda & R.A. Mundell (Eds), Monetary problems of the international economy. Chicago: University of Chicago Press.

Kitcher (2012). Quoting and trading in WAMZ currencies: Challenges and way forward. WAMI Occasional Papers Series No.3, Ghana.

Krugman, P. (1990). Policy problems of a Monetary Union. In P. De Grauwe and L. Papaenmos (Eds.), The European monetary system in the 1990s. London and New York: Longman.

Kose, M. A., Prasad, E. S., Rogoff, K., & Wei, S. J. (2010). *Financial Globalization and Economic Policies*. Handbook of Development Economics, 5, 4283–4359.

Kose, M. A., Prasad, E. S., & Terrones, M. E. (2003). Financial Integration and Macroeconomic Volatility. IMF Working Papers 03(05).

Larkin, B., Meyer, B., & Akyeampong, E. K. (2006). Pentecostalism, Islam & Culture. *Themes in West Africa's history*, 286-312.

Llanes, M., & A. Barbour (2007). Self-Employed and Micro-Entrepreneurs: informal trading and the journey towards formalization, London: Community Links.

Levine R. (2001). International Financial Liberalisation and Economic Growth. *Review of International Economics*, 9, 688-702.

Lewis, Karen (1999), Trying to Explain Home Bias in Equities and Consumption, *Journal of Economic Literature*, 36, 571-608.

Maze, K (2015). Land Conflict, Migration, and Citizenship in West Africa: Complex Diversity and Recurring Challenges: A Desk Study. World Bank Group.

Marano, V., Cuervo-Cazurra, A., and Kwok, C. 2013. The impact of conflict types and location on trade. International Trade Journal, 27, 197-224.

Medina L., & Schneider F (2018) Shadow economies around the world: What did we learn over the last 20 years? IMF Working 18(17): 1.

McKinnon, R.I. (1963). Optimum currency areas. American Economic Review, 53 (4), 717–725.

Mckinnon, R. Mundell, (2000). The Euro, and Optimum Currency Areas". Standard University, Department of Economics. Working Paper

Mundell, R.A. (1961). A theory of optimum currency areas. America Economic Review 51 (4), 657–665.

Mogaji, P. K. (2017). Evaluation of Macroeconomic Indicators and Dynamics for Monetary Integration of West Africa: The Case of the WAMZ. MPRA Working Paper 98943. Downloaded from *https://mpra.ub.uni-muenchen.de/98943/.*

Nnyanzi, J. B., Kavuma, S., Sseruyange, J., & Nanyiti, A. (2022). The manufacturing output effects of infrastructure development, liberalization and governance: evidence from Sub-Saharan Africa. Journal of Industrial and Business Economics, 49(2), 369–400.

N'Zué, F. F. (2011). Les perspectives economiques de la cedeao faceaux crises financieres/economiques europeennes.

N'Zué, F. F., Olayiwola, W. & Jalloh, M. (2012), Mobilisation des Ressources Intérieures dans quelques pays de la CEDEAO/Domestic Resource Mobilization in Selected ECOWAS Countries, Abuja: ECOWAS Commission, xxiv.

Obstfeld, M. (1994). Risk-taking, Global Diversification, and Growth. *American Economic Review*, 84, 1310-29.

Ofori-Abebrese., G., (2006). The Eco and the economic development of West Africa, Journal of Science and Technology, 26, 2.

O'Mara, J., & Richter, A. (2011). *Global diversity and inclusion benchmarks: Standards for organizations around the world.* O'Mara and Associates.

Ogunkola, O. (2005). An Evaluation of the Viability of a Single Monetary Zone in ECOWAS. African Economic Research Consortium (AERC), Nairobi, Research Paper 147.

Osagie, E. (2005) "ECOWAS, Globalization and the Alleviation of Poverty in Nigeria": The Second Distinguished Annual Lecture of the Faculty of Social Sciences, Ambrose Alli University, Ekpoma: 28th July, pp. 6.

Oshikoya, T.W., (2010). Monetary and Financial Integration in West Africa. Routledge.

Quinn, D. (1977). The correlates of change in international financial regulation. *American Political Science Review*, 91, 531-51.

Rogan, M., & Skinner, C. (2017). The nature of the South African informal sector as reflected in the quarterly labour-force survey, 2008–2014. REDI3 Working paper 28.

Russell, C. (2002). Overturning Mundell: Fiscal policy in a monetary union. *Federal Reserve Bank of Minneapolis.*

Stavárek, D. Řepková, I. Gajdošová, K.(2011). Theory of financial integration and achievements in the European Union. In Matoušek, R. – Stavárek, D. (eds.) *Financial Integration in the European Union. (Routledge Studies in European Economy)*. London: Routledge.

Schraeder, P. J. (2000). African Politics and Society: A Mosaic in Transformation. Boston: Bedford/St.

The World Factbook, Central Intelligence Agency (2022), retrieved 2022-09-10

Tollnek, F., & Baten, J. (2017). Farmers at the heart of the 'human capital revolution'? Decomposing the numeracy increase in early modern Europe. *The Economic History Review*, 70(3), 779-809.

Tralac, trade law centre. "African Continental Free Trade Area (AfCFTA) Legal Texts and Policy Documents". tralac.org. Retrieved March 28, 2018.

Trichet, J.C. (2005). Financial markets integration in Europe: the ECB's view. BIS Review, 39: 1-5.

Uche, C. (2019). The politics of the African Continental Free Trade Agreement. African Studies Centre Lieden blog post.

Umofa, N., Orji, K. E., & Worika, I. L. (2018). Infrastructural development and the Nigerian industrial sector performance. International Journal of Scientific Engineering and Research, 9(6), 331–335.

UNCTAD (2020). United Nation Conference on Trade and Development Report

United Nations (2022). World Population Prospects 2022. Retrieved on 6th November, 2022 from: *https://population.un.org/wpp/.*

Voz di Paz & Interpeace (2010). *Root causes of conflict in Guinea-Bissau: The voices of the people.* Guinea-Bissau: Voz di Paz/Interpeace.

WAMZTIR (2020). West African Monetary Zone Trade Integration Report (2020). Annual Publication of the West African Monetary Institute (WAMI). Special Edition Accra, Ghana.

West Africa Monetary Institute (2002). Questions and Answers on the West African Monetary Zone.Accra, Ghana.

West African Monetary Institute (2020). A current assessment of the state of preparedness of the member states of the West African monetary zone for the ECOWAS single currency programme 2020. Accra, West African Monetary Institute.

West African Monetary Institute (2022). WAMZ Payments

System Development Project. Retrieved from: *https://wami-imao.org/en/integration-projects/payment-systems.*

Williams, C.C. (2006). *The Hidden Enterprise Culture: Entrepreneurship in the underground economy.* Cheltenham: Edward Elgar.

Williams, C.C., & S. Nadin (2012). Tackling entrepreneurship in the informal economy: evaluating the policy options. Journal of Entrepreneurship and Public Policy, 1(2), 111- 24.

Williams, C.C. (2013). Tackling Europe's Informal Economy: A Critical Evaluation of the neo-liberal deregulatory perspective. *Journal of Contemporary European Research*, 9(3), 261- 79.

World Bank (2016a). Population of West African Countries for 2015. Retrieved from databank.worldbank.org/data/download/POP.pdf.

World Bank (2016b). Gross Domestic Product of West African Countries for 2015. Retrieved from databank.worldbank.org/data/download/GDP.pdf.

Zeidy, A. I. (2020). The Role of Trade Finance in Promoting Trade: The Implications of COVID 19 on Trade Finance in Africa. Special Reports, Zambia: COMESA Monetary Institute.

Made in United States
North Haven, CT
06 November 2026

21875926R00224